1970

This bo   may be l   t

COLLAGE

PERSONALITIES   CONCEPTS   TECHNIQUES

Juan Gris: Tea Cups   1914   Oil, charcoal and collage on canvas
25¾ x 36¼ inches

G. David Thompson Collection

PERSONALITIES

CHILTON BOOK COMPANY

HARRIET JANIS and RUDI BLESH

COLLAGE

CONCEPTS TECHNIQUES

PHILADELPHIA NEW YORK LONDON

Second Printing, December, 1969

ACKNOWLEDGMENTS

This book and its authors are heavily in debt to the generosity and long patience of literally hundreds of sources of help—artists and writers, museums and museum officials, educational institutions, art dealers and art collectors, photographers, and publishers and publications, all over the world. Artists from each of the modern generations have taken time to give interviews or to answer laboriously detailed correspondence; art dealers have furnished photographs, facilitated interviews, supplied exhibition details and other data; and so on through the list—the extent and variety of cooperation over a period of several years testify both to a generous spirit and to the apparent desire and need for a book on this subject. Being in the debt of so many for so much, adequate thanks become manifestly as impossible as even merely to give detailed thanks to all.

From the artists and writers we would like first to single out those of earlier generations: Alexander Archipenko, Jean Arp, Gabrielle Buffet-Picabia, Joseph Cornell, Sonia Delaunay, Jean Dubuffet, Marcel Duchamp, Suzanne Duchamp-Crotti, Max Ernst, Naum Gabo, Hannah Höch, Marcel Jean, Gyorgy Kepes, Man Ray, E. L. T. Mesens, Sibyl Moholy-Nagy, Hans Richter, Franz Roh and Dr. Juliane Roh, Xanti Schawinsky, Kurt Seligmann, Walter Spengemann, Jr., Tristan Tzara, and Nellie van Doesburg.

We have been assisted by artists, writers, and composers, among more recent generations, including: Will Barnet, William Baziotes, Alberto Burri, John Cage, César, Karl A. Dickenson, James Dine, Ronnie Elliott, John Ernest, Jimmy Ernst, Francisco Farreras, Gonzalo Fonseca, Walter Gaudnek, Ernst Geitlinger, William Getman, Adrian Heath, Anthony Hill, John Hoppe, Allan Kaprow, Yves Klein, Conrad Marca-Relli, Kenneth Martin, Mary Martin, Manolo Millares, Robert Motherwell, Louise Nevelson, Claes Oldenburg, Victor Pasmore, Marcel Polak, Robert Rauschenberg, Bernard Schultze, Richard Stankiewicz, Harold Town, Wilhelm Wessel, Robert Whitman, Jr.

Among the critics, historians, and museum officials who have assisted us we must mention: Alfred H. Barr, Jr., Henry R. Hope, Daniel-Henry Kahnweiler, Lawrence Alloway, Douglas MacAgy, Bernard Karpel, Librarian of the Museum of Modern Art and his staff, William S. Lieberman, Curator of Prints, and Willard Tangen and Pearl Moeller in the Photograph Department of the same institution; Dorothy Morland, Director of the Institute of Contemporary Arts, and W. Sandberg, Director of the Stedelijk Museum.

Art dealers, whose contact with art, artists, and collectors is intimate and continuous, have helped us immeasurably as shown by the length of the list: in New York—The Alan Gallery, David Anderson Gallery, Bodley Gallery, Leo Castelli Gallery, Galerie Chalette, D'Arcy Galleries, Downtown Gallery, Robert Elkon Gallery, André Emmerich Gallery, Rose Fried Gallery, Allan Frumkin Gallery (also in Chicago), David Herbert Gallery, Martha Jackson Gallery, Sidney Janis Gallery, Judson Gallery, M. Knoedler and Company, Kootz Gallery,

Pierre Matisse Gallery, Betty Parsons Gallery, Stephen T. Radich Gallery, Reuben Gallery, Saidenberg Gallery, Bertha Schaefer, Stable Gallery, Allan Stone Gallery, 10/4 Gallery, Tibor de Nagy Gallery, Howard Wise Gallery (also in Cleveland), and World House; and elsewhere — Galleria d'Arte Naviglio, Milan; Galerie Beyeler in Basle; Galerie Claude-Bernard, Paris; Galerie Iris Clert, Paris; Simone Collinet, Paris; Galerie Daniel Cordier, Paris; Dilexi Gallery, San Francisco; Galerie Europe, Paris; Richard Feigen, Chicago; Ferus Gallery, Los Angeles; Gimpel Fils, London; Hanover Gallery, London; Kestner-Gesellschaft, Hanover; Louise Leiris, Paris; Lord's Gallery, London; Galerie Maeght, Paris; New London Gallery, London; Galleria Odyssia, Rome; Rabin and Kreuger, Newark; Galerie Rive Droite, Paris; Galerie le Soleil, Paris; and Arthur Tooth and Sons, London.

Photographers helped us both with original work and with photographic reproductions of works of art. We must single out a few for the amount and importance of the help they rendered: Aaron Siskind, Hans Namuth, Marvin P. Lazarus, David Gahr, and John Craven, for original material; Oliver Baker, Rudolph Burckhardt, Robert McElroy, Eric Pollitzer, and John D. Schiff for reproductions.

Museums, colleges, and educational institutions whom we must specifically thank, include: the American Federation of Art; the Art Institute of Chicago; the Baltimore Museum of Art; Cape May Historical Society; Peggy Guggenheim's Art of This Century, Venice; Solomon R. Guggenheim Museum, New York; Institute for Contemporary Arts, London; Landesmuseum, Hanover; Mercer Museum, Doylestown; Metropolitan Museum of Art, New York; Minneapolis Institute of Arts; Museo de Bellas Artes, Caracas; Museum Haus Lange, Krefeld; the Museum of Modern Art, New York; Newark Museum; New School for Social Research, New York; Philadelphia Museum of Art; Phillips Collection, Washington, D.C.; Stedelijk Museum, Amsterdam; Washington University, St. Louis; Whitney Museum of American Art, New York; Yale University Art Gallery, New Haven.

We are grateful for the assistance of the following editors, publishers, and publications: James Fitzsimmons and Art International, Zurich; Art News, New York; Editions de l'Oeil and Editions du Seuil, both of Paris; René P. Métras and Correo de las Artes, Barcelona; Charles-Henri Ford and View magazine, New York; Wittenborn and Company, New York; and finally to Random House, Inc., New York, for permission to quote James A. Michener's account of Hokusai in his history of Japanese prints, The Floating World.

Finally, we thank the many collectors who have generously allowed us to reproduce works from their private collections: Various anonymous lenders, Mme. M. Arp-Hagenbach, François Arp, Jean Arp, Richard Brown Baker, Mr. and Mrs. E. A. Bergman, Mrs. Elizabeth B. Blake, Mr. and Mrs. Leigh B. Block, Mrs. Raymond J. Braun, André Breton, R. Cabral, Leo Castelli, Mrs. Talbot W. Chambers, William N. Copley, Mr. and Mrs. John deMenil, Kenward Elmslie, Mrs. Henry Epstein, Mr. and Mrs. Thomas Folds, Mr. and Mrs. B. H. Friedman, Miss Eve Garrison, Wreatham Gathright, Mrs. Edith Gossage, Mr. and Mrs. M. H. Grossman, Miss Peggy Guggenheim, Mrs. Mortimer B. Harris, Mr. and Mrs. Ben Heller, Joseph Hirshhorn, Mrs. Martha Jackson, Dr. Riccardo Jucker, Mr. and Mrs. Samuel Kootz, Mrs. Katharine Kuh, Mr. and Mrs. Arthur Lejwa, Mr. and Mrs. Julien Levy, Mr. and Mrs. Albert A. List, Mrs. Horatio Gates-Lloyd, Wright Ludington, Mr. and Mrs. Arnold H. Maremont, Mr. and Mrs. Pierre Matisse, Gianni Mattioli, Mr. and Mrs. Robert E. Meyerhoff, Mr. and Mrs. Morton G. Neumann, Mr. and Mrs. Constantino Nivola, Dr. Giuseppe Panza, Mrs. Silvia Pizitz, Mrs. Lee Krasner Pollock, Stephen T. Radich, Mrs. Paul Scott Rankine, Dr. E. Rathke, Mr. and Mrs. Bernard J. Reis, Dwight Ripley, Mme. Pierre Roché, Mrs. James Roemer, Baroness Edmond de Rothschild, Herbert and Nanette Rothschild, Mr. and Mrs. Robert C. Scull, Mr. and Mrs. Joseph R. Shapiro, Leon Polk Smith, James Thrall Soby, Mr. and Mrs. David Solinger, Miss Laura Lee Stearns, Karl Ströher, Mrs. Kay Sage Tanguy, Mrs. Manuela Piña de Torrés-Garcia, Mrs. Eleanor Ward, Mrs. George Henry Warren, Dr. Frederic Wertham, Mr. and Mrs. Max M. Zurier.

FOREWORD

A history of collage in the serious art of this century properly begins, as does the meaning of the word, with the cutting and pasting of paper into pictures. Almost immediately, however, the history, like the meaning—if it is to realize the importance of its subject—must become the story of the great phenomenon of modern art: the movement of the picture out into space and its eventual merging or dissolving into action and/or forms in the time-space continuum. Though this process, inescapably involving the rejection of old values and traditions, has often been considered destructive, it is essentially logical, factual, and realistic.

Significantly, it began not with art but with an infant science when, three centuries ago, a German Jesuit priest in Rome projected the first magic lantern pictures on a screen. Here for the first time picture and real space were wedded as the two-dimensional painting on glass was imprinted as it were in light and then (with light's speed) transported and reassembled on a distant screen. *For*

every inch of its travel however, the picture existed in an expanding three dimensions in light-filled space. It is significant that the picture after being dissolved into light-in-space was eventually reconstructed again in a two-dimensional form whose continued existence was contingent not upon solid matter but upon energy in the space-time continuum. It is significant too that with the very name "magic lantern" it became evident that science was inheriting the magical properties previously attributed to art.

There was one missing attribute of the picture in its new time-space habitat. This was motion, and immediately experiments began, to make pictures that would move. Motion came to the magic lantern in the nineteenth century with the cinema. It is not necessary to point out the potent magic exerted by the motion picture and its people for the next half-century until this magic began again to be transferred, this time to that even more mysterious creator of "living" pictures in space, the television.

Art only began to address itself to this magical reality of the picture in space in the early years of this century, and then only by gradual experimental stages, each one of which was bitterly opposed by the same public that had so eagerly and uncritically embraced the magic lantern and then flocked to the nickelodeons to see the moving pictures.

Ever since the cubists' first collages

with their almost impalpable added thicknesses of glued paper, painting has steadily moved out into reliefs and constructions, then into objects, and now finally into paintings (or at least *painting-ideas*) that have flowed out as objects and people in motion in real spatial areas in the development of the esthetic creations of today called Environment-Happenings. The spatial area, whatever it may be—room, stage, garden, street— is the screen; the moving objects and people are the picture-in-solution reconstituted as a transient entity in time and space. With this final development the public is suddenly and startlingly acquiescent: it is finally evident to them that modern art has become factual and realistic, having at last retrieved from science the stolen mantle of its own proper magic.

So this drama of picture into space (which is also the drama of artists' struggle to recapture usefulness and importance) is the subject of this book which, it must be confessed, began as a simple chronicle of cut-and-pasted paper and then, like the pictures themselves, compulsively and inescapably expanded into the larger space of philosophy—of real meanings and the meanings of reality, of artists' motives and of human needs.

CONTENTS

COLLAGE

PERSONALITIES   CONCEPTS   TECHNIQUES

"The waste of the world becomes my art"
(Der Abfall der Welt dient Mir zur Kunst)

KURT SCHWITTERS, 1935

Inscription on the back of his collage, "Für Bieleny"
Collection: Martha Jackson, New York

1 Picasso: *Violin and Fruit* 1912–13

1

COLLAGE IN
FOLK ART

Collage was once only the simple, pleasant folk art or pastime of cutting and pasting bits of paper into pictures or ornamental designs. It was no concern of serious artists. The height of its aspirations was more or less measured by the naive and nostalgic, often mawkish but always delightful, sentiments of the lacy valentine. It was a folk art once practiced almost everywhere that paper might be found, and its origins began so many centuries ago that they cannot be pinpointed as to time and place. It is only with this century and the advent of modern art that this quondam delight of schoolgirl and housewife came to the attention of serious artists grappling with the revolutionary ideas that eventually effected one of the most complete esthetic reorientations in history. Today, fifty years after its first serious use, collage is a major art medium whose techniques have expanded, range of materials immeasurably broadened, and use become almost universal. Collage together with its many offshoots emerges today not only as a major me-

dium, but as a germinative idea that, once planted, has pointed and even led to some of the most significant as well as astonishing developments in the astonishing art of our time.

Yet its first use—the inclusion of humble scraps of newspaper within the once-sacred confines of the easel picture of oil on canvas—had an intentional element of shock that derived in part from the seeming impertinence and incongruity of this folk art device in serious art. There were other elements of shock involved, of course—particularly the baffling intrusion of objects—simple, real, and honest—into what for centuries had been unquestioningly accepted as the stage of illusion. This, as we shall see, precipitated a dialogue between reality and illusion, a dialogue whose purpose, like that of the Socratic dialogues, was to establish the real and expose the false. It was thus that the art of the valentine became the philosophic tool of new esthetic ideas.

However, since the original folk art aspect was an integral part both of its shock to the public and of its reality as conceived by the artists, a quick survey of its popular employment will be useful.

The playful pastime of cutting and pasting paper which originated so long ago was not confined to any one age level or sex or to any particular class, nationality, or race of people. Its practice in the United States in the nineteenth century resulted in much delightful folk art: tinsel pictures, valentines, elaborate paper cutouts (frequently featuring the American eagle trumpeting victory), cigar bands symmetrically pasted on glass bowls and dishes, boxes, and even articles of furniture, and arrangements of Indian arrowheads glued to panels that were framed and hung like pictures. Then too there were the Victorian screens covered with their gay hodgepodges of lithographed scenes, personages, children, and animals. Also allied to collage was the ubiquitous scrapbook that in every household hoarded on its pages colorful advertisements, box and bottle labels, visiting cards in florid hand penmanship, and many other paper mementos and curios. A particularly useful and durable kind of collage was the homemade children's picture book, its illustrations culled from magazines and catalogues and pasted on soft muslin pages with hand-stitched edges. Many and inventive were the uses of the facsimile ephemerae that began in our culture with Gutenberg and in the centuries since have assumed the proportions of a snowstorm of heterogeneous paper images. The souvenir and curio mania of the last century has even proved of considerable historical value. Great commercial and manufacturing firms have often had to scan old scrapbooks in order to verify what their own labels and even trade names were eighty, ninety, and a hundred years ago; and costly law suits for infringement of patent and copyright have been settled in cases where the chief witness was a scrapbook assembled long ago by a housewife for her own naive pleasure in color and design.

In the nineteenth century collage led to some rather extraordinary pictures of people and scenes constructed entirely of pasted-up fragments of advertising or postage stamps, pictures that in their whole effect seem almost like prophecies of surrealism.

A strong psychological element of folk collage seems always to have been the urge to save things. At the fringe of this normal instinct there are instances where collage pasting became an obsessional activity. There are large vases, for example, completely covered with glued-on heterogenies of buttons or paste jewels. Among the saddest and most haunted of this class of objects are the "memory jugs" whose surfaces are packed communities of tiny naked china dolls. With such collaged objects as these, sentimentality shades into an irrational area similar to that which James Thrall Soby has called the "memorable antireason of surrealism." In France, where objects of this sort that reach a certain degree of crude, harsh, and obsessional morbidity are called *art brut,* this haunting imagery has inspired the paintings and collages of an artist of stature, Jean Dubuffet.

Folk collage falls into several types that in general survive or are paralleled in the serious art collage of this century. One folk type employs pasted materials to form a decorative design, generally geometric, e.g., star and rosette. In this type a natural form like rose or tulip is arbitrarily stylized from pasted fragments, resembling the decorative peasant painting of rural France, The Palatinate, or Dutch Pennsylvania.

A second type of folk collage consists in an illusion or metamorphosis in which objects of one sort are assembled in an aggregate representing something entirely different. The flowers and trees constructed from horsehair and, in the Victorian mourning pictures, often from human hair, are typical examples of the metamorphosis of the primary image into the secondary image.

A third type uses the collaged objects to represent themselves, particularly in instances when the object would be difficult to delineate, or in other instances where the illusionist chiaroscuro of light and shadow is rejected in favor of a bold corporeality. In folk paintings one frequently encounters such things as actual branches or seashells used in these roles. In the one case the folk artist, lacking professional technique, gratifies the image-making urge by using the object as image-in-itself; while in the other case we have the rather extraordinary double reversal of reality to create the illusion of illusion.

A fourth type of folk collage is the curious sort of object, generally three dimensional that, like the doll-covered vase, is plastered over with irrelevant things. These objects, which are often disturbingly obsessive, form one class of the objects in which the surrealists were deeply interested. A well-known object of this sort from our century is the 1936 work popularly called *The Fur-lined Teacup* by the Swiss surrealist Meret Oppenheim.

Finally, there is that quality in folk collage and in folk art in general which is called "naive." Specifically this means an ignorance of artistic credos, tenets, and theories; and practically it means that this ignorance frequently results in an esthetically productive freedom of expression. The folk artist, not hampered by preconceptions that a painting must be executed on a flat two-dimensional plane, blithely sticks on objects, builds up bas-relief, or even creates free-standing "pictures" in three dimensions. This "naive" freedom was purposefully adopted by modernists from the beginning, and we will have ample and dramatic evidence of how, through its knowing employment, they have altered art and expressed the challenging new concepts of our time. We will find at the core of this revolutionary process the papier collé or cut and pasted paper of folk art.

There is some justification for believing that folk art's use of object-in-itself as image is actually a naive imitation of the *trompe-l'oeil* or "fool-the-eye" tradition of extremely naturalistic painting. There is even to be found highly sophisticated precedent in seventeenth-century Dutch paintings with real butterflies glued among the painted blossoms. The sophistication in this instance, of course, derives from the fantastically dexterous painting that made the butterflies appear to be painted effigies among real flowers, whereas the folk artist appeals to the real object to lend veracity to his painting. The particular magic of *trompe l'oeil* lies in the mythology of life in the simulacrum, which is the basic illusionist concept most decisively rejected in this century, whose artists have instead tended to embrace the indisputable common-sense reality of the thing-in-itself.

Dutch and Flemish fool-the-eye still-life painting from the sixteenth century on had a strong influence on nineteenth-century American artists. A Raphael Peale masterpiece of this sort, dating from 1802, depicts visiting cards, lottery and admission tickets, and invitations meticulously delineated against a painted background that simulates cracked and torn paper (Fig. 2).

The vogue of fool-the-eye paintings continued in Europe and America well into the early decades of this century, enlisting here the efforts of painters as technically skilled as William Harnett, John Peto, John Haberle (Fig. 3), and Jean Dubreuil. A typical Harnett or Peto still life shows objects such as a pottery stein (rendered with actual relief textures simulating the stoneware surfaces), a pipe with burning coals, and a folded newspaper, all with a chiaroscuro so heightened that they seem really to project from the canvas and invite the touch of skeptical fingers. The technical mastery of these artists and their European colleagues got wide distribution through remarkably faithful colored lithograph reproductions that enjoyed enormous popularity. These paintings so close to the people depict many of the elements that the French

2 Raphael Peale: *A Deception* 1802

cubists were to use in introducing collage into serious art—such characteristic elements, for example, as wood-graining simulated in painting or in facsimile papers pasted-on, as well as scraps of newspaper, actual or simulated.

This folk art and genre art activity, in fact, is historically sandwiched between earlier classical prototypes and the far differently oriented adaptations by twentieth-century modernism. There are, for example, the curious sixteenth-century metamorphic paintings by the Italian Arcimboldo that, while realistically depicting fruits, vegetables, cereal grains, or even landscapes, metamorphose into human portraits. There is such basic human delight in the magical properties of everyday things that one must acknowledge the possibility that Arcimboldo's painting was itself preceded by folk art which worked its magic with fruits and vegetables—all the things-in-themselves. Nevertheless the nineteenth century brought Arcimboldo back to earth in its flood of metamorphic production: the hair flowers, the floral wreaths constructed from feathers and seeds, the cut-up postage stamps that changed into vases of flowers (Fig. 4). Today metamorphosis has disappeared in most of the pictures and objects made from extrinsic things of preserved particular identity. Metamorphosis nevertheless is potent magic: it vivified much surrealist work including both found and made objects and is at its most haunting today in Dubuffet's *assemblage* collages of dried leaves (*éléments botaniques*) forming landscapes inhabited by animals and humans.

Nineteenth-century American women in New England or the Midwest who patiently assembled seashells and coral into floral bouquets also had imposing precedents. For one example there is the large and fabulous bouquet made for Maria Theresa, Empress of Austria. Fashioned entirely of gold and precious stones—liberally featuring diamonds in all hues and sizes—this costly conceit represented full-size lilies, roses, tulips, and other blooms, while, in the blaze of facet-reflected light, there hovered bees and butterflies made of equally costly gems. Though few American housewives are likely ever to have seen this fantastic gem sculpture in Vienna, still, with all its skill and sophistication, it sprang from the same essential vein of magical naïveté as their leaves and feathers, buttons and shells.

Nowadays much of the popular urge to create these magical images out of materials at hand has been diverted into the easy semimechanical device of photography. This is certainly one reason that amateur camera work enjoys so overwhelming a vogue. The snapshots taken today in the hundreds of millions, of every possible subject and place, are those human-made images for which we have so perpetual a hunger and so deep a need.

However, if a machine has all but wiped out a fascinating folk art that once had many forms and ramifications, it has not eradicated collage on the level of fine art. Serious and important

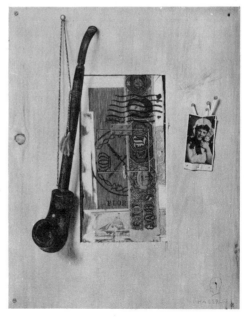

3 Haberle: *Still Life* Early 20th Cent.

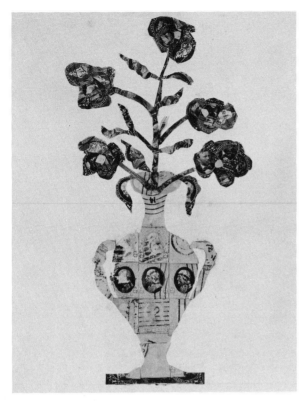

4 Anonymous: *Vase with Flowers* Late 19th Cent.

port back into society; the preservation of the castoff fragments of daily life squares his conscience with our materialist orthodoxy of the Good Life from Waste while investing discontinuity with a sense of continuity; its metamorphosis of sad earthy shards into spiritual entities is a grant of hope for him and for us in the midst of a desert of matter and machine.

work is being created wherever modern art is understood: all of western Europe, Scandinavia, the British Isles, Japan, and other East and Near East countries, and the entire western hemisphere. Everywhere, and particularly perhaps in America, collage's quick and direct method meshes with our quickened sense of time; the use of technological matériel serves the artist as a worker's pass-

4A Anonymous: *Memory Jug.* c. 1900

8

2
CUBISM—
PROTO-COLLAGE

6), includes a pasted piece of paper imprinted with the words *AU LOUVRE.* At about the same time in the painting *The Match Holder,* Braque painted a folded copy of the newspaper

Modern collage began with Braque and Picasso several years prior to 1914. Before the shot at Sarajevo that precipitated world war and signaled the end of the old political and social order the two great cubists were pasting bits of newspaper into pictures. Nothing could be more misleading, however, than the comparison that leaps to mind—it would be a grave mistake indeed to stigmatize as trivial the two painters' activity. In its profound effect upon the course of art this folk concept and technique, though acting slowly, would in the long run be as revolutionary in art as an assassin's gun in politics. Whatever the headlines on the pasted clippings—even if of war or impending war—they were irrelevant to the matter in hand; what they really signified was the end of the art that had endured for centuries and the beginning of a new art.

As early as 1908 there were premonitions of what was to come. In Picasso's case an ink drawing, *Baigneuses* (Fig.

5 Cézanne: *Portrait of the Artist's Father* 1860–63

9

6 Picasso: *Les baigneuses* 1908

GIL BLAS showing only the block letters GIL B.[1] We will discuss these two pictures later.

It is generally considered that the immediate forerunner of Braque's collage work is a shadow cast across a cubist painting—the painted shadow of a painted nail created through *trompe-l'oeil* illusionism in the 1909–10 *Still Life with Violin and Pitcher*. Above the kaleidoscopic tumble of dissected forms and glinting brown and silver-gray facets, there intrudes this strangely foreign fool-the-eye thing: a nail painted as if driven into the canvas and casting its angular painted illusion of shadow. Amid the cerebrated seriousness of cubism there sounds a whisper of folk art, mundane yet poetic—a simple homely thing working the magic of the image.

This slight inclusion proved strangely provocative. As Henry Hope has written: "It might have been a somewhat intuitive act but as soon as completed it caused much speculation. . . . The nail was an innovation that caused much discussion among Braque, Picasso, and their friends."[2] Hope relates that the painters' dealer Daniel-Henry Kahnweiler "argued that this revealed a new significance in their painting. It was held to be a sudden evocation of reality, in the midst of their bold departure from material appearances."

A half-century of subsequent development has proved Kahnweiler right: the tiny painted nail quietly indicated what the total revolution of modern art was to be—the long convulsive effort of artists to bring a primitive reality back

[1] Hope dates *The Match Holder* as of 1910. (See Hope, Henry R., *Georges Braque*. New York, The Museum of Modern Art, 1949, p. 48.) However, this painting is stylistically more in accord with earlier canvases, 1908–1909, and is included and dated by Christian Zervos as 1908 in *Cahiers d'Art*, No. 1–2, 1933, p. 13.

[2] Hope, Henry R., *ibid*.

to art. An illusion heralded a truly factual realism; the painted nail, seeming to project into the spectators' space, pointed the way; soon pictures would follow, thrusting themselves bodily into the real space of the real world. The pictures thus would objectify the artists' desires. Even before the turn of the century certain late Victorian artists, like Toulouse-Lautrec, had begun to rebel against "fine" art, wanted to drop the useless, onerous adjective altogether. The fauves sought to destroy the adjective by eliminating the "fine art" quality from their paintings. Artists, uneasy and estranged in a false romantic isolation, had begun, as Marcel Duchamp has said, "to feel like animals in a cage." They wanted people to need them and need their art; they wanted to merge with society.

Much of cubism's strength came from the close partnership of two creative but basically different personalities. Braque's nature, philosophical and contemplative, quiet and essentially modest, was balanced by that of the fiery Andalusian, bold, adventurous, and intensely factual even while almost wildly imaginative. After they turned toward a common goal in cubism, the same anti-art motives and the same urge to make contact with reality drove them to the strongly iconoclastic act that collage represented at that time. Picasso characteristically leaped forward, pasting the island of paper in *Baigneuses* but then waited several years before going all the way to collage. More cautiously, Braque *painted a newspaper* in a picture several years before he used scraps from a real one. But each in his way moved toward the beginnings of a new reality: the image-in-itself. In Braque's case there is no room for doubt. Breton quoted him: "The papiers collés in my drawings have given me a feeling of certainty."[3]

In any event, Braque's philosophical temperament coupled with an early training close to folk craft made him an artist capable of posing sophisticated and significant contrasts between fine art and folklore magic, as well as between pictorial reality and genuine reality. In 1899, at the age of seventeen and while an evening student at the École des Beaux-Arts, he became apprenticed to a house painter. While working in the serious academic vein in oil painting, landscape, and figure, he was learning with great enjoyment "the special skills . . . the stock in trade of French house painters . . . the ability to make imitations of the expensive materials found in houses of the wealthy bourgeois: gilt, polychrome, marble, rare wood and masonry . . . by the skill of his brush. A good apprentice also had to know hand lettering and sign painting."[4]

By 1902 Braque was concentrating exclusively on art study; by 1905 he was a professional "fine" artist showing fauve paintings in the explosive *Salon d'Automne* exhibition. But he had not lost the humble skills of painter-decorator nor forgotten the delight in their exercise. Soon in one of his cubist paintings appeared the sign painter's plebeian little trick of painted nail—both affectionate memory and significant gesture.

Given the time and the needs of artists everywhere, it was the right gesture, helping to open the door to a flood: first a trickle of collage, then a stream, and finally today a deluge of objects and symbols from the real world. The Victorian dream was over; artists began to re-enter the world by embracing its artifacts; anti-art became art and art strove to become a part of life.

Primitivism was the key to the return, but not merely the alien or exotic, as in Gauguin's Tahitian paintings or

[3] Breton, André, *Georges Braque*. Paris, *Cahiers d'Art*, No. 1–2, 1933.

[4] Hope, Henry R., *op. cit.*

in the faceted African masks that Picasso with miraculous insight collated with Cézanne's planar painting to create the prototype of cubism. In the climate of that day any object from European daily life was primitive. The vain preciousness of Victorian art ideals lingered on: a painted nail, a scrap of newspaper, the signs in the street—even the marvelous trade signs, the giant cigars and pipes, scissors and knives, horse and ox heads—were things the esthete ignored as gauche and crude. The new artist welcomed them all.

Braque in his day had done honest lettering; he did not abhor signs and letters, on the contrary he knew their force. So the painted letters GIL B are thrown across the canvas in a gesture of anger and disdain: for *GIL BLAS* was the Paris newspaper most violently opposed to cubism in those years of its crucial struggle for recognition. The gesture said to this critic: "Since you don't or won't understand cubism, here I give you the name of your newspaper. Can you read this?"

Beyond the knowledgeable sign painter was Braque the philosopher who must surely have sensed the far-reaching meanings that would attach to the use of letters in this way in painting. Unlike other representations, letters have a life outside the painting. The printed letters of a living language have ineradicable overtones of meaning; separately or combined into words they cannot merely be looked at—they insist upon being read.

By 1911 the two artists were using isolated letters as well as words in their cubist canvases, not polemically as in *The Match Holder* but woven functionally into the compositions as notes of reality to be read by the spectator. In some paintings they become calligraphic lines or abstract forms more difficult to read; in more abstract paintings, by contrast, they sometimes become more explicit by being stenciled in. In its dual role of abstract elements of composition and simple arguments *ad hominem*—functioning, that is, in two different kinds of reality—painted lettering swiftly opened the door to pasted-in pieces of newspaper.

In this sense of the dual function of the letter, both pictures, Picasso's *Baigneuses* and Braque's *The Match Holder,* made a place in art for both worlds: that of esthetics and that of everyday life. Conceivable now was the strange dualism of collage, whose component parts live two lives. The collaged object participates in a picture only by its own consent, for its memory of the world it came from is unimpaired. The psychological, emotional, and signifying enrichment of art implied by the introduction of a scrap of paper or four block letters can only be measured in the amazing developments in art that have in such strong measure derived from this germinal idea.

The cubists realized that long before their time the camera had made the illusionisms of a naturalistic art both pointless and ridiculous. Not rejecting the real existence of subject matter, they began searching more deeply for its reality. Their search was made in several steps. First, they "analyzed" the subject (model or still life) as simultaneously seen from several angles of view (front, side, from above, below, etc.). Then, eschewing all naturalistic devices (traditional modeling, perspective, and pictorial depth), they expressed these various views, simultaneously superimposed in flat planes of monotone painting.

By 1909 they had achieved the aim of revolutionary artists from Courbet and the impressionists on, namely, to make the picture real in itself. They searched for the significant, rather than the idiosyncratic, form; they distorted or concealed the idiomorphic appearances of wine bottle, glass, or guitar, in drawing, contour, and detail; in light and shade; in color narrowed down to browns, blacks, grays, and whites. They denied the space of the real world and refused to re-create it in illusion; whereupon their subject matter, already distilled into esthetic essences, came to life in the flat pictorial world of two dimensions.

Strangely enough, once this transmuted reality began to live within the picture it did not want to stay there. In the voyage from one world to another some sea change had occurred. Just as the Form of Plato's table became idea not object, so the cubists' still life became the objectification of the esthetic ideas—even the personalities—of two revolutionary painters. Their search for reality had led aside to another, or surrogate reality. It was one of the great turning points: the end became the beginning.

Subject for them had been only the point of departure for imagination while they assayed and revalued their own part in the drama of art. Images drawn from without became inner images of the artist. As never before the observer had to contribute creatively: a picture was no longer a child's book of kindergarten pictures but a difficult text to be "read." The original subject was dim and misty, the emphasis elsewhere, and this "elsewhere" is the real concern of art in this century.

Reading of course consists in the interpreting of graphic symbols in terms of meaning. Recognition of the symbols is a prerequisite to the process. Recognition was no problem in naturalistic art, but the power and validity of the images as symbols faded. Religious symbolism was once a living visual vocabulary that made interpretation clear and cogent, but religious symbolism in art was outworn long before our time. And what enduring symbols can our swift-changing materialist technology give us to express, for example, the concept of speed? The futurists tried, but locomotive image faded into automobile, automobile into airplane, and now airplane

fades into rocket—no realistic image-symbol from our time can have the permanence the mythical Pegasus once had. But realism demands reality, not myth. So modern art, being basically a true epistemology, concerned with reality not appearances, searches, as science has searched, for indivisible basic elements. The symbol—if there is one—behind locomotive, motor car, rocket, and all the rest, might be energy: the fire in prehistory's cave, steam, electricity, nuclear fission, and behind all this, basic energy. But if so, then in what units and what forms can artists portray basic energy? They have wisely left that to the scientists. The cubists found the new image of energy in life, in themselves, in the inner image of man.

Half a century later, through a dozen isms, the projection of inner image has developed into visual vocabularies that people "read" with increasing ease. However unfamiliar new works may be, never again in our culture is there likely to be the dark, shattering, almost cataclysmic strangeness of cubism's first unveiling over fifty years ago. Yet with it came a new humanism. Through all the strenuous subsequent history of isms and counter-isms threads the warm humanistic strand that came into art with the first collages of Braque and Picasso. What was the essential meaning of this quondam folk play that still engages creative artists?

Surely it must be this: when a painting, painted for itself, has achieved its own autonomous existence, then the object from the real world can come bodily into the picture, not as illusion or adjunct of illusion but in its own reality. On a remarkable double stage there then ensues a drama of two realities enacted on two levels of experience.

On this stage, art suddenly boiled with new possibilities. The stage door, however, opened both ways: from world into picture and from picture into world. Easel painting per se, both as métier and

13

as technique, became for the first time since the Renaissance no longer adequate to all legitimate creative needs.

Pictorial extensions beyond painting, both in idea and in an actual spatial sense, became necessary to express wide new ranges of subject from the inner vision. All those intangibles of artist's psyche and feelings, his reactions to the outer world, extrasensory experiences, in short, all the preoccupations of the human mind and spirit, entered in through contrast versus identity in a startling new vocabulary of material things from the everyday world. There was no known precedent for this in painting. This was collage.

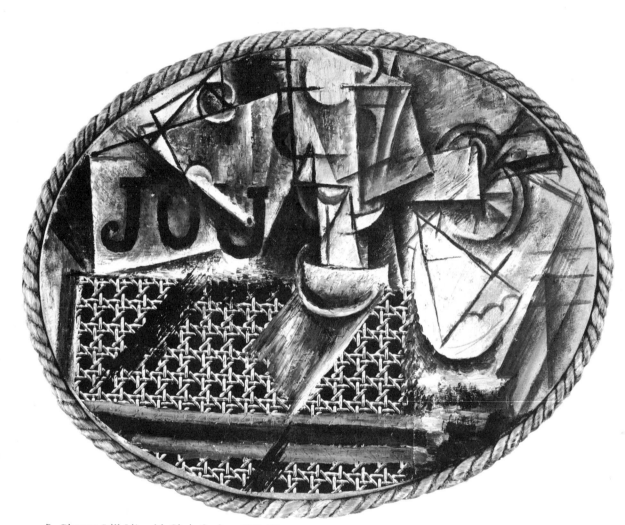

7 Picasso: *Still Life with Chair Caning* 1911–12

3

CUBIST COLLAGE

The cubists' free and frequent use of painted letters might lead us to expect that the printed word, perhaps in a newspaper cutting, would be present in the first true collages. In Braque's first collage, however, the pasted elements consist of wallpaper that represents wood-graining, and in Picasso's, a piece of oilcloth that simulates chair caning. Thus timidly and almost deceptively as it were, the real object enters the world of the picture, as though illusionism were its essential passport. Nevertheless, though disguised, the quondam enemy is safely inside the walls in two 1912 pictures: Picasso's *Still Life with Chair Caning* (Fig. 7) and Braque's *Fruit Bowl* (*Compotier*) (Fig. 8).

Which picture came first? Or, in other words, who made the first collage? The question may never receive a final answer. Although both artists are still alive and active as this book is written, their memories differ; early works were undated at the time; the opinions of art historians differ; there is not even agreement as to what, actually, would con-

stitute the first collage, i.e., an initial tentative inclusion of a scrap of pasted paper in a drawing or painting or a more completely realized papier collé, not to mention creative priorities such as that of idea before fact. Though not historically crucial, it will be illuminating to review the facts available.

In this period 1908 to 1912, the two artists' intensely close collaboration, which once made even stylistic differentiations difficult, still obscures a more precise pinpointing of comparative dates. Kahnweiler writes:

It is obvious that it was a joint discovery if one calls it a discovery. These two painters were then working so closely together that it is not at all certain that the one who did the first "papier collé" had really had the idea first. They might have talked about it before. . . . It is generally admitted that the first one was "Compotier," done by Braque in summer 1912 at Sorgues.[1]

There could be no doubt at least concerning the intense, adventurous excitement surrounding their work in those years. A climax—at least so far as collage is concerned—was reached in the summer of 1912 at Sorgues near Avignon in southern France. Picasso experimented with painted metal sculpture while Braque made paper constructions that Hope describes as having been "like certain geometric details in his painting," adding that while "none of these

[1] Kahnweiler, Daniel-Henry, in a letter to Harriet Janis, Feb. 4, 1961.

8 Braque: *Fruit Bowl* 1912

has survived . . . we can guess what they looked like from the fact that Picasso . . . addressed Braque as *'mon vieux Vilbure!'* referring to Wilbur Wright."[2]

The older Wright brother had just died. His name, filling the headlines, is a key to the excitement of the cubists. The world, generally, was intensely excited by flying. Kitty Hawk lay only nine years before; Blériot's flight across the English Channel only three years; and his fragile monoplane of bamboo, wire, and silk was still suspended out over a busy sidewalk from the front of a Paris building. No more excitement or hero worship can ever attend the first flight into outer space than was accorded man's first ventures into the air in primitive kitelike machines.

The two cubists, buoyed on the general current of optimistic excitement, imagined themselves—and became—bold pioneers in art. It was in this recklessly imaginative mood that the two men twisted metal, mixed sand in paint, and pasted paper into aerialistic shapes. They were collating painting with unheard-of materials, expanding into three-dimensional construction—which is another way of saying that they were bent on some kind of synthesis between two kinds of reality and two kinds of space: the pictorial and the real.

That summer Braque saw in a shopwindow some wallpaper of the sort used for wall panels and wainscot dadoes. The paper simulated the grain of quartered oak; it stirred the memory of the erstwhile painter-decorator; on an impulse he bought a few rolls. Almost immediately he translated impulse into action:

The first composition he made with this papier collé or glued-on paper, was on a sheet of drawing paper . . . upon which he pasted the strips of the wood-grain paper. . . . He then drew a simple composition in charcoal . . . sketched a bunch of grapes, a goblet, and beneath the grapes a suggestion of a compote dish upon a table. One of the strips was placed at the bottom where it suggests the table drawer. Another was neatly cut out to fit the curve of the fruit bowl. The drawing was extended across some of the pasted strips and the letters ALE and BAR were added. . . . But who knows what discussions preceded it, what mutual ideas and inspiration, what forgotten remarks or sketches led to the discovery?[3]

The *Compotier* is clearly Braque's first collage. Picasso's first, however, is a matter of definition. By one definition it could be the 1908 drawing *Baigneuses* (Fig. 6) ; by a stricter one it would be the *Still Life with Chair Caning* (Fig. 7) which Alfred H. Barr, Jr., Christian Zervos, and Picasso himself assign to the winter of 1911–12. Barr relates that Picasso did not consider the earlier picture a collage. It does seem obvious, however, and Barr agrees, that it could be considered at least a technical step toward collage.[4]

However, was the *AU LOUVRE* scrap, as generally considered, a revision? Why, for example, is the pasted paper separated from the main drawing by lines added to indicate its shadow? Revisions, like patches, are blended into the whole, not glaringly emphasized. Above all, why is a piece of paper bearing commercial lettering used *upside down*, when the artist must have had, if not matching paper, at least a clean scrap?

We suggest that if this collaged bit of paper be considered a planned inclusion then certain significant associations will come to light. Suppose that we consider another phenomenon of that era almost as new as human flight: the cinema, which once exerted so powerful a visual fascination on artists. Can

[2] Hope, Henry R., *op. cit.*

[3] Hope, Henry R., *op. cit.*

[4] Barr, Alfred H., Jr., in a letter to Harriet Janis, July 26, 1960, and in subsequent conversation.

9 Picasso: *Bouteille et verre* 1912

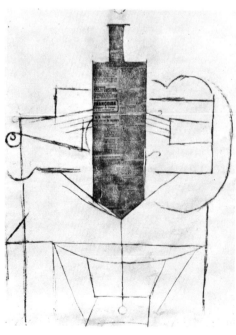

10 Picasso: *Bottle and violin* 1912

there be a connection between the idea of the cinema and this pasted inclusion?

The inclusion is rectangular like a screen; it is centrally located as in a theater; it is on paper lighter in tone than the surrounding paper. Perhaps equally important: Picasso has turned the letters *AU LOUVRE* upside down so that they bear a singular resemblance to the words on the song slides that once were screened to lead audience singing while reels were being changed. The great nickelodeon joke of that period was the accidental screening of a slide backwards or upside down. Could Picasso be alluding to this general joke?

In any event he certainly did not intend so crass or ridiculous an idea as a slide literally projected outdoors among bathers. Here we must follow our clue a little further: from the physical image projected on screen, to the reality within another reality, and finally, by extension of these ideas, to the flashback episode. This might be called a psychological vignette or visualized memory of a past event. Picasso had already employed this device, e.g., the large Blue Period canvas of 1903 variously called *Couple nu et femme avec enfant* or *La Vida,* painted in Barcelona.[5] These inclusions, whether painted or collaged, seem clearly parallel to the kind of invasion of one order of time and space by another order that the stereopticon and the cinema represent. As visual phenomena with deeper implications, the influence of such inventions on artists can hardly be overestimated.

In Picasso's work this invasion was explicitly accomplished in the *Still Life with Chair Caning* in which oilcloth representing chair caning is integrated into the structure of an oil painting. The letters *JOU* from *LE JOURNAL* are painted; the chair caning, though a foreign inclusion, is also a simulation; only the hemp rope framing this oval picture is a real artifact. In 1911, painted bits of rope appear in a number of Picasso's cubist paintings: here the real thing has ventured almost, but not quite, into the painting. The oilcloth itself enters almost furtively: by continuing the painting over its cut edges Picasso makes it seem the background material upon which the entire painting has been done. It is hardly there in its own right; its ready-made pattern merely substitutes mechanical illusion for painter's illusion; though the material is foreign it is not yet the image-in-itself—the defiant scraps of newspaper soon to come.

Astonishingly enough, newspaper had already symbolically entered painting a full half-century before in a remarkably prescient Cézanne painting. In his early twenties, long before the canvases that forecast cubism, Cézanne painted his fa-

[5] Cf. Zervos, Vol. 1, Plate LXXXIII.

11   Picasso: *Éléments d'étude*   1914

11A   Picasso: *Femme assise . . .*   1914

ther reading the newspaper with its flag-head title *L'Événement* boldly painted (Fig. 5). If the use of lettering and newspaper was controversial in 1911, one can only judge how defiantly unorthodox it must have been in the Second Empire.

By 1912, embarked upon collage in its full sense, Braque and Picasso made heavy use of the medium until 1915. Midway in this period Juan Gris adopted the medium. Gradually the paintings of all three began imitating the typical patterns of their papiers collés, to the extent that certain paintings could almost be construed as realistic "portraits" of collages, down to painted representations of news clippings, grained papers, and patterned wallpapers. By the early 1920's the three leading cubists had virtually ceased collage work but its imprint remained permanently in their painting. Long before this, however, they had firmly established collage

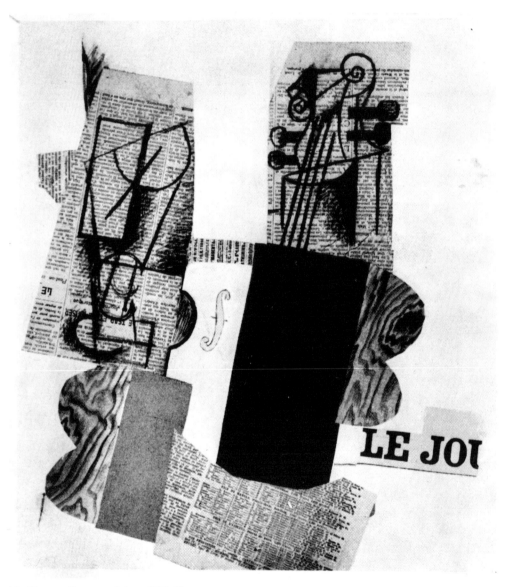

12 Picasso: *Verre et violon* 1912–13

as a separate medium; between them had stylistically formulated what is now called "classic collage"; and had prophetically experimented with many techniques and materials.

Of the three, Braque was primarily the stylist, Picasso the experimentalist, Gris the one of romantic vision. James Thrall Soby writes: "It was Braque's distinction to have arrived quickly at an integrated solution of collage's abstract possibilities." Soby contrasts "the temperamental differences between Braque and Picasso" in terms of the former's "serene calculation" and "exceptionally pure formal order," and the latter's "intuitive willful search for a new plasticity." Then he observes: "The drawing in Picasso's pictures is more energetic and inventive than in Braque's . . . and we sense beneath it a pressure of humanistic subject. . . ." Soby points out that Gris created independently, "owing nothing intrinsic either to Picasso or Braque, but affirming a distinct and valid personality . . ." Finally, "all three cubists," Soby observes, "used collage with the utmost seriousness. They did not use it . . . as a stage in the development of more ambitious works as is sometimes claimed."[6]

The actual works confirm Soby's judgments. After the initial prototypal collages, Picasso's innovations far exceed those of Braque. The latter confined most of his work to classic papier collé with corrugated packing board the most unorthodox material. On the other hand, during 1912–14, Picasso made at least 15 relief constructions with wood, paper, cardboard, and tin; several polychromed objects of tin as well as bronze; and miscellaneous collages containing sand, cloth, and other foreign materials —all of this in addition to at least 70 papier collés of the classic type and a number of paintings that incorporate collaged paper. Gris meanwhile, by his characteristically warm use of bottle labels, newspapers, and patterned papers suggesting interiors, was evoking a vivid nostalgia of time and place.

It was in this period that the new medium received the general name "collage" and the more specific one "papier collé." Both names indicate the way collage began: with pasted paper. Since then many terms have come into use designating special methods. If the paper is cut, for example, we have *découpage*; if it is torn we have *déchirage*. As the collage idea expanded the list grew, until today it forms a lengthy list. An up-to-date glossary will be found at the end of the book.

The word collage is derived from *coller* (to paste or glue) and means pasting and, by extension, that which is pasted. The name, like the pictures, had carried a shock, the word collage having the slang meaning of an illicit love affair, which must have delighted Braque and Picasso with its inferences of shameful cohabitation between nobly born oil paint and the streetwalker newspaper. Beyond this, the past participle *collé* (pasted or glued) used as slang means faked or pretended.

Of all the paper used in collage, newspaper in that day was the most shocking —the nose thumbed at art history and the conventional mind. Behind the shock was wit: first in the basic form of disparates coupled in surprising and revealing combinations, and second, the use of newspaper clippings as verbal or visual puns. Even the casual eye finds visual puns: a corrugated-paper clarinet (Fig. 21) or the torso-to-hips curve of a cutout-paper guitar (Fig. 18) .[7]

Part of the humor of verbal puns derived from newspaper copy came from a contradiction: cubist theory used

---

[6] Soby, James Thrall, *Modern Art and the New Past*. Norman, University of Oklahoma Press, 1957.

[7] Both Picasso and Braque exploited the feminine shape of violin and guitar. Gris said: "In the guitar Braque has found the new Madonna."

13 Picasso: *Journal et violon* 1912–13

14 Braque: *The Clarinet* 1913

pieces of newspaper as abstract elements but like postcards they of course were doomed to be read by everyone. The journalistic scraps in cubist collages indicate events, places, and even date or sign unsigned, undated pictures. In the 1913 *Journal et violon* (Fig. 13), Picasso trimmed the heading of *Le Journal* down to the exclamation *E Joi,* above a news item reporting that a chauffeur had killed his wife. "Oh, joy!" exclaims Picasso. In *The Clarinet* (Fig. 14) by Braque the clarinet makes a visible echo, excised from the flag-head of *L'Echo d'Avignon.* By the use of his shears Gris signed the collage *Breakfast* (Fig. 15) with his surname excised from a subhead in the ever useful *Journal.* In another collage (Fig. 16) Gris lets the clipped words *Le vrai et le faux* point up the extraordinarily equivocal vibration between reality and illusion inherent in collage.

In fact, besides functioning in the abstract plastic structure, collaged paper may be said to function in a visual play that expresses the paradox between the true and the false in a way that pure painting cannot, and this extends expression to fit the vast complexities of the modern world. In one collage, Picasso's *Tête d'homme au chapeau* (Fig. 17), this counterpoint of ideas includes not only true and false but also the metamorphosis of one reality into another. A newspaper rectangle forms the lighted side of the face, plain dark paper the shadowed side, and the curve of a guitar side becomes the facial contour.

An early virtuoso demonstration of the manifold possibilities of collage is the 1913 Picasso *Guitar* (Fig. 18), which

23

15 Gris: *Breakfast* 1914

consists of papiers collés with crayon drawing. Dark patterned wallpaper forms the shadow half of the guitar, pure white paper the light side, and newspaper the sound hole. The two halves are split and forced out of alignment by the cubist analysis derived from the light-refraction distortions Cézanne had employed. The white half of the guitar casts its shadow in gray paper, transformed from feminine curves to geometric squareness. All of this play with form constitutes what are essentially visual-constructive elements. The play of meanings is another thing. The guitar halves, as previously mentioned, refer to the female torso; in this case the white half is nude, the other is encased in a tight-fitting lace undergarment by virtue of the wallpaper pattern and the power of wallpaper to suggest concomitantly a domestic interior.

We are already far past what pure painting could suggest, yet by pasting in a piece of Barcelona newsprint Picasso could leap to another meaning still. The flag-head fragment *DILUV* is a phonetic equivalent of *du Louvre*. To artists of that day the Louvre was literally a place of the dead since no artist's work could appear there until twenty years after his death.

The violent shock has faded from cubist collage and a kind of mellow beauty has taken its place—a measure of the revolution in seeing that it helped to win. Today it is classic in every sense, yet has not become dated as its newspaper clippings have. It constantly yields new meanings. Its principles and patterns are constantly being discovered by new generations of artists. Its drama of *vrai et faux* is the eternal drama engaging the generations. Georges Braque was clear about this. He knew that the bits of glued paper and imitation wood were compositional facts. But, he said, illusions too "are simple facts, but they have been created by the mind, by the spirit, and they are one of the justifications of the new spatial configuration."[8]

[8] Quoted in Maurice Raynal, *Modern French Painters.* Translated by Ralph Roeder. New York, Brentano's, 1928.

16 Gris: *Still Life* 1914

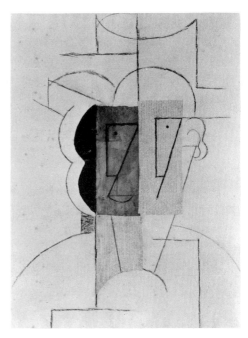

17 Picasso: *Tête d'homme au chapeau* 1912–13

18 Picasso: *Guitar* 1913

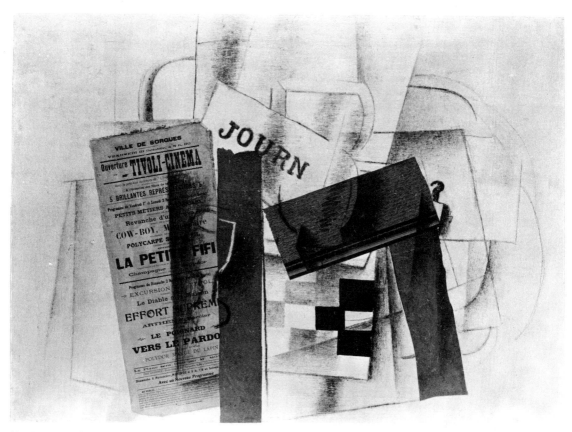

19   Braque: *The Program*   1913

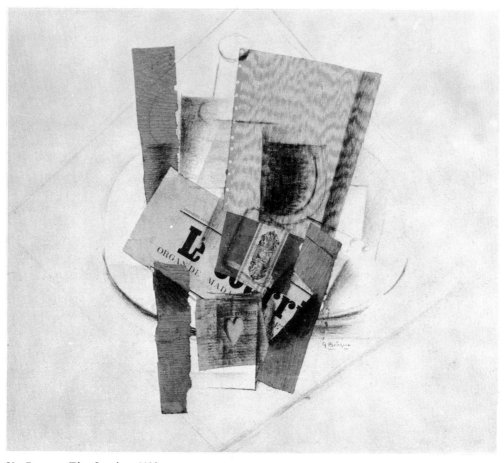

20   Braque: *The Courier*   1913

21 Braque: *Musical Forms* 1918

28

22 Braque: *Guitar* 1913–14

23 Braque: *Le Quotidien* 1913–14

24 Picasso: *Still Life with Guitar* 1913

25   Picasso: *Glass and Bottle of Bass*   1913

26   Picasso: *Glass and Bottle of Suze*   1913

27 Gris: *Collage* 1914

28   Gris: *The Marble Console*   1914

29   Gris: *La bouteille d'anis del Mono*   1914

30 Gris: *Man in Café* 1914

31   Laurens: *Head of a Woman*   1916

32   Robert Delaunay: *Drame politique*   1914

33   Sonia Delaunay: *Prisme solaire* . . .   1914

34   Carra: *Manifestazione Interventista*   1914

4

FUTURISM AND COLLAGE

COMPRESSION: CENTRIPETAL

SOUND

DYNAMISM

ELASTICITY

STATES OF MIND

TRANSPOSITION OF THE ARTIST OR SPECTATOR

DENSITY OF ATMOSPHERE

DYNAMICS OF LIGHT

LINES OF FORCE

SMELL[1]

Once cubism initiated collage other art movements began to utilize it. Among the earliest to do so was futurism, the Italian movement that was cubism's chief rival from 1909 to 1914. Though it faded then, true to its name it prophesied some of the most striking developments after mid-century.

While cubism confined itself to plastic art, futurism spreadeagled the arts— painting, sculpture, architecture, literature, music, and drama—meanwhile casting a Machiavellian weather eye toward government. Futurists were supposed to blend art and life, to make art as important as science and politics. There has never been an art movement more grandiose and visionary, more wildly optimistic. To achieve painting that would involve all humanity, the futurists aimed to capture in paint all of the following qualities or states:

SPEED

SIMULTANEITY

KINETIC CONTINUITY

INTERPENETRATION OF PLANES AND OF SOLIDS

PLASTIC EXPANSION: CENTRIFUGAL

The futurists' gods were the racing car and the airplane; in their remarkable cosmos speed was a physical entity through which the unseen could be graphically illustrated. They claimed that total 360° vision was possible; they discovered a new "motion"—that of stationary objects; they described lines of force emanating from objects and forming "continuities in space" beyond them; they argued for a dynamism that was universal energy, physical and metaphysical, that was in essence life itself "in its infinite, uninterrupted becoming."[2] They proposed concepts even more abstruse and difficult.

Futurism was a blend of the real and the visionary, the practical and the impractical. Though its reach exceeded its grasp, in art vision is more important than feasibility and the sheer energy of intense obsessive desire can sometimes stretch unstretchable limits. For this is

[1] From exhibition catalogue: *Futurism*. March 22–May 1, 1954, Sidney Janis Gallery, New York.

[2] Umberto Boccioni in the pro-futurist periodical *Lacerba*, Florence, January 1, 1914. Quoted and translated by Rosa Trillo Clough in *Looking Back at Futurism*, New York, 1942.

a century when the wildest imagination need only wait for events. Take, for example, the futurists' concept of illustrating the unseen through speed, and then consider the revolutionary electronic microscope of today which photographs not atomic particles but their orbits. Einstein himself postulated lines of force as an invisible grid throughout the universe upon which travel at the speed of light may some day be possible. As for universal energy, science in its own terms has long since confirmed the futurists' poetic prophecy of "dynamism."

Among their esthetic concepts, that of the relationship of artist and public to the picture was probably the most revolutionary. Rejecting the traditional idea of a picture as fixed upon a "predetermined . . . surface placed before

us," the futurist leader Umberto Boccioni formulated the concept of the picture as "a radiating structure whose center is the artist and not the object."[3] The artist was not to be alone, however; in 1909, in their first manifesto, the futurists had already declared their intention to transport the spectator from the periphery into the center of the picture, "which reaches out explosively towards the edge of the canvas as it attempts to contain all the strands of natural and human life."

It was impossible for them: the futurists failed to make pictures that were environments. Yet today the idea is suddenly vital and all over the world artist groups have given up painting and are creating environments that "attempt to contain all the strands of natural and human life." It took almost exactly a half-century for this futurist idea to come to fruition.

To interpret motion, dynamism, and light, as well as emotions and states of mind, the futurists derived visual imagery from the machine. In a sense they mechanized man, e.g., Boccioni's *Dynamism of a Football Player;* and humanized the machine, e.g., Carra's *What the Streetcar Told Me.* Thus futurist paintings in general tend to a more mechanistic appearance than those of the cubists. And machine forms, rhythms, and sounds, form a large proportion of futurist subject matter. It seems fair to say that futurism was the first movement to embrace the machine esthetic.

All of this is apparent in a thoroughly futurist collage like Carra's *Manifestazione Interventista* of 1914 (Fig. 34) with its violent, dynamic, centrifugal expansion to edges of the picture in lines that to futurist eyes would continue out into space. Here is the "periphery whose center we occupy,"[4] and, equally,

35 Carra: *Bottle* 1914

[3] *Ibid.*
[4] Boccioni, Umberto, *Pittura scultura futurista.* Translated by Rosa Trillo Clough. Milan, 1914.

36 Balla: *Forza e volumi* 1914

the "expanding image" of American abstract-expressionist painting from the mid-1940's on. The *Manifestazione* is more explosion than structure, originating below center with the *sole bruciaticcio*—the "scorching sun" where dynamism originates in heat, light, and movement.

The imperious din of modern life—not the wit and innuendo of the cubists—is in the hurtling traffic streams of lettering: dogma, slogans, and verbalizations (as in futurist poetry)—EEEE, EVVIVAAA, TRRRRRR, O/oo/O/oo—of the high-pitched mechanical sonics of the city. Futurist preoccupations appear in various phrases: the modernization of Italy, *città moderne*—"the modern city"; the electric light, *taie volontà di Edison*—"by the will of Edison"; science, *cos-*

tellazioni per nuovi piu acuti astronomi—"new constellations from a more exact astronomy." There is still more in this pictorial futurist manifesto: technical means, *incidente*—"chance," and *accidente*—"accident"; cockcrow defiance by argumentative, assertive, gifted young artists, *noi siamo primo*—"we are first"; excited plaudits of the crowd, *folle eccitato;* a visual furore of noisy salutes to friends, relatives, sweethearts, a friendly Milan newspaper, bicycles, the *Piazza;* and at the bottom the signature *Carra, leggiero, duraturo, FUTurista*—the strong and lighthearted!

For all its packed symbolism, the *Manifestazione* by no means comprises futurist expression in collage. There are striking differences between the work of the futurists, Carra, Boccioni, Seve-

37 Severini: *Blue Dancer* 1912

rini, Balla, Prampolini, Soffici, and Rosai.

Carlo Carra was not limited to a rigid rays-of-light composition. He expressed centrifugal force quite differently, for example, in the collage *Bottle* (Fig. 35), where the bottom of the bottle operates as the "sun" but the diagonals are shuffled into tilting thrusts operating in a deep chiaroscuro that shuffles them back and forth in space.

Giacomo Balla, by contrast, employs scrolls, arcs, and segmental curves with curved and straight diagonals to express planar and volumetric developments in space as in the 1914 collage, *Forza e Volumi*, "Force and Volumes" (Fig. 36).

Gino Severini celebrated a lighter side of life than racing cars, machinery, and rising cities. His 1912 *Blue Dancer* (Fig. 37), a painting collaged with blue sequins, is a version of a recurrent Severini theme: the dynamism of a dancer in motion. A later collage, *Still Life with Bottle and Playing Cards* (Fig. 38), celebrates chianti, café, and cards. In between these extremes Severini painted prismatic pointillist oils portraying the

40

expansion and contraction of light. In a similarly light and cheerful vein Enrico Prampolini often employed nontechnological materials like lace and feathers, ostrich plumes and plaited straw. Prampolini also employed plain-colored papers in cartoon-collages for the weaving of tapestries, as in the oval *Still Life No. 13* (Fig. 39).

At the opposite extreme in materials and plastic organization are certain early collages by Ottone Rosai that are like fragments of paper whirling in the wind of the streets. *Composition d'une rue* (Fig. 40), for example, is like a prophecy of the great dada collagist Kurt Schwitters, who wove forlorn, discarded things into evocative visual poems.

Ardengo Soffici's subject matter often paralleled the cubists'—wine bottle, glass, and newspaper—as in the *Natura morta con piccola velocità* (Fig. 41) of papiers collés with gouache.

Gifted leader of futurism's painters and sculptors as well as one of its most influential theorists and polemicists was Umberto Boccioni. His paintings—like *The City Rises, Elasticity,* and *Dynamism of a Football Player*—are energized by charged dynamics combining straight lines and curves to express futurist continuities of energy and moving mass in space. His complex visual counterpoint interweaves paths of physical movement, ratiocination, and psychological states. In paintings like the 1911 series devoted to states of mind (*Those Who Say Farewell, Those Who Stay,* and others), Boccioni attempted to express climates of emotion. Though his success in this was at best inconclusive, nevertheless since Boccioni was first and last a significantly creative artist the paintings are superb in themselves.

His highly personal organization of forms—trailing and tattered, sharp and explosive—calls for real space and thus comes to full realization in the bronze sculptures in-the-round so strongly stamped with his autonomous personal-

38 Severini: *Still Life with Bottle and Playing Cards* 1917

ity that their authorship is unmistakable. Boccioni furnished a list of sculptor's materials remarkably prescient of inclusions to come in collage, including some that would not be employed until the advent of so-called neo-dada in the late 1950's. Boccioni sanctioned wood, cement, cardboard, iron, copper, mirrors, cloth, as well as electric bulbs and other unorthodox materials.

Boccioni had implemented his words in advance in a 1911 sculpture, *Fusion of a Head and a Window,* in which he placed a plaster head on an actual window frame, fixing real locks of human hair to the head. Not only was this one of the earliest uses of "ready-made" materials, but it prophesied the surrealist

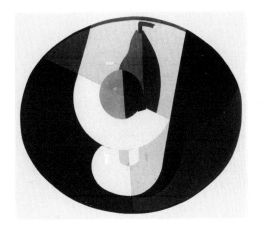

39 Prampolini: *Still Life: Tapestry Design*

41

40 Rosai: *Composition d'une rue* 1914

object of the 1930's and the mid-century "combine–paintings" of the American artist Robert Rauschenberg, who interweaves painting with stuffed birds and animals and many discarded objects.

Others began to put these materials to work. The cubist sculptor Alexander Archipenko—though not given to writing manifestoes—was both adventurous and imaginative. His remarkable figure construction, the 1912 *Medrano I,* of polychrome glass, wood, and metal wire, says Alfred Barr, "put into practice that defiance of traditional materials recommended by Boccioni in his Futurist Sculpture Manifesto of April 1912."[5]

A half-century has proved the validity of the anti-art materials recommended by Boccioni in his search for his "unique continuities." The incongruous, the *outré,* the discarded, the mundane or trivial, these do indeed form "unique continuities" with our heedless, swift-changing, wasteful times. They are true symbols of our century, found and recognized by the intuitive flash of prophetic vision. Durable ephemerae, they leaped

[5] Barr, Alfred H., Jr., *Cubism and Abstract Art.* New York, Museum of Modern Art, 1936.

across disruptive war years to form the disillusioned core of dada, and now in our time have become so realistically specific that they could not conceivably refer to any other period in man's history. Anti-art, in an anti-art time, becomes art.

It is strange that Boccioni's collages are less adventuresome than the other work of this adventurous artist. *Still Life*: *Glass and Siphon* (Fig. 42) is typical, essentially a painting-drawing executed on a background of papiers collés —newspaper, a bit of a futurist manifesto, scraps of envelope lining paper. As a painting, however, its "lines of force" work on powerful diagonals that remind us of Carra's statement that the acute angle is "passionate and reveals volition and aggressive onslaught."[6]

Prophetic as they were, the futurists were too early to be pacifists when war came. In Nietzschean fashion they glorified armed combat. Boccioni's 1915 collage, *La Guerre* (*Charge of the Lancers*) (Fig. 43), is painted over frag-

[6] From *Lacerba,* I. Florence, January, 1913.

41 Soffici: *Natura Morta con piccola velocità* 1914

ments of battle communiqués. No overtones linger here of the trivial or discarded: the bits of newspaper assume grim, explicit factuality. All the futurist philosophical abstractions, conceived by young and enthusiastic men to portray benign universals—lines of force, dynamism of light, "life's uninterrupted becoming"—suddenly become savage, angry, ruthless. The lines of force have become bayonets; the dynamism, destruction; the tattered fragments that once in Boccioni's sculpture trailed a kind of spiritual glory, battle flags and galloping horses. Boccioni is now serving in his country's cavalry.

A year later he was violently dead. Soon, the cubist sculptor Raymond Duchamp-Villon and the poet-doctrinaire Guillaume Apollinaire followed. With or without their loss, however, war had cleft an immeasurable, final gulf athwart those years, separating two epochs forever. The wonderful, reckless, fruitful, unshadowed time was gone.

After the war cubism went on, integrated into the work of its great masters. Cubist painting and especially cubist collage were formative influences in most modern art into the late 1930's.

42 Boccioni: *Still Life* 1912–13

43 Boccioni: *La guerre* (*Charge of the Lancers*) 1915

Futurism picked itself up, went into a second period. But something had been lost—perhaps the fresh enthusiasm, perhaps the prophetic vision. Only the recklessness survived, flamboyant and pointless now without the other two. Futurism had had its short day. Or so it seemed.

Another world war came and after it another epoch with different esthetic ideals—first abstract—expressionism and then an art dealing with action in a space that engulfs both artist and audience. For those with the long view there is something vaguely, nostalgically familiar about the enthusiastic, gifted young men who today boldly and confidently discard all painting—even the cubist masterpieces—to create their continuities of object and thought in space and time. It is art and talk that Umberto Boccioni would have understood. Perhaps this is the future that, fifty years and two world wars ago, the futurists were saluting.

5

DADA AND COLLAGE

In 1916 at Zurich a French dictionary was opened and a finger blindly placed upon a page. The fingertip landed on a word. Someone read it aloud: an onomatopoetic child's word meaning hobbyhorse. Through this tongue-in-cheek sortilege a name was found for the first art movement of international locale, one that sprang up spontaneously in a number of cities in both hemispheres. The word of course was "dada," and it designates the strangest and for a long time least understood of all modern art movements.

Dada on the surface was a carnival of wild nonsense. Seemingly scores of artists of secure international reputation had suddenly gone mad. It was a shameless, shocking public vaudeville of exhibitionist acts, from mild "happenings" like three poets simultaneously reading three gibberish "poems" and artists with stovepipes for hats acting out nonsense plays, to unsettling events like stirring up an audience to the cataclysmic din of "Protest Noise," rudely flagrant acts

like a dada lecturer publicly disrobing while shouting obscenities, or the notorious exhibition in Cologne that could be entered only through the men's toilet.

No wonder an affronted public called the dadas madmen. The artists returned the epithet. Actually their actions concealed the despair of highly intelligent human beings. With dada, Breton observes that "the attack on the past became far less platonic. An attitude of disrespect became universal, the negation of previous values was complete. . . . The despair that prevailed could

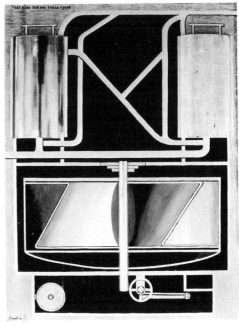

44   Picabia: *Very Rare Picture Upon the Earth*
1915

45 Arp: *Collage* 1915

46 Arp: *Collage with Squares Arranged According to the Laws of Chance* 1916–17

only be overcome by a kind of dismal jesting, a 'black humor.' "[1]

Dada was not merely anti-art. As if heeding the futurist call to political action, the dadas were anti-society, violently opposed to a materialist culture that could unleash the bloodiest and most destructive war in man's history. Anti-art, the cubist and futurist weapon, extends as an iconoclastic symptom back into the 1890's—implicit in Lautrec, the gross deliberate brutishness of Alfred Jarry's *Ubu,* and the sadly derisive disillusion of Satie's little piano *morceaux.* Anti-art had been a reaction, the rebellion against art's uselessness in a Philistine society. With dada it became not apology but accusation. The *épater le bourgeois* is the slap that answers the slap. Society had arrogantly slapped the artist: "We deal in important things—manufacture, banking, munitions, war. Art is only entertainment. Entertain us."

[1] Breton, André, *Art of This Century,* catalogue of the Peggy Guggenheim Collection, New York, 1942.

Dada slapped back: "You are useless and worse, destructive. *We* are not entertained." Then it lashed out with its "black humor" at the criminal cruelty it saw everywhere.

The dadas could hardly have known that by destroying they were building—a function no creative artist can escape. Nor could they have foreseen that society would triumph anyway—when collectors would begin avidly collecting a dada art they scarcely understood. It is materialist society, not the artist, that is essentially anti-art.

Dada was forecast before 1914 in the proto-dada work of Marcel Duchamp and Francis Picabia in Paris. Picabia's satiric machine paintings are in the dada spirit even to their titles, like that of the

47 Arp: *Collage*

48 Duchamp: *Tu M'* 1918

grotesque machine called *Daughter Born Without a Mother*. Duchamp is an artist who has lived the dada role: an international celebrity at twenty-six through the *succès de scandale* of his *Nude Descending a Staircase* at the 1913 Armory Show in New York, he was already rejecting painting in the decisive anti-art gesture of ready-made art, signed by the artist. His ready-mades began that same year with a bicycle wheel and in 1917 they would reach a sardonic climax in the urinal labeled *Fountain* that he submitted to the Independent Show in New York.

The *Bicycle Wheel*—a plain wire wheel mounted on a wooden stool—received belated recognition in the retrospective exhibition, Dada—The Documents of a Movement, in the Düsseldorf

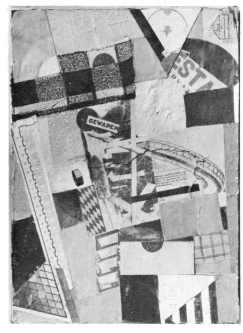

49 Van Doesburg: *Collage* 1921

50 Picabia: *Femme aux allumettes* 1920

Kunstverein in 1958. The first construction made entirely from ready-made components, it stood in the place of honor, a disarming simplicity belying its varied historic significance. (In this respect it resembled its creator.) The prototype of all mobile sculpture, whenever the attendants were not looking the gallery-goers reached out and set it spinning.

Like Calder's mobiles, the *Bicycle Wheel* is a kind of collage in space and even more truly collage in feeling, because not only are its elements brought in from the outside world but they also proclaim the new esthetic ideas that were explicitly announced by collage. Beyond all this, Duchamp's *Bicycle Wheel* forecasts the mid-century sculpture that assembles discarded machine parts.

Duchamp and Picabia were not men to don uniforms with the futurists' qualmless ease. By 1915 they were in New York, avowed antiwar expatriates. A similar group had gathered in Zurich in neutral Switzerland. An unexampled four decades of peace having only led into senseless war, all were now ready to unleash a potent fulmination of bitter disillusion. Dada was born. It was destructive of all established values: social, political, and esthetic.

Jean Arp, a leader of Zurich dada, has written, "Disinterested as we were in the slaughterhouses of the world war, we gave ourselves to the fine arts. While the cannon rumbled in the distance, we pasted, recited, versified, we sang with all our soul." To society, deep in the irresponsible deadly business of its self-destruction, this could only seem the irresponsible idle play of useless artists. Play, yes—but neither idle nor irresponsible, the kind of play, rather, that tries the conscience.

Mme. Gabrielle Buffet-Picabia observed that "the atmosphere of New York during the years 1915–18 was heavily charged as the result of the un-usual gathering together of individuals of all nationalities . . . an exceptionally favorable climate for the development of a certain revolutionary spirit in the domain of the arts and letters which, later on, became crystallized in Europe under the name of *Dada*. . . . It was destined to go beyond the limits of esthetics, to grow venomous and charged with blasphemy and harshness. . . . It was to manifest itself with unforeseen violence, [a] systematic plan of disturbance and demoralisation [that] assailed . . . all commonplaces, all collective and official hypocrisies."[2]

Duchamp and Picabia immediately attracted a small group of artists who shortly became the New York dada cell: painters Jean Crotti and Morton Schamberg, painter-photographer Man Ray,

[2] Buffet-Picabia, Gabrielle, article in *Transition*, No. 27, April-May, 1938.

51 Baargeld-Ernst: *The Red King* 1920

52 Suzanne Duchamp: *Radiance of Two Lonely Far Away Beings* 1916–18–20

poets and writers Walter Arensberg, Mina Loy, and Louise Norton (Varèse), and painter-constructionist John Covert. By this time international dada was launched on its brief, spectacular, unsettling history. America soon lost interest in it as we enthusiastically plunged into our first international war. Elsewhere it was a thorn in society's side. Before the war was barely over it is recorded that 8590 shocked articles about dada had already appeared in more than 50 cities throughout the world. It flourished in Zurich with a large group that included artists and sculptors Arp, Janco, Van Rees, Hans Richter, Sophie Taeuber (Arp), futurist Prampolini, photographer Schad, and literary figures Tristan Tzara, Hugo Ball, Huelsenbeck, and Serner. Bitterly iconoclastic, strongly antisocial, they kept Zurich's Cabaret Voltaire aboil with collage and painting, poetry and drama, ballet, and satiric photography.

Berlin dada, no less antisocial, was also boldly and subversively political. Collages, cartoons, photomontages, and writings, by Baader, Citroën, George Grosz, Hausmann, Herzfelde, Hannah Höch, Huelsenbeck, and others attacked the crumbling Central European military monarchies.

Berlin dada stressed collage and developed the polemical use of documentary photomontage. Kurt Schwitters broke with the Berlin dadas from the conviction that they overstressed political actionism. He returned to his native Hanover. There his collages which had begun as protest ended as poetry, and in the end assured him of a position as one of the greatest of all artists in the medium. Nevertheless, later events would lend irony to his rejection of the Berliners' political bent: Schwitters himself had to flee Germany because of anti-Hitler denunciations that he began interspersing with his public readings of dada poetry.

Everywhere, even in Spain, dada burned on like a fuse attached to the tail of the body politic. In Cologne from

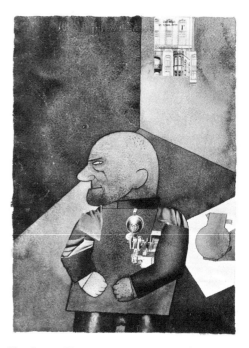

53 Grosz: *The Engineer Heartfield* 1920

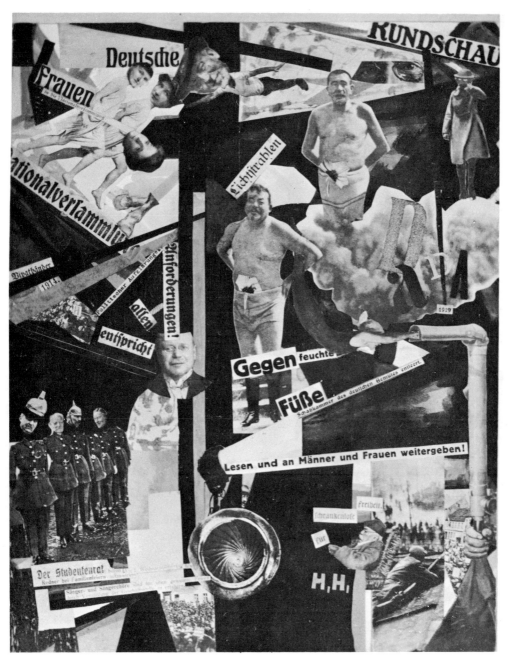

54   Höch: *Rundschau DADA*   1920

55   Man Ray: *Transatlantique*   1921

1918 to 1922, it centered around artists
Arp, Max Ernst, and Johannes Baargeld. In Hanover writer Paul Spengemann joined Schwitters. Going briefly
to the Netherlands Schwitters was joined
in local dada demonstrations by the
Dutch De Stijl leader Theo van Doesburg who took as his dada name the
pseudonym I. K. Bonset. Paris dada,
though including artists like Suzanne
Duchamp and intermittently Picabia and
Ernst, laid considerable stress on music
through composers Erik Satie and the
young American George Antheil. The
Parisians excelled at dada ballets, motion pictures, and provocative public
demonstrations. Paris dada was most
heavily weighted, however, on the literary side with a large active group including René Crevel, Ribemont-Dessaignes,

Jacques Vaché, Paul Éluard, Philippe
Soupault, Luis Aragon, André Breton,
Tristan Tzara, and others.

Beyond its protest dada was a response
to crisis. The crisis was society's loss of
valuable goals, of the unity that comes
from established moral and ethical values. Moral synthesis is the answer to
this loss. For the cubists the crisis was
only one of art, an unthreatening drama
in a studio. Cubists expressed synthesis
in the esthetic idea of simultaneity: a
still life seen from all sides as the artist,
calmly puffing his pipe, moved unhur-
riedly around it. The cubists however
were far from unaware of the world.
By initiating collage, they made the first
rapprochement between the two worlds,
art and reality.

Nevertheless, the futurists sensed
more keenly the overtones of their time:
anxiety and menace. Urgent dynamism
entered their work; real life strove to
enter their pictures; studio broadened
out into world; simultaneity now meant
interpenetration of artist with public,
picture with environment.

War made the futurist ideas suddenly
and frighteningly real. It was already
too late: crisis had become catastrophe.
Society stood exposed: a lunatic fabric
of lofty ideals—justice, goodness, beauty
—woven together with absurd irrationalities and the manias of destruction.

So dada's synthesis was to exorcise
madness with madness, to weave a
matching lunatic fabric of unrelated, incongruous, contradictory materials,
ideas, and concepts—an *Absurdum ad
Absurdum Reductio.*

This was an art to which collage was
completely apposite. The cutting, gluing, and patching together of a hundred
disparate fragments into a new unity was
exactly the technique by which to weave
a meaningful fabric out of madness. We
can say that *all* dada activity was in a
sense collage, and even dada as a whole,
with its patchwork of centers—New
York, Berlin, Cologne, Zurich, Paris, and

56 Citroën: *Metropolis* 1923

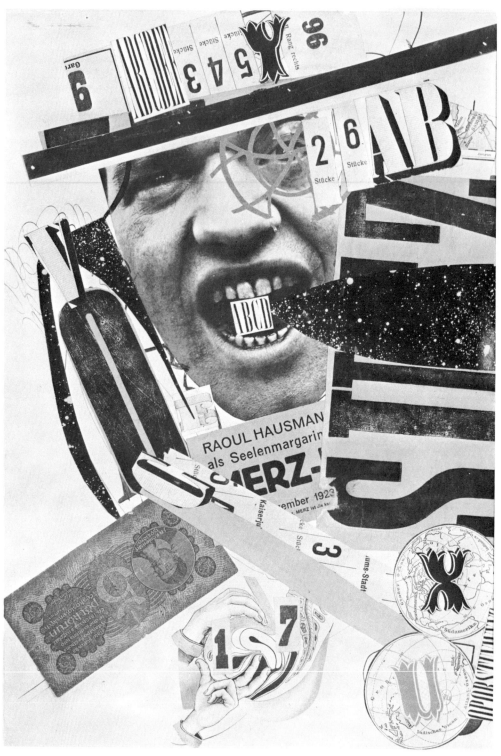

57   Hausmann: *Fotomontage*   1923

58   Arp: *Plate, Fork and Navel*   1923

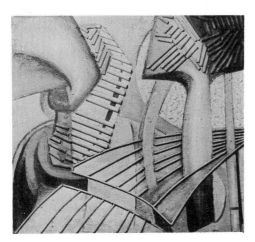

59   Covert: *Vocalization*   1919

60   Dove: *Monkey Fur*   1926

the rest—a collage like that of cities cut from a map. This comes close to being the basic dada art form, this spontaneous, simultaneous, knowing madness: poems chanted simultaneously; noise-music discordantly collaging unrelated sounds; the pooling of efforts, from the wild charades in stovepipe hats on to the *Fatagaga* collages made by Arp and Max Ernst together; the supreme simultaneity of this wild chaos of individual anarchies patched and pasted together by the amazing acquiescence in group activity.

Tristan Tzara once wrote a poem telling how to write a poem by making a collage:

To make a dadaist poem
Take a newspaper.
Take a pair of scissors.
Choose an article as long as you are planning
    to make your poem.
Cut out the article.
Then cut out each of the words that make
    up this article and put them in a bag.
Shake it gently.
Then take out the scraps one after the other
    in the order in which they left the bag.
Copy conscientiously.
The poem will be like you . . .[3]

Concealed within dada's impetuous spontaneities was a strong and realistic intellectualism. Ideas were "clipped" at seeming random from the unconscious and "pasted" together with the adhesive of an apposite illogic. With dada itself a kind of collage, it is not surprising that the movement developed two major collage artists, Schwitters and Ernst. To each of these we will devote a separate chapter.

Dada's nihilism included the idea of its own self-destruction. By 1922 it had run its brief, shattering course and Breton, with surrealism in mind, was busy picking up the fragments. As an art movement dada was uncompleted; as a philosophy its ideas have remained germane.

Dada's idea of destruction, for example, runs parallel to the suicidal idea implicit in materialist machine technology. This dada allusion, that had begun with Duchamp and Picabia, became explicit a third of a century after dada's demise. On a cold, rainy March day in 1960, in the sculpture garden of the Museum of Modern Art, a great protest machine called *Homage to New York* (Fig. 61), designed to make music and create paintings, destroyed itself according to plan. A player piano plunked three notes over and over, while mechanical drums beat an idiotic rhythm; a weather balloon made unheeded weather reports; a drawing machine drew Chinese mountains; empty Coca-Cola bottles rolled endlessly down a rack to smash into bits; typed reports about nothing issued from within while another part of the machinery simply flapped aimlessly. . . .

An audience of the art world elite sat and watched while Jean Tinguely's blasphemous machine exploded by script, burst into orange flame, and destroyed itself. The veteran dada Huelsenbeck stood in a puddle of rain, watching. Someone said, "It's the end of civilization as we know it." Someone else said, "This is like an unfinished nightmare."[4] Dada's durability, hinted at by Huelsenbeck's presence, was confirmed by the attendance of dada's giant, Marcel Duchamp. Duchamp evolved in celebration a fantastic punning sentence that whirred like Tinguely's machine: *"Si la scie scie la scie et si la scie qui scie la scie est la scie que scie la scie il y a un suissscide métallique."* Duchamp watched the proceedings with an equanimity touched perhaps by boredom. Half a century before he had had the

[3] Tzara, Tristan, *Sept manifestes dada. Quelques dessins de Francis Picabia.* Paris, Jean Budry & Co., 1924. Translated by Ralph Manheim in *Dada Painters and Poets,* edited by Robert Motherwell. New York, Wittenborn, Schultz, Inc., 1951.

[4] Reported by Dore Ashton in *Arts and Architecture,* May, 1960.

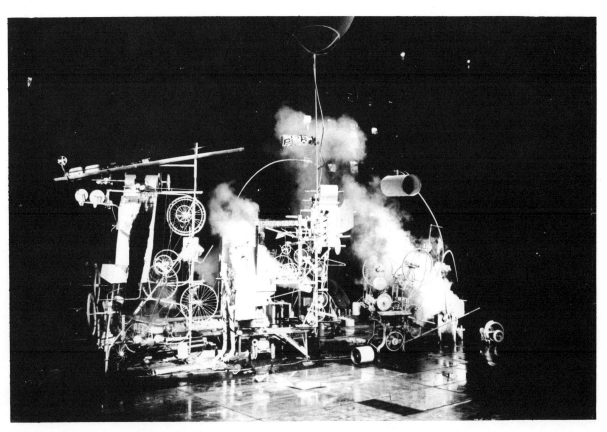

61 Tinguely: *Homage to New York*   March, 1960

horrid vision, had glimpsed the mechanized apocalypse of the machine society destroying itself.

The theme was real; it was in the air. A few months later an opera, *Amara,* premiering at the Royal Opera in Stockholm, sounded it at least as eerily. The scene: a spaceship rushing to Mars with 8000 émigrés fleeing the radiation-poisoned earth; its heroine, Mima, a calculating machine equipped with a soul and a conscience. Mima sang "her" lead-ing role, *Life* magazine said, in "weird electronic harmonies and snatches of human speech recorded on tape."[5] Shooting stars deflected the rocket; Mima expired; and then came the endless ending: a macabre *Outward Bound* with no Heaven or Hell ahead awaiting a spaceship going "on forever with a cargo of corpses."

Undeniably, the world is catching up with Marcel Duchamp's vision.

5 *Life* magazine, March 3, 1961.

6

KURT SCHWITTERS

With Kurt Schwitters, poet, painter, and sculptor, collage at last developed into an art medium important enough in its own right to stand alongside painting. In the twenty-nine years of his activity in the medium—from 1919 until his death in 1948—Schwitters produced a vast quantity of collages that in style, variety, method, materials, and expressive bent, all but pre-empt the field creatively. Even today in the midst of an unparalleled interest and activity in collage there is scarcely a material, manner, or meaning that Schwitters did not either invent or prophesy.

It has been said of him that if the dada movement had never happened, he would have been a dada anyway. Born in Hanover, Germany, in 1887, Schwitters belonged to that first artistic generation that bridged the great gulf between nineteenth-century academism and the modern idea, drawing strength equally from rejection of older modes and exploration in new and unknown ones. Like Picasso, Braque, and Matisse, Schwitters began with traditional art training. He studied until 1914 at the Dresden Academy. As early as 1918, however, an exhibition in Berlin traced his precipitate development—almost a leap —from ultraconservative representationalism to complete nonobjective abstraction.

Almost immediately thereafter Schwitters found his medium, in fact his own personal idiom, in collage. He began collecting from sidewalk, dustbins, wastebaskets, and trash heaps, all their dusty, tattered, castoff materials to paste into the extraordinary little pictures upon which his towering present reputation so securely rests. Granted that these mun-

62 Kurt Schwitters 1927

Schwitters: *Merzbau*

dane fragments can be transmuted through poetry and pure invention into important art works—and the smallest Schwitters collage, scarcely larger than a postage stamp, proves that they can[1]— then a mere cataloguing of the castoffs he retrieved from the streets will show what an amazing variety of new materials he used, many of them for the first time in modern art:

stickers, stamps, bus transfers, corrugated paper, torn paper, cut paper, transparent papers, postmarks, addresses from envelopes, commercial trademarks and slogans from newspapers and packages, numbers and letters from many sources, coins, cork, cloth, washers, buttons, nails, photographs in whole or in part, magazine illustrations, lithographic art work, brown paper bags, return addresses from friends and from government agencies, etc., words and phrases used for literary or autobiographical meaning, parts of words used as puns, crushed silver foil, seals, pieces of wood, rubber stamps, candy wrappers, tarred protective paper, stenciled wood from crates, subway or bus tokens, burlap, perforated tin, art papers, sealing wax, wire, mirrors, matches, wheels, wood shavings, and many other things.

It is little wonder that oil on canvas began to seem limited, stiff, and outdated to Schwitters. By 1920, a year after beginning his first work in collage, he would be writing: "When I adjust materials of different kinds to one another,

[1] Like Paul Klee, Schwitters' scale is usually small, from the exceptionally tiny and aptly named *Klein aber Mein* to "large" works the size of a sheet of typewriter paper. The usual Schwitters collage is a little smaller than a postcard although there are occasional large works, e.g., *Radiating World*, which is more than 2x3 feet. Most of these large works date from Schwitters' earliest collage period when he frequently combined oil and collage.

I have taken a step in advance of mere oil painting, for in addition to playing off color against color, line against line, form against form, etc., I play off material against material for example wood against sackcloth."[2]

Beyond a material enrichment of art, moreover, Schwitters saw in collage a liberation of the creative impulse from the last remaining shackles of orthodoxy, conformity, and hardened tradition. Though he saw collage as revolutionary, he also saw it as logical and reasonable. "Every artist," he wrote, "must be allowed to mold a picture out of nothing but blotting paper, for example, providing he is capable of molding a picture."[3]

"In fact," Schwitters wrote in another place, "I did not understand why one could not use in a picture, in the same way one uses colours made in a factory, materials such as: old tramway and 'bus' tickets, washed-up pieces of wood from the seashore, cloak-room numbers, bits of string, segments of bicycle wheels, in a few words, the whole bric-a-brac to be found lying about the lumber room or on top of a dust bin. From my standpoint, it involved a social attitude, and, on the artistic level, a personal pleasure."[4]

In this first year Schwitters had already hit upon a monosyllable without previous specific meaning which he forthwith used to designate his collage pictures. He has written:

I gave to my new manner of work, based on the use of these materials, the name of MERZ. This is the second syllable of the word KOMMERZ [commerce]. This name was born out of one of my pictures: an image on which one reads the word MERZ, cut out of the KOMMERZ UND PRIVAT-BANK advertisement and stuck among ab-

stract shapes. . . . When for the first time I exhibited these images made of paper, glue, nails, etc. . . . at the Der Sturm Gallery in Berlin, I had to find a generic name to designate these new species. My work, indeed, did not answer to the old classifications such as: Expressionism, Cubism, Futurism and all the others. Therefore I called all my pictures . . . MERZ pictures, the name of the most characteristic one. Later, I extended this denomination, first to my poetry—because I have written poems since 1917—and finally to the whole of my corresponding activities.[5]

The strange little word so like a bit of slang, and as derivable from the German word for pain, *Schmerz,* as from the cold business term, *Kommerz,* seemed to have some deep, cryptic, all-inclusive significance for Schwitters as though in one syllable it compressed many important

[5] Schwitters, Kurt. Merz in *Der Ararat,* Munich, 1921. Translated by Ralph Manheim in *Dada Painters and Poets, op. cit.*

65   Schwitters: *Merz 13-A* 1919

[2] From Schwitters' foreword to his 1920 exhibition, MERZ. Translated and quoted in *Dada Painters and Poets, op. cit.*
[3] *Ibid.*
[4] Schwitters in his magazine *Merz,* No. 20. Hanover, 1927.

66 Schwitters: *Radiating World* *c.* 1920

meanings. In the same way the word dada had wide, hidden meanings for the artists involved in that movement. In any event, Schwitters went on to say: "I myself am now called MERZ."[6] *Merz*, in short, was a way of life.

Schwitters could truthfully call his 1919–20 collages a "new species," for Schwitters was in the truest sense of the word an original. His Hanover apartment in Waldhausenstrasse became a *Merzbau* (Figs. 63, 64, 413), an incredible grotto of old lumber, weirdly molded plaster, and a dozen other materials combined into a rambling, stalactitic, uterine cavern that eventually was extended into the upper story by the simple expedient of evicting the tenant. Moholy-Nagy, artist-sculptor, theorist, and one-time Bauhaus member, and his wife Sibyl often visited the Schwitters family in the *Merzbau* den. Mme. Moholy-Nagy has related that the fantastic architecture was subdivided into plaster grottos dedicated to Schwitters' friends. She remembered an occasion when her husband discarded a worn pair of socks, Schwitters retrieved them, dipped them in plaster of Paris, and added them to the Moholy Grotto. On that same occasion their host similarly "preserved and dedicated" a brassière of Sophie Taeuber-Arp, another overnight guest.[7]

Schwitters was an unforgettable personality. Hans Richter, Zurich dada, has described him: "He was six-foot-two, with an enormous voice like a trumpet, and recited his poetry wherever he went. His acting ability was amazing." Bauhaus faculty member Xanti Schawinsky contrasted the junk-collecting proclivities of his friend with his incongruously bourgeois attire: "Kurt was always correctly,

67   Schwitters: *Merz 20-B Das Frühlingsbild*   1920

immaculately dressed: blue suit, white shirt."

Attire was no index to the contents of his luggage. On a trip with Schawinsky—Schwitters was an inveterate traveler ready to leave at any time for any place —his valise flew open while the two friends were running up the station stairs to catch a train. "People stopped," Schawinsky said, "and gathered around in amazement. Scattered all over were hundreds of scraps of paper as well as wire, tin, and other junk, also a pot of glue and a large brush." Schawinsky laughed and added: "As for the extra clothing—only one shirt."

Richter recalled that Schwitters always carried two portfolios filled with collages which he sold to all comers at a standard price of twenty marks each. These were the devalued post-World War I marks but, of course, before the extreme inflation that a little later made German currency so valueless that Schwitters might almost have picked up thousand-mark notes with the other scrap paper he found on the sidewalk. But a few dollars apiece bought pictures that

[6] *Ibid.*
[7] These reminiscences by Mme. Moholy-Nagy, as well as those following by Hans Richter, Richard Huelsenbeck, and Xanti Schawinsky are from notes made by Harriet Janis at an evening dedicated to Kurt Schwitters at the Sidney Janis Gallery, New York, October 13, 1952.

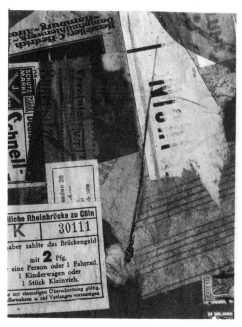

68 Schwitters: *Merz 88 Rotstrich* 1920

helped to change the course of art. Schwitters never lived to see his humble, pasted-up *Merzbilder* selling as they now do for thousands of dollars each.

They were, in fact, not an essential part of his plan of livelihood. All his life Schwitters supported himself in part by painting academic portraits, seeing nothing inconsistent or humiliating in this. On the contrary, by this choice he made a sharp even if implicit distinction between his academic "art *for* commerce" and that other "art *from* commerce," the commercial castoffs that he retrieved, poeticized, and rededicated to an art cleansed of the mundane, a ludic art pure and completely purposeless in any practical sense. *Merz*, born of *Kommerz*, was so purged of commerce, so freed from its venal origins, so transmuted in very fact, that for it eventually to become a prize commodity in a boom art market could only have struck its creator as one of dada's highest reaches in irony.

All of these things, of course, are part of the extraordinary light-into-shadow reversal of meanings by which the word *Merz* had been plucked out of the par-

64

ent word *Kommerz* in order to title a new art species. Schwitters' meanings, as well as the meaning of *Merz* as a way of life, are to be found in the reversals, behind the fact.

Kurt Schwitters operated on a creative plane so divorced from hampering practicalities that only the creative idea retained intrinsic importance. Both artist and picture were unimportant as compared with the idea creating the form. For all his dada nature, Schwitters the artist was the purest of Platonists. "The medium," Schwitters wrote, "is as unimportant as I myself. Essential is only the forming."[8] Art at this level is comparable with pure philosophy, pure science.

Still, the materials had to be gathered. Not all were bits of ownerless flotsam retrieved from sidewalk and ashcan. Richter recalled one instance at least when, he said, Schwitters, using "artist's license," had availed himself of a piece of public property:

Kurt was at the very back ·of a streetcar. He was standing with his hands behind him. Accustomed as I was to his peculiarities, I was nevertheless curious as to why he kept wriggling so. He looked like a shimmy dancer. Suddenly he leaped off the car at a stop. I followed. After the car had gone on, he showed me a sign, "*Rauchen verboten,*" which he had removed from the car with a small screwdriver he always carried. Nothing could stop the man once he wanted some piece of material for his work.

Schwitters made no strong distinctions between his various media—collage, painting, sculpture, constructions, architecture—and his literary efforts: all were *Merz*.

Schwitters wrote many poems. Moholy-Nagy was a great admirer of them, calling them "verbal collages" and defining his work as "an outburst of subconscious pandemonium." Moholy-Nagy has described a public performance of 1924:

[8] In *Merz*, No. 20. Hanover, 1927.

69   Schwitters: *Merz 312 MÜDE*   1921

70 Schwitters: *Schwimmt Merz 14-C* 1921

. . . he showed to the audience a poem containing only one letter on a sheet:

Then he started to "recite" it with slowly rising voice. The consonant varied from a whisper to the sound of a wailing siren till at the end he barked with a shockingly loud tone. This was his answer not alone to the social situation but also to the degrading "cherry-mouthed," "raven-haired," "babbling-brook," poetry.[9]

As always with Schwitters, behind the bare fact lay the reversal or the double meaning. Here it lay in the circumstance that the German name for W, *doppel weh* also means "double sorrow."

[9] Moholy-Nagy, László. A letter quoted in *The Dada Painters and Poets, op. cit.*

66

The longest Schwitters poem was the famous *Ursonate* or *Primordial Sonata,* an extraordinary, wordless sound effect of rhythms and shifting timbres that lasted thirty-five minutes and despite its abstractness was strangely moving to audiences.

Schwitters' first volume, *Anna Blume,* published in Hanover, 1919, contained his poems from 1917 on. In his second volume, published about 1924 in Berlin, Schwitters made the pun explicit by reversing the title to *Die Blume Anna (The Flower, Anna)* with a play on the familiar proper name Blum. Schwitters called the mythical Anna "the mad beloved of my twenty-seven senses."

Georges Hugnet calls the earlier *Anna Blume* volume Schwitters' most important literary work, describing it as "a written transcription of all that is eccentric in his sculpture." Hugnet terms Schwitters' personal accent "a force that sweeps up the ready-made phrase, vulgarity and bad taste," but Hugnet stops short of what would seem an almost inevitable comparison of this literary junkpicking of clichés with his retrieving and collaging of paper scraps from the street. *Anna Blume* seems to Hugnet to

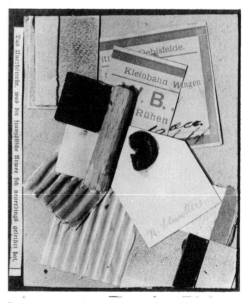

71 Schwitters: *Das Unerhörteste* 1923

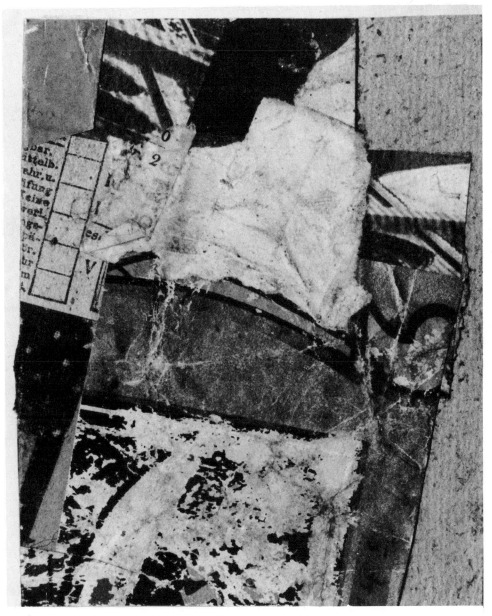

72   Schwitters: *V*   1926

73   Schwitters: *Trein*   1934

74 Schwitters: *Das Gustav Finzler Bild* 1926–36

75 Schwitters: *Pariser Frühling* 1936

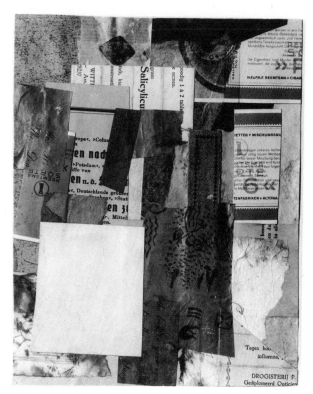

76 Schwitters: *Wrisbergholzen* 1937

77   Schwitters: *Urki K*   1939

78 Schwitters: *Dark Semi-Circle* 1941

79 Schwitters: *Number 17* 1942

personify "the sentimental German girl with all her absurdities" and he says that Schwitters' "description of her is a grab-bag of clichés, newspaper clippings and popular songs, advertising copy, and expressions of innocence."[10]

Among the excursions into prose were two fantasies written for popular newspaper serialization: *The Private Life of a Streetcar* and *Public Auction Sale of a Menagerie*. Sir Herbert Read has called Schwitters' poetry developments of "abstract vocal rhythm . . . parallel to James Joyce," and considers that he invented a new literary form.[11]

During his Hanover period Schwitters edited and published the review, *Merz*, which appeared at irregular intervals from 1923 to 1932, attaining a total of twenty-four numbers. *Ursonate* appeared in the last issue. The Belgian surrealist, E. L. T. Mesens, describes these little magazines as "captivating documents," observing that "they illuminate the path of the poet, artist [and] man of action."[12]

If not a political or a practical man, Schwitters was one of intensely sympathetic human feeling. He thought in terms of creative esthetic action rather than political action. Isolated in his gentle *Merz* world within the extraordinarily hectic, hysteric, neurotic, postwar, pre-Nazi Berlin that launched a social artist-polemicist like George Grosz, Schwitters even resigned from the local dada group in protest against political activity. But he was soon to be awakened.

Walter Spengemann, Jr., of Hanover relates that Nazi excesses finally drove Schwitters to action. He began enlivening his poetry lectures with a most dangerous kind of audience participation. Opening that strange, omnipresent, cabalistic portmanteau of his, he would remove a photograph of Hitler and place it at the platform's edge. Before launching into the long *Ursonate*, with its prelude, four movements, and cadenza, he would invite his audience to spit at Hitler's likeness whenever they felt so inclined. This, he implied, would be an acceptable substitute for applause.

Such things could not continue long in a Gestapo state. Schwitters soon had to leave Germany quickly and secretly. He fled with his grown son to an island off Denmark, and from there to Norway. When Hitler invaded Norway, Schwitters reached England on a boat carrying Norwegian officials into exile. After the required stay in an English alien camp, he was freed. This was in 1941. He lived the rest of his life in England, and died in Ambleside in Westmoreland in 1948.

There are both continuities and disparities between his English collages and the earlier ones done in Germany. He had once made a prediction to a fellow Berlin dada, Richard Huelsenbeck, "If I ever move from Hanover where I love and hate everything, I will lose the feeling that makes my 'world point of view.'" A true Schwitterism, this, to find in the most provincial of provinces a "world view," but then, of course, Schwitters may really have meant his world of *Merz*.

Established in the English Lake District, Schwitters tried faithfully to re-establish his life as it had been. An English neighbor having given him the use of a barn, he promptly filled it with a jumbled grotto. The continuity, even so, was flawed when Schwitters named the new cavern not *Merzbau* as formerly, but *Merzbarn*, out of deference to the English locale. The original *Merzbau* was destroyed by bombing in 1943, and there existed even more serious ruptures

[10] Hugnet, Georges, *The Dada Spirit in Painting* (*L'esprit dada dans la peinture*) in *Cahiers d'Art*, No. 8–10. Paris, 1932.

[11] Read, (Sir) Herbert, Foreword to a Schwitters exhibition at the Modern Gallery in London, December, 1944.

[12] Mesens, E. L. T., *A Tribute to Kurt Schwitters*, in *Art News and Review*, Vol. X, No. 19. London, October 11, 1958.

80   Schwitters: *Aerated VIII*   1942

81 Schwitters: *Number 9* 1943

acter of Schwitters' work, comes a wavering, unsettled, drifting appearance, as though what might have been an occasional mood in Germany, were now the permanent climate of his life. The English collages in a way confirm the prediction he had once made to Huelsenbeck.

While the German collages vary from massive, stable compositions to violent, explosive futurist diagonals, they all reflect certitude. They are sanguine in mood—remarkably so in view of the innate sadness of the castoff, rejected, lost materials. In the German works this sadness for the main part sounds an echoing scale of overtones that heighten the essential optimism.

In many of the English works the overtones swell into the main theme. Intrinsic melancholy is no longer muted, is heightened, rather, by the unsettled instability of compositions that drift like wastepaper in the wind. They are tumbled, feverish, like memories of a *Merzbau* that no longer exists. They are flur-

with the past. Schwitters' wife had remained in Germany by choice. He never saw her again. The real rupture, nevertheless, was outside Schwitters, between two worlds, two eras. Schwitters' Germany no longer existed.

The collages of the German period, of course, had gone through changes and developments. Elements of cubism, and even more of futurism (e.g., the strong diagonals thrusting out of the edges of the pictures) furnished some of the infinite variety of Schwitters' structuring of forms. After a visit to Holland in the winter of 1922–23 with Theo van Doesburg, his collages underwent further structural changes, utilizing some of the De Stijl geometrics. In some cases these consist of the horizontal-verticals at right angles characteristic of Mondrian; in others this framework revolves through forty-five degrees into the diamond grid formation developed by Van Doesburg and Mondrian.

Many of the English works have a shredded look: long slim pieces of material (paper, cloth, etc.) pasted on in the same direction, vertical or slightly diagonal. From this device, which now in the new locale became a dominant char-

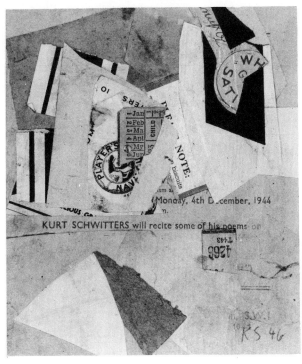

82 Schwitters: *Kurt Schwitters Will Recite* 1946

ried, nervous, restless, and infinitely sad, as in a collage made a year before his death, with the advertising slogan "Watt's the use of living" (Fig. 85). But from beginning to end one central informing quality never changed: a brooding magic, a fleeting elusive poetry, a gentle wit, a close, warm sense of personality that lives on in these small pictures.

Charlotte Weidler, from firsthand observation, evokes the image of the man at work:

He spread flour and water over the paper, then moved and shuffled and manipulated his scraps of paper around in the paste while the paper was wet. With his fingertips he worked little pieces of crumbled paper into the wet surface; also spread tints of water color or gouache around to get variations in shadings of tone. In this way he used flour both as paste and as paint. Finally he removed the excess paste with a damp rag, leaving some like an overglaze in

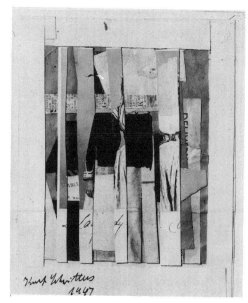

84 Schwitters: *Able* 1947

places where he wanted to veil or mute a part of the color.[13]

Pioneer constructivist Nahum Gabo adds to the picture of the man:

In the early '20's I had the opportunity of living close to him and seeing how he worked. We used to take long walks together. . . . In the midst of the most animated conversation he would stop suddenly, sunk in deep contemplation. . . . Then he would pick up something which would turn out to be an old scrap of paper of a particular texture. . . . He would carefully and lovingly clean it up and then triumphantly show it to you. Only then would one realize what an exquisite piece of color was contained in this ragged scrap.

It needs a poet like Schwitters to show us that unobserved elements of beauty are strewn and spread all around us and we can find them everywhere in the portentous as well as in the insignificant, if only we care to look.[14]

In these pasted-up pictures, unpretentious and inches-small, we can find our

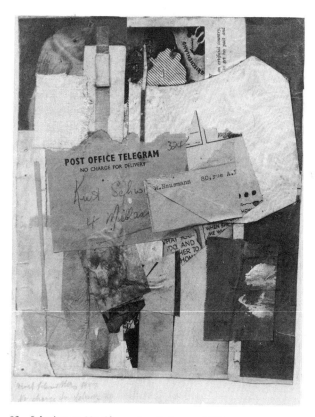

83 Schwitters: *No Charge for Delivery* 1947

[13] In a personal interview, 1959.
[14] From the foreword of the catalogue of the first Schwitters one-man exhibition in the United States, at Rose Fried's Pinacotheca, beginning January 1948, only eleven days after Schwitters' death.

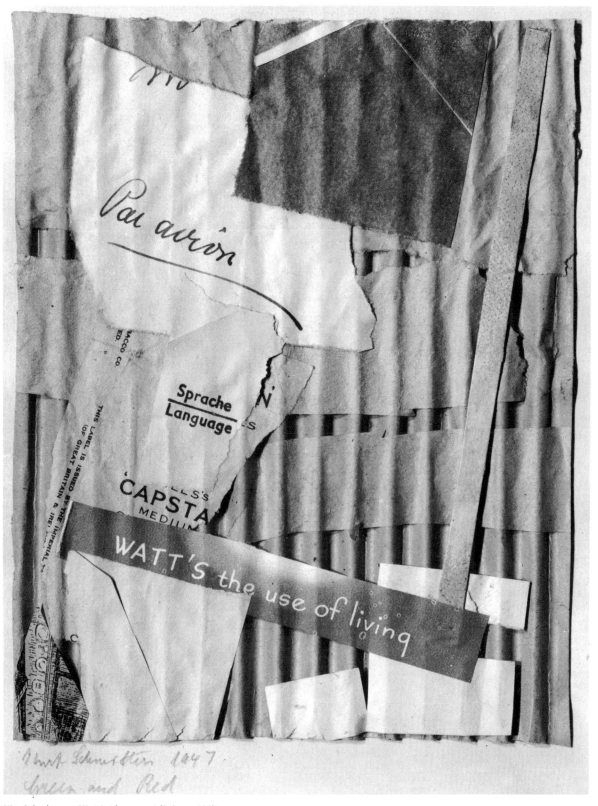

85   Schwitters: *Watt's the use of living*   1947

world, our time, and ourselves. The world of *Merz* is not really alien to our own world. *Merz* even rectified ancient errors in logic by acknowledging the potency of chance and denying the validity of absolutes. If Schwitters recognized any absolute, it was form, double-visaged, the multiple paradox of truth.

His world of the sidewalk was pre-existent collage—an expanding image, vast in space and inexhaustible in variety. His immediate vignette of pavement ran on, street joining street, city way joining country road, veined in the whole network of the world. This is the world that survives political changes and schisms in individual lives. Its endless fortuitous variety became in the end a kind of order with infinite variation as its foundation. So each bit of paper came to his hand magnetized with invisible relationships to all other bits, wherever or whenever he might or might not find them. Schwitters made one with this world so that for all his art and canny taste he became the orderly channel of endless mutation. So it came

about that even his smallest picture seems so vast in scale. There are no limits to the imagination when it finds the object or the world that it loves.

The *Merzbilder,* however abstract their construction, are realistic in a way that the most academically representational painting can never be. Natural collages exist everywhere around us; they are the artifacts of our time. The scraps of paper, labels, ticket stubs—all the sad detritus that Schwitters dutifully, thoughtfully, obsessively picked up from the streets, were parts of natural collages before he ever salvaged them—discarded, lost, glued by rain to dirty sidewalk under hurrying oblivious feet. Natural collages, too, are the layers upon peeling layers of posters and commercial bills pasted upon tenement walls and the flagrant hoardings that flank our superhighways. Any observant eye can see them on every hand. Schwitters is gone, but his was the poet's eye that first saw them, saved them, "formed" them, and reported them to us—true realistic histories of his time and ours.

7

SURREALISM AND COLLAGE

In the early 1920's when dada ended, the nightmare of war was already over and in the daylight of peace its despair seemed faintly absurd. Optimism was the fresh note; science was in a rapidly rising perihelion of popularity and everyone was ready to believe that it could measure, direct, and accomplish anything. A new science, the modern psychology of Freud, Adler, and Jung began to appear to at least one man as a possible bridge between science and art.

The man was André Breton, who forthwith put his ideas into forming a new art movement. Surrealism's formal beginning came in 1924 in a manifesto adopting the name which Breton devised from the subtitle *drame surréaliste* of Guillaume Apollinaire's 1917 play, *Les Mamelles des Tirésias*. Breton then defined the name:

Surrealism, subst.: Pure psychic automatism, by which it is intended to express, verbally, in writing or by other means, the real process of thought. It is thought's dictation, all exercise of reason and every esthetic or moral preoccupation being absent.[1]

Breton's early interest in psychology led him to try to utilize the powers of automatism, a creative force known and commented on since ancient times. Many writers had described the trancelike state during which their writings seemed to pour out fully formed without previous planning. It had always seemed a force, a source, or a personality outside their own; some believed that God (or the gods) spoke through them, or, perhaps, the spirits of the dead. Now, at last, there seemed to be scientific authority and exegesis for the mysterious process. Freud explained it in cold scientific terms as overt manifestations of the unconscious mind operating behind or below the conscious mind.

Breton's idea of harnessing this power opened up the tempting prospect of sharpening one's skills and vision through science. The idea was timely, cogent, and appealing; many dada artists—Ernst, Arp, Picabia, Man Ray— joined the movement; others, like Duchamp, allied themselves without final commitment; brilliant new talents like Dali, Masson, Miró, Tanguy, and, later, Magritte, Brauner, and Delvaux, joined; pioneers of modern art like Picasso, Klee, and De Chirico accepted honorary, retroactive memberships. The surreal-

[1] Breton, André, *First Manifesto of Surrealism*, 1924. Translated and quoted in exhibition catalogue *Fantastic Art, Dada, Surrealism*. New York The Museum of Modern Art, 1936.

ists even reached back into history to "elect" Uccello, Hieronymus Bosch, Arcimboldo, Füssli, Böcklin, and others who, they felt, had unknowingly used surrealist principles.

The dominant personality, phenomenal energy, and organizing abilities of Breton were evident everywhere: in proselytizing artists dead and alive, in organizing and combining artistic and literary activities, and especially in the sanguine spirit and the fever of creative excitement that propelled surrealism during its first twenty years into the most prominent and sensational activity in contemporary art.

Though dada characteristics, like shock techniques for example, were retained, surrealism represented a strong change of objective. Anti-art as goal was replaced by a renewed drive toward permanent art values. The emphasis shifted from destruction to construction as ways were explored through "controlled automatism" to use anti-art techniques in constructive ways. Dada's nonsense and sardonic humor contrast with surrealism's *humour noir* and patent seriousness; dada's relentless war against all human systems is at the opposite pole from surrealism's proposed systematizing of creative methods.

Yet it is easy to overemphasize the differences between the two movements. In a real sense surrealism was a "new model" of dada, redesigned to fit the changing atmosphere of a changing time. Even seemingly essential differences, closely scrutinized, reverse themselves in a bewildering ambivalence that is nevertheless typical of ideologies based upon dualism. Behind dada's attacks upon logic there lay logic; disgust and disillusion are *normal* human reactions to abnormal conditions; even further, to systematically create chaos is to create a system. On the other hand, surrealism's logic resided in the use of irrational elements of the human psyche. For a further example: dada's individualistic

nihilism was basically activated by thwarted gregariousness and was basically concerned with public values, while surrealism's systematic group activities, being concerned with each artist's individual psyche, were essentially introvert and solitary, even recessive.

Thus scanned, the two attitudes appear strikingly like the opposite sides of the same coin. In any event there is this basic sameness between the two movements: both sprang from the irresistible human need for maintaining identity under the stresses of modern life. Both—knowingly or not—were shaped by the irrational, unconscious mind. Dada chaotically, and surrealism systematically, derived esthetic expression from subliminal paranoid imagery and the hypnagogic areas of metamorphosis and magic.

With surrealist poets like Tristan Tzara, Luis Aragon, Paul Éluard, Philippe Soupault, and Breton having collaborated in dada, it is unquestionably true, as Georges Hugnet has written:

. . . their poetic temper led them rather toward the marvelous, toward the unfathomed depths of the unconscious recently revealed by Freud and hitherto completely neglected, than toward total disorder. . . . It appears more and more clear that, for them, Dada was only a *state of mind*, . . . a liberating, shocking force.[2]

Under the circumstances of its literary birth surrealism at first stressed literature more than the plastic arts, and through its history supported its painting and sculpture with unparalleled propaganda and polemics.

As early as 1921, while both were still dadas, Breton and Soupault had collaborated in writing *The Magnetic Fields* through automatist inspiration which—anticipating surrealism—was paradoxically subjected to control.[3] Many

[2] Hugnet, Georges, *The Dada Spirit in Painting.* In *Dada Painters and Poets, op. cit.*
[3] Breton, André and Soupault, Philippe, *Les champs magnétiques.* Paris, Au Sans Pareil, 1921.

80

years later, in the foreword to the catalogue of *Art of This Century,* Breton wrote:

The Surrealism in a work is in direct proportion to the efforts the artist has made to embrace the whole psycho-physical field, of which consciousness is only a small fraction. In these unfathomable depths there prevails, according to Freud, a total absence of contradiction, a release from the emotional fetters caused by repression, a lack of temporality and the substitution of external reality by psychic reality obedient to the pleasure principle and no other. Automatism leads us straight to these regions.

In *The Magnetic Fields* this process had yielded imagery like this:

A great bronze boulevard is the shortest road. Magical squares do not make good stopping places. Walk slowly and carefully; after a few hours you can see the pretty nose-bleed bush. The panorama of consumptives lights up . . .

which is not at all stranger, more brilliant, or more inspired than the imagery of Poe, Coleridge, or others. Through its deliberate exploitation of dream illogic, however, it does have a strong feeling of indwelling madness. Breton and Soupault were simply directing dada's avowed chaos toward pro-art ends by the use of controls.

The surrealists systematized these controls. For example, they recorded remembered dreams in full detail. Upon rising from sleep they immediately recorded their uncensored free-associational thoughts and sensory images, in order to utilize the hypnagogic state. This is the state that accompanies both the period of awaking and the period of falling asleep. In hypnagogia the unconscious mind is near-ascendant, dreams linger, merge, or form like crystals of consciousness; hallucination and reality blend and melt and fuse.

Controls actually make sense because of the fact that the unconscious and the conscious minds are not completely

86 Picasso: *Glass of Absinthe* 1914

separate and autonomous but are parts of one entity and, being connected with the needs, desires, or plans of the individual, are always subject to some degree of control. When coherent form and pleasurable emotion or ecstasy are a poet's desire then the unconscious pours out creations that, however marvelous and unexpected, will not unreasonably baffle, shock, or terrify. When the surrealists, however, chose to baffle, shock, and terrify, their unconscious minds obliged.

Breton was never a complete dada, as Duchamp, for example, has always been. Embracing disorganization, he nurtured formidable organizing powers; attacking the follies of human leadership, he eventually became the autocrat of surrealism. A psychologist-turned-poet, his basic method was analysis, not intuitive synthesis. He was a paradoxical poet, a most methodical dada. Nevertheless, such are his complexities of character that his imprint on surrealism was as imaginative as methodical, and the balancing of such seeming irreconcilables helped to give the movement seriousness and permanent value. Without them, it might have been little more than a naive transposition of psychological jargon and methodology into esthetic terms.

Irreconcilables like system and inspiration or madness and logic stimulated and challenged creative, imaginative personalities such as Ernst, Arp, Picabia, Dali, and the rest. As dadas, artists like these had already created a proto-surrealism, as in the remarkable *Fatagaga* collaborative collages (Fig. 90) done at Cologne in 1919 by Ernst and Arp, as well as in semi-automatist drawings (Fig. 51) by Ernst and Baargeld. Breton, however, did more than follow signposts, he surveyed and laid out a road, and by pointing out possibilities, inspired a highly creative group of artists.

Breton's "impossible" idea—to direct and systematize the unconscious—worked in practice. It unloosed a sustained flood of creation; became a useful tool in the artists' hands. Automatism, as principle and method, was an esthetic revolution almost as basic as cubism. Cubism broke the hold of the past, reformed vision, and altered age-old concepts of pictorial space—automatism freed the creative impulse itself. It gave artists confidence in their own inspiration. Though it did not make great artists out of inferior ones (along the lines of Breton's promise of "every man a poet" or Ernst's semi-ironic "inspiration to order"), it helped to break Picasso's hypnotic spell over the art generations.

With the automatist method Breton proved to all that the same kind of wells of inspiration that activate Picasso exist in some degree and kind in every man's unconscious. More: he tapped the flow.

By introducing psychic states and dream symbolism as subject matter, surrealism restored representation and storytelling to art. This in turn revived interest in painting. Collage per se tended toward de-emphasis, even as the collage idea was widening into strong interest in constructions and objects.

Dali, for example, while adroit in collage techniques, used its elements sparingly, and then only to enhance the dream feeling in a few early paintings. Miró, though producing important collages—some witty, some serious—and like Dali, a number of important objects, is also primarily a painter. Max Ernst, however, though also committed to painting, utilized dada and surrealist ideas to become one of the most original of all collagists. The chapter following will be devoted to his important work and theories.

Nevertheless, the collage idea—with its essentially dreamlike marriage of strange disjuncts—is almost startlingly apposite to surrealist ideas. The development of these, not only in painting and object but in poetry, drama, ballet, and art film, provided the immediate springboard for the upsurge of collage at midcentury. Surrealism led also to the development of unorthodox ideas and techniques related to collage theory. These, too, helped spur present activity. It will be useful to examine four of these central to surrealist art: Chance, Double and Multiple Imagery, the Object, and Metamorphosis of the Object.

Chance

Marcel Duchamp pioneered ideas and techniques based on the laws of chance in his 1913–14 proto-dada work *3 Stoppages Étalon* (Fig. 87). Chance has been an idea of enormous influence ever since. Duchamp's aim was double: to extend the artist's personality and creativeness by this fortuity while simultaneously protesting the frozen sterilities of academism. The *3 Stoppages* are three "meter" measuring sticks constructed from patterns evolved through chance. Duchamp dropped three threads, each exactly one meter long, from a height of one meter, to land on three glass panels. He then glued each thread to its glass panel in the free form it assumed. Each line then served as pattern for a "measuring stick." The curved sticks have become symbolic units of measure less arbitrary and preposterous than they once seemed, now that we know that Einstein was already envisioning in his general theory of relativity a time-space continuum in which straight lines are impossibilities.

Jean Arp used chance to drop the shapes in his *Collage with Squares Arranged According to the Law of Chance,* 1916–17 (Fig. 46). The use of chance as technique, by removing the artist's conscious control of his material, represents a decisive step away from design by logic and a long step toward automatism.

Double and Multiple Imagery

The phenomenon of double and mulple imagery is a well-known paranoid manifestation that happens to normal people in moments of fatigue or stress, during illness and fever, and in the hypnagogic periods between sleep and wakefulness. Dali developed the theory and technique under the name of *paranoiac-critical method* in 1930, and wrote:

> The way in which it has been possible to obtain a double image is clearly paranoiac. By the double image is meant such a representation of an object that is also, without the slightest physical or anatomical change, the representation of another entirely different object, the second representation being equally devoid of any deformity or abnormality betraying arrangement.[4]

Dali defined his paranoiac-critical method as a "spontaneous method of irrational knowledge based upon the interpretive-critical association of delirious phenomena."

Double imagery or the metamorphic image is an old device. Arcimboldo became a surrealist posthumously through his familiar metamorphic paintings of the sixteenth century—still lifes of fruit, cereal grains, or flowers that change into human heads. Familiar, too, are the old German engravings of landscapes which, tilted and viewed obliquely, become personages.

"The double image," Dali wrote, "may be extended, continuing the paranoiac advance . . . to make the third image appear . . . and so on until there is a number of images limited only by the mind's degree of paranoiac capacity."

The Object

The surrealists' idea of the object depends upon a magical view of reality that revives the faith of the primitive idol makers. It is animistic and, like Dali, holds the "belief that the animate and the inanimate are interdependent in

[4] In *Le surréalisme au service de la révolution,* No. 1. Paris, 1930.

87   Duchamp: *3 Stoppages Étalon*   1913–14

88   Rrose Sélavy (Duchamp): *Why Not Sneeze?* 1921

significance and function, with the inanimate taking its vitality from its relation to the living or from a strange capacity to come alive."[5]

As early as 1913 Marcel Duchamp began selecting objects not to paint but to present as works of art in themselves, given esthetic validity through his creative selection. The *Bicycle Wheel* of that year was followed in 1914 by a milk bottle drying rack called *Ready Made*. *Why Not Sneeze* of 1921 (Fig. 88), a small cage filled with white marble "sugar lumps" and a thermometer, is technically a construction. Like other modern constructions—whether by dadas like Duchamp, or by Russian constructivists like Tatlin, Gabo, and Pevsner, or by Braque and Picasso—*Why Not Sneeze* is a kind of three-dimensional manifestation of collage.

The increasing psychological orientation of dada objects, particularly those

of Duchamp, is apparent in his *Unhappy Ready-made* of 1922–23, "a geometry book that Duchamp had mastered as a child . . . opened and held in the air by taut strings tied through holes in its four corners and then stretched and fastened like guy wires . . . out-of-doors on a balcony. . . . Through the long winter the book . . . hung there, its pages turned or torn out by the fingers of the wind, its printed lore of theorems and equations slowly dissolving in the rain and sleet."[6] From an object such as this to the construction of objects that appear in dreams—Dali's "images of concrete irrationality"—is just a step. That step came with surrealism and Breton's proposal to actually construct objects that appear in dreams. Éluard termed them "physical objectifications of poetry."

The object falls into many categories. In addition to objects fabricated in toto, there are those created by combining ready-made elements or simply by choosing a single ready-made thing. There is, additionally, the "aided ready-made" bearing the artist's added touches. Natural objects form a distinct class. *Objets trouvés* or "found objects" are strange, evocative bits of nature: gnarled bark or driftwood, eroded rock, or fantastic mineral formations. They are the traditional tourists' "curios" given point and haunting poignancy by their animistic ability to change identity. Found objects can also be "aided" by added touches. A strange, affective class is the "perturbed object," which is a ready-made distorted by accident or disaster. An example of this was a half-melted and strangely contorted wineglass found in the ashes after the eruption of Mount Pelée on Martinique in 1902.

With surrealism, the juxtaposing of disparate and even hostile elements became a prime objective. The shock and

[5] Soby, James Thrall, *Salvador Dali*. New York, The Museum of Modern Art, 1941.

[6] Blesh, Rudi, *Modern Art U.S.A.* New York, Alfred A. Knopf, Inc., 1956.

89 Giacometti: *The Palace at 4 A.M.* 1932–33

90 Ernst-Arp: *Here Everything is Floating* 1920

91 Cornell: *De Medici Slot Machine No. 1* 1941

Among the most magical of surrealist objects are those by the American Joseph Cornell. Engrossed in old silent movies, toys, and nostalgic mementos, he assembles objects like the stages of raree peepshows: "magic windowed boxes filled with strange, memoried things—old photographs, theater tickets, sea shells, fragments of jewelry, and colored sand, and other things less explicit, more muted."[8] *De Medici Slot Machine* is typical of Cornell's niched objects (Fig. 91).

Cornell's work, which began in the early 1930's, is a strong influence on many present-day American artists. His importance to them lies in the "presence" of his objects. This derives from the rejection of replicas or imitations in favor of object-in-itself. As a part of its obvious relation to collage, it seems evident that questions of identity and re-

surprise secured through these techniques of illogic and irrationality created the desired animistic overtones. By 1936 objects had become so important that an exhibition revealed the extraordinary variety possible in the basic idea.[7]

[7] The International Surrealist Exhibition at the New Burlington Galleries, London. Breton listed the categories of objects in this exhibition as follows: *Objets mathématiques. Objets naturels. Objets sauvages. Objets trouvés. Objets irrationels. Objets ready made. Objets interprétés. Objets incorporés. Objets mobiles.*

[8] Blesh, Rudi, *op. cit.*

92 Dali: *Accommodations of Desire* 1929

93   Dali: *Illumined Pleasures*   1929

ality are involved: where the object as fetish was once the abode of foreign spirits, now it is where the faceless individual in an alienated society can find his own identity.

Metamorphosis of the Object

This is clearly represented in Dali's 1929 painting-with-collage, *Accommodations of Desire* (Fig. 92) . Freudian Oedipus symbols, father images, birth traumata, and sexual phantasies are woven together in a dream landscape. The lion, symbol of father and of sexual aggression, is both painted and collaged into the scene from cutout prints. Heavymaned and snarling he flashes episodically across a series of egglike forms: here complete and there with face removed; on one egg, jaws only in a white silhouette, and on another, blank red silhouette only. In the distance an egg is spotted with small replicas of the noble, feral head. The most shocking episode of all is the torn egg with gaping hole

where the beast has burst forth in a parturition of lust, hate, and rage.

The colored prints together with the skilled painting carry frightening conviction through the realism that Dali called "handmade photography." The universal symbols shock the beholder whether consciously understood or not.

The surrealists reveled in rich fields. From the materials of dream symbolism and sexual phantasies, they developed a whole mystique of science and superstition, mathematics and magical revelation. They formulated obsessions, hallucinations, irrationalities, delusions, delirium, and the haunting, shifting world of dreams into a grand metaphor. As a popular and fashionable art movement surrealism faded in the mid-1940's. Its ideas have continued potent, however, and can be traced in a large part of the art of today. They are, in fact, a key to even the most puzzling of the present movements.

94 Miró: *Collage* 1929

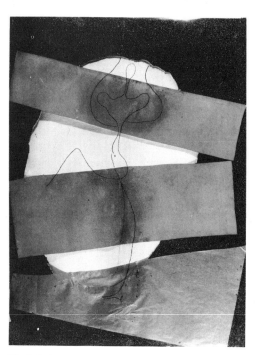

96 Miró: *Collage* 1929

95 Miró: *Spanish Dancer* 1928

97   Miró: *Collage*   1934

98 Miró: *Composition* 1933

99 Miró: *Object* 1936

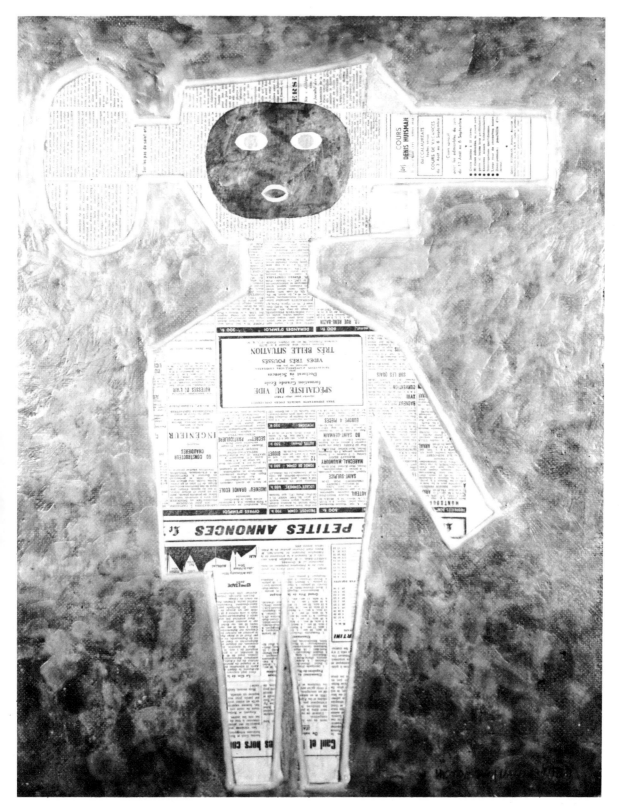

100   Brauner: *Petites annonces*   1959

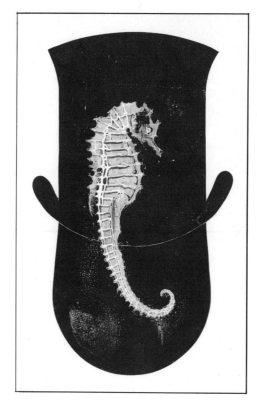

101   Brauner: *Faux-col-âge*   1938

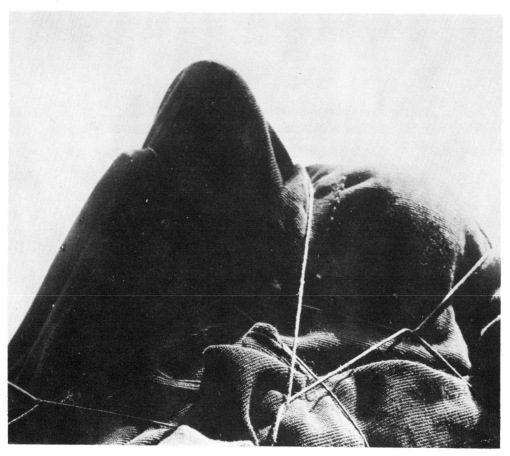

102   Man Ray: *The Riddle*   1920

103   Mesens: *L'instruction obligatoire*   1927

104   Kubicheck: *Collage*

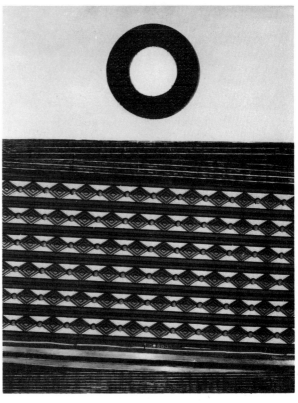

105   Ernst: *Moon and Sea*   1929

106   Arp: *La planche d'oeufs*   1930

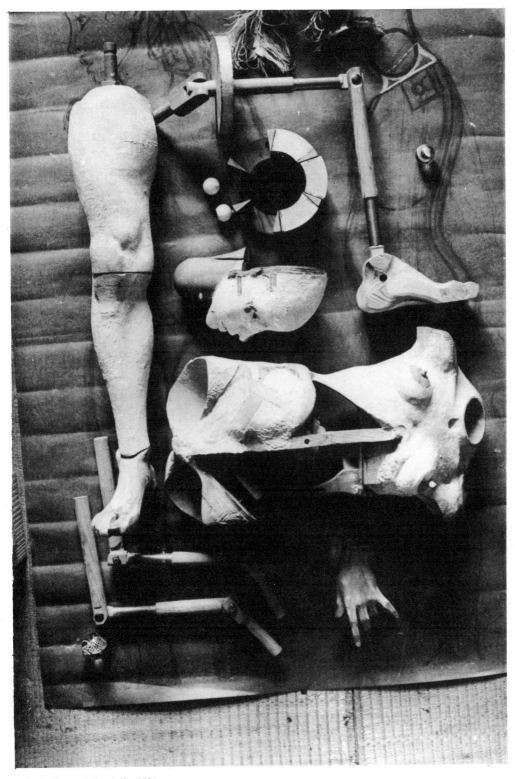

107 Bellmer: *The Doll* 1936

108   Penrose: *Camera Obscura*   1937

109   Masson: *Street Singer*   1941

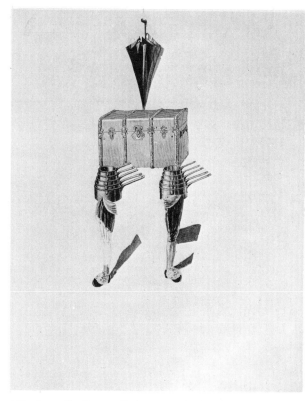

110   Surrealist Group: *Cadavre exquis, figure*   *c.* 1928

8

MAX ERNST

With Schwitters collage became a major art medium. With Max Ernst it became a philosophy. He grasped the idea that this almost-play of cutting-and-pasting (with its folk art background) was a concept deeply germane to our time. Ernst discovered "collage thinking," and explicitly formulated the "collage idea."

The manipulation of ideas—conscious and unconscious—typifies the creative work of Max Ernst. His ties with science and philosophy are strong and prior to art, though art has always been his outlet. Basic differences exist between Ernst's collages and the contemporaneous oeuvre of Schwitters. In the broadest terms the latter was a romantic arriving intuitively at a philosophy only partly formulated; using machine products, he gave his *Merzbilder* a strong "handmade" feeling; whatever the philosophic overtones, his pictures end in pure plasticity. Ernst is both Romantic and as Gothic as Gruenewald. To this complex diversity he adds a paradoxical obsession with modern science and technology. His collages though resulting

from hand techniques look machine-made; in some of them literature or psychology almost overpower plastic composition.

Max Ernst turned keen analysis and judgment upon the real meanings of collage. In doing this he came close to defining nearly all contemporary modern art as one kind of collage or another. In addition, he invented new techniques and a new type of collage. The latter, fool-the-eye assemblages of book illustrations—old steel engravings and scientific plates and diagrams—is one of the definitive surrealist expressions. The techniques, as tools of automatism or of chance, have had a strong influence on art and artists.

Max Ernst was born in 1891 in the small Rhineland city of Brühl. His father, Philipp Ernst, was a painter. His formal education, however, did not include art instruction, and from 1909 to 1914 he studied philosophy at the University of Bonn. His interest in art was nevertheless intense—he had begun drawing by the age of five and painting by nine—and in 1913 he visited Paris and also exhibited his painting at the first German Autumn Salon in Berlin.

As yet uncommitted to art, Ernst was deeply committed to his time, absorbing the new ideas and rigorous skepticism of the rapidly advancing sciences. Then war came. "Max Ernst died the 1st of August 1914," he later wrote, adding, "He [was] resuscitated the 11th of November

111   Ernst: *Dadamax* . . . (Self-portrait about 1920)

1918 as a young man aspiring to become a magician and to find the myth of his time."[1] In the four-year interim he had served as artillery engineer in the German army at the front.

In 1919 he made his choice, joining Arp and Johannes Baargeld in founding the Cologne dada group. He immediately began to demonstrate how he had reconciled his scientific and philosophic studies with art, both by the nature of his work and by initiating a lifelong interest in devising techniques. For Max Ernst dada was the open door to esthetic freedom and a future free of the stifling past. Reorienting his genius, it released

[1] Ernst, Max, *Beyond Painting*. Translated by Dorothea Tanning. New York, Wittenborn, Schultz, Inc., 1948.

an astonishing fecundity of esthetic and literary ideas.

Ernst immediately plunged into making his first collages. He called his initial one-man showing, which Breton arranged in Paris, a "collage exhibition," even though it also included paintings. The collage method fascinated him both as a technique and as a medium whose visual constituents could embody wit, irony, and above all, literary narrative. As a result, even his earliest collages are strongly proto-surrealist. It was precisely in its development along these lines, which Ernst later described as "beyond painting," that collage would expand into the esthetic philosophy that has proved so important for our time.

Kurt Schwitters and Max Ernst were profoundly different collagists. Ernst was not one to retrieve wastepaper from dustbin and sidewalk. In his first collages, which begin almost simultaneously with those of Schwitters, he discovered a mine of materials thoroughly personal and as inexhaustible as Schwitters' streets. From books and catalogues Ernst clipped scientific line illustrations, engineering working drawings, advertising illustrations (e.g., men's hats, etc.), and also, according to Arp, by 1920 he had already discovered the rich vein of Victorian steel-engraved book illustrations, with their absurd dramatics and disturbing psychological overtones. These would soon culminate in collage-scenarioed books like *The Hundred-Headless Woman* (*La femme 100 têtes*), *Une semaine de bonté*, *Rêve d'une petite fille qui voulut entrer au Carmel*.

Ernst remembered his discovery of the possibilities in scientific engravings:

One rainy day in 1919 finding myself in a village on the Rhine, I was struck by the obsession which held under my gaze the pages of an illustrated catalog showing objects designed for anthropologic, microscopic, psychologic, mineralogic, and paleontologic demonstration. There I found brought together elements . . . so remote that the sheer absurdity of that collection . . . brought forth an illusive succession of contradictory images, double, triple and multiple images, piling up on each other with the persistence and rapidity . . . peculiar to love memories and visions of half-sleep.[2]

Pursuing the possibilities of prints and engravings in collage, Ernst soon came upon old novels with steel-engraved illustrations. The overdramatization (as typified by a Gustave Doré engraving) appealed to his sense of the absurd, while the Victorian morbidity aroused the black humor of his Gothic heritage.

His first collage constructed entirely from steel engravings seems to have been *The Preparation of Glue from Bones,* 1921 (Fig. 112), a picture that could be a visualized Wellsian description of Doctor Moreau's island laboratory. Whatever the gruesome operation being performed on the bandaged human figure, the title itself, as Ernst has indicated, refers to the glue used in collage.

Ernst grasped immediately a technical advantage of line engravings, that their lines can be utilized to conceal the pasted joints. In this way parts from different engravings can be assembled to produce a new picture, complete from edge to edge. The subject matter can be altered, wildly disparate objects put together as in a dream. With all this, an air of verisimilitude, as of an illustration of a real happening, can be achieved. This "realism of the unreal" was the ideal vehicle to convey surrealist imagination and symbolism.

Through almost incredibly skillful manipulation of these novel elements (it is nearly impossible to detect the sutures without a magnifying glass), as well as through blending fable, myth, and marvel with the visible appanage of dreams, Max Ernst achieved a new art species just as Schwitters had with the *Merzbilder.*

[2] *Ibid.*

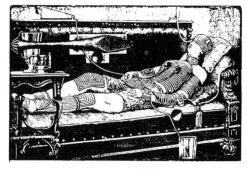

112   Ernst: *Preparation of Glue from Bones*   1921

Wonder and horror, mystery and fantasy, foreboding and sadness, grotesque, sardonic humor, all stalk through these extraordinary evocations, culled and orchestrated into the altogether remarkable illustrations of Ernst's books. *La femme 100 têtes,* for example, tells the strange, almost incoherent story of Loplop, the imaginary bird—sometimes raptorial, sometimes columbine—with which Ernst identified himself. The narration is entirely through a sequence of one hundred and forty-nine of these marvels of adroit craft and unleashed imagination, with only the slight literary aid of captions.

A print-collage from *La femme 100 têtes* with typically Ernstian title is *Plus légère que l'atmosphère, puissante et isolée: Perturbation, ma soeur* (Fig. 113) —*Lighter than air, mighty and secluded: Perturbation, my sister.* It is a dream of levitation made visible and all the more astonishing because factually documented like an historical event—two figures holding enigmatic objects and stepping lightly and fearlessly into the twilight air from an upper story window while the naked goddess of a Greek myth stands by oblivious.

In these pictures the visual counterpoint shifts in so dreamlike a way that, after this visual necromancy, Ernst's strange titles seem only the normal literary counterparts of metamorphosis. Even the name of this particular book is a pun: *La femme 100 têtes* read

113   Ernst: Illustration from *La femme 100 têtes*   1929

aloud sounds the same as *la femme sans tête*, or "the woman without a head." From these puns and the verbal "collaging" of random ideas, as well as the inevitable literary allusiveness of engravings once used to illustrate fiction, come the literary overtones which still further mark Ernst's engraving collages as a new art species.

It was the material itself, however, and the techniques involved that spurred Ernst's imagination. The new and the experimental were the lifeblood of surrealism. Creative excitement had seized all: new techniques and media emerged and were adopted so suddenly that (just as with cubism) it is hard to find who invented or discovered some particular process. Techniques like *décollage, le coulage, déchirage, fumage, grattage, éclaboussage,* and *décalcomanie* were discovered, invented, developed, or borrowed from nonesthetic technologies during an intense two-decade span.

Décollage, for example, might be defined as the opposite of pasting, that is, the opposite of collage, for it means to peel off. Pasted paper may be partially or wholly stripped away, leaving a coating of paste or glue; if part of a cardboard background should be roughly torn away in the process, so much the better. *Déchirage* means tearing, and the irregular, haphazard deckle edges of torn paper are its esthetic result. *Grattage* is the ancient process of *sgraffito* or scratching a design, borrowed from architecture and applied to the abrasion and torturing of paint or paper surfaces by penpoint, razor blade, broken glass, or any kind of strigil or stylus. *L'éclaboussage* is a scattered explosion of paint achieved by dropping it from a goodly height onto the surface of a picture. A variation of this is accomplished by spattering paint from an overloaded brush. All these processes, characteristically, are accidental or destructive acts turned to esthetic use.

Other new techniques were construc-

114 Ernst: Illustration from *Rêve d'une petite fille . . .* 1928–29

tive in method as well as in intent. Such a technique is *fumage*. Closely allied to effects obtainable by airbrush, *fumage* is the actual smoking-up of a picture by using a candle, burning grease, or a smoky lamp so that the smoke becomes amalgamated with the surface. *Décalcomanie* is only partly allied to the familiar everyday process of transferring design from one surface to another. Decalcomania in the art sense seems to have been discovered by Oscar Dominguez and extensively developed and employed by Ernst. It is akin to the Rorschach blot idea. Not folded paper is used, however, but two sheets of canvas made into a sandwich with wet paint between, and peeled apart to reveal strange and unexpected forms and designs. Then, just as the psychologist interprets symbolically the identities ascribed by the patient to the Rorschach blots, Ernst develops through further

101

115 Ernst: Illustration from *Rêve d'une petite fille* . . . 1928–29

116 Ernst: *Untitled Collage* c. 1920

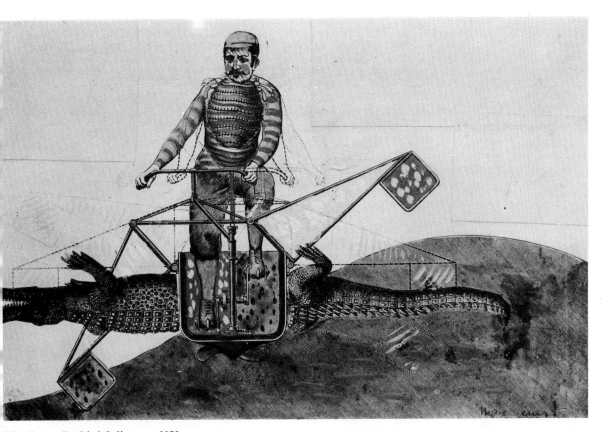

117   Ernst: *Untitled Collage   c.* 1920

painting the paranoid imagery he discovers in the accidental configurations.

Following the original choice of materials in his early collages, Max Ernst soon discovered creative possibilities in a very old process that he calls "a mechanism of inspiration." *Frottage* is the name of the technique, the familiar method of taking rubbings of surface designs and textures. Schoolboy's pencil rubbing on paper of the surface of a penny, or archaeologist's rubbing from a sculptured tomb inscription are both ways to reproduce existing patterns. Ernst, however, saw strange, hallucinatory forms in the grain of a wooden floor and from this began to utilize *frottage,* not to record but to prompt his imagination. It became one of his major techniques.

. . . in an inn at the seaside . . . I was struck by the obsession being imposed on my irritated gaze by the floor, the cracks

of which had been deepened by countless scrubbings. . . . To examine the symbolism of this obsession and to assist my meditative and hallucinatory powers I obtained from the floor boards a series of drawings [on] pieces of paper . . . rubbed with black lead. . . . The drawings thus obtained steadily lose . . . the character of the material being studied and assume the aspect of unbelievably clear images. . . .[3]

Ernst called his *frottage* system the "optical *provocateur* of a vision of half-sleep," transforming the mere grain of wood into

. . . human heads, animals, a battle that ended with a kiss (the bride of the wind), rocks, the sea and the rain, earthquakes, the sphinx in her stable, the little tables around the earth, the palette of Caesar, false positions, a shawl of frost flowers, the pampas.[4]

[3] *Ibid.*
[4] *Ibid.*

103

LE MASSACRE DES INNOCENTS   MAX ERNST

118   Ernst: *Massacre of the Innocents*   1920

Ernst subsequently extended the process from rubbing on paper to a new oil painting technique. Pressing the canvas down upon a textured surface, he coated an area with paint and then scraped away with palette knife at this coat of paint which, despite the scraping, tended to adhere to the canvas, corresponding to the texture underneath. So altered is the technique as adapted to oil painting that it is called *frottage* by courtesy, and actually is a variant of the scraping method called *grattage*. Also, in a kind of reverse way, through utilizing raised surfaces under pressure as though they were type faces, it is a kind of printing.

Printing by hand or by press was a favorite dada method. Arp, Tzara, Picabia, and his wife Gabrielle Buffet had

made a cover for the February 1919 issue of *Anthologie Dada* by taking an old alarm clock apart, bathing the parts in ink, and imprinting them at random on paper. The same year the Berlin dada Baader was doing *Schrift Montagen* (Fig. 155), collages of cut-out headlines and letters. Max Ernst—besides approaching printing through *frottage*—used the actual process in ways undreamed of by Gutenberg. One Ernst process is described as "dipping a leaf, a piece of tin kitchenware, an embroidered tablecloth, toys, or broken plates in liquid paint and then stamping them on the canvas."[5] Pied type being the

5 Revel, Jean-François. In the New York *Times*, December 13, 1959.

printer's nightmare, Gutenberg must have turned in his grave at another Ernst invention (also in 1919), which consisted of assembling printers' line-cut plates of scientific diagrams, mechanical devices and the like, at free angles in galleys. These were then pulled in rough hand-press proofs and altered and "aided" by gouache or pen and ink. As a part of Ernst's collage-oriented thinking, particularly in this period, the corollary of collage is to be found in the preprinting assemblage of plates.

Ernst's technical inventions and technical extensions parallel the imaginative use to which he puts them. The *grattage* variants of striating wet paint by drawing a comb or revolving the edge of a painter's spatula, a ruler, fork, or other object through it in order to form shell and flower shapes were primarily "mechanisms of inspiration." Vision, not craft, is the true goal of the craftsman, Ernst.

Another Ernstian technique first appeared in a picture at the Betty Parsons Gallery in New York. Ernst had punc-

tured the bottom of a tin can with small holes, filled the can with very liquid paint, and suspended it like a pendulum at the end of a string above a canvas. He then put the pendulum into motion, imposing "changes of direction through the movements of the hand, the arm, the shoulder, the entire body." The lines of paint, he said, made their designs on the canvas. Then, he added, significantly, the play of mental associations superimposed theirs. Here, as always, the collage idea is in the forefront of Ernst's thinking: design upon design, idea upon idea—and the glue? The actual glue, Ernst has said, does not make the collage. The adhesive that does, of course, is the adhesion and attraction of ideas pertinent to the creative orientation.

It has been said that certain New York painters adopted this technique. Actually only one American, Jackson Pollock, made serious use of the "drip" technique, and with him it became one of the important manifestations of ab-

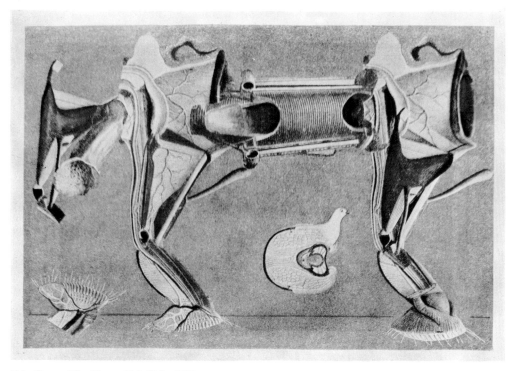

119   Ernst: *The Horse, He's Sick*   1920

stract-expressionism. Control far outweighed chance with Pollock, who threw paint from a loaded brush upon canvases stretched on the floor, his method involving exquisite control in the direction of the flight of the paint. In any event the Ernst "drip" painting of 1942 may have revived Pollock's memory, inasmuch as this technique tentatively appears in certain Pollock canvases of the late 1930's.

Having invented a technique, Max Ernst would then invent—or develop - variations of it. In *décalcomanie,* for example, he employed many methods, chiefly those that invite marriages of method and chance, like the use of sponge or crumpled paper. Or he might use paper for the top half of the sandwich, with the paint applied to the bottom, or canvas half. Other possibilities were discovered by applying paint to the paper which he caused to adhere to the canvas before peeling it away. Among other alternatives, he is known to have put paint on both canvas and paper, certain colors on the first, other colors on the latter, creating fantastic polychromes.

Always in *décalcomanie* the magic moment came with the peeling apart. This was the moment of truth when the paint was found in complex, unexpected, provocative configurations—the moment when, for Ernst himself, painting in the true sense began, enticing and directing his imagination through physical equivalents of the spiritual plasticity of dreams. All this daring invention was only the springboard for an imagination so Gothic that from childhood (with or without surrealism) Max Ernst's world has al-

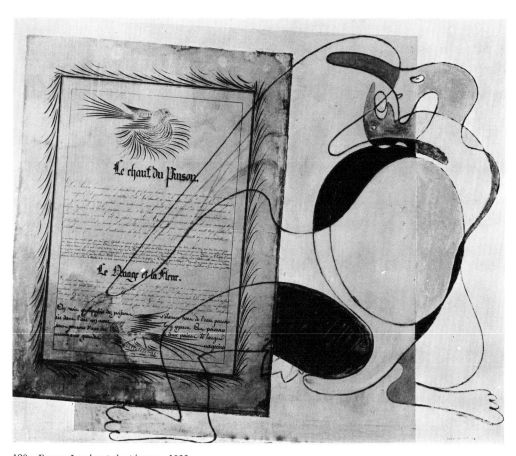

120   Ernst: *Le chant du pinson*   1933

121 Ernst: *Loplop Introduces* 1932

ways been a world of "marvels, chimeras, phantoms, poets, monsters, philosophers, birds, women, lunatics, magi, trees, eroticism, stones, insects, mountains, poisons, mathematics . . ."

This extraordinary grouping of desires, dreams, impulses, and visions can only be called a mental collage. Ernst himself thought so, developing from it what he has described as the collage idea. Though collage had been used before, to him it amounted to "a bewitching of either reason, taste, or the will," and collage, he believed could, in effect, produce a "photograph . . . on paper [of] the amazing graphic appearances of thoughts and desires."[6]

Not merely is collage an idea, but

ideas themselves (even those originating with different personalities) can be "glued," as Ernst has clearly indicated: "When the thoughts of two or more authors were systematically fused into a single work (otherwise called collaboration) this fusion could be considered as akin to collage."[7]

The *Fatagaga* series (Fig. 90) done collaboratively by Ernst and Arp in 1919 (some of which are collages in a technical sense) are all collages according to Ernst's philosophy. These and the semiautomatic dada collaborations with Baargeld lead directly into proto-surrealist literary collaborations, like the poems and tales composed in successive portions by writers who were shown only the

[6] Ernst, *Beyond Painting, op. cit.*

[7] *Ibid.*

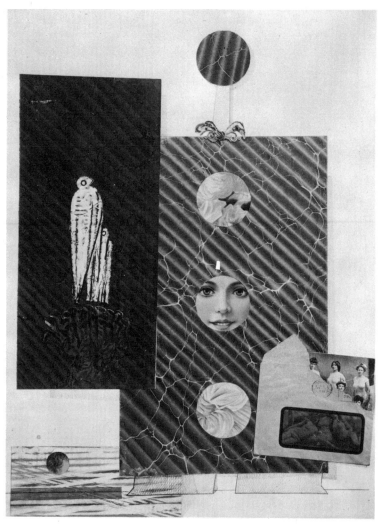

122   Ernst: *Le facteur cheval*   1931

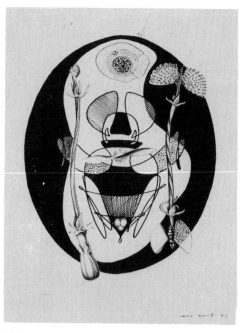

123   Ernst: *Untitled Collage*   1949

final sentence of the preceding portion. The pictorial equivalent of these were the pictures called *Cadavres Exquis* or Exquisite Corpses, pictures drawn collaboratively by various surrealists (Fig. 110).

In all of this there is clearly much more than the development of art techniques, or literal applications of Freudian theory to art. There is a basic philosophical concept. What is this concept, that seems to Max Ernst to be so well expressed by the term collage? In its most basic form, it is dualism and pluralism replacing nineteenth-century monism. The real struggle of scientist, philosopher, and artist had been to shatter the monolithic Victorian concept of the Absolute. The impressionists began it in art and the divisionists—breaking up solid colors into their components (as green into blue and yellow)—made dualism explicit. The fauves then broke the monolith "Beauty" into twin entities, Beauty and Ugliness, thereby releasing the changeling powers of metamorphosis. Next, the cubists began breaking up form into many aspects in a pluralistic time-space continuum. Meanwhile, philosophers like Bergson were attacking old monoliths such as Truth, and Freud and the new psychologists were shattering rationalism into Reason and Unreason (or conscious and unconscious mind).

To Max Ernst, with his Gothic imagination, all of this appeared completely reasonable. Dualism had fertilized the Gothic mind: good became more real when battling the dragon; pluralism lurked in the gargoyle-haunted jungle. Dualism rules all the ages of overweening faith.

Now, in the third and fourth decades of our century, a new religion had come, science, commanding and receiving unquestioning faith. With it, inevitably, came anti-science—poetry, intuition, inspiration, dreams, revelations—in the new art. Three-quarters of a century earlier, poet Lautréamont had foreseen these collaged, Siamese-twin-joined, disparate coexistences in his celebrated description of "the chance meeting upon a dissecting table of a sewing machine with an umbrella."

The opposites have revolutionized art: the trivial and serious, the beautiful and ugly, the valuable and nonvaluable, the permanent and nonpermanent, the logical and illogical, the sane and mad, the constructive and destructive—the list could be strung on endlessly or be as short as "art and anti-art."

Max Ernst, a personality deeply aware of our total contemporary world, calls it all "the collage idea." His words bear listening to, in fact explain much about the thorny art of today. In our complex shifting time, hurrying beyond haste toward ultimates, reality seems to reside in the penumbra between opposites. So it is not too unlikely that it might lie somewhere between a scrap of pasted newspaper and a Winged Victory.

9

CONSTRUCTIONS

The collage philosophy, as Max Ernst formulated it, explains a great deal about the course of modern art. The collage idea, in fact, is related to the construction of objects, to the tendency of paintings to project into the third dimension, and with many contemporary concepts of sculpture including that which involves welding metal.

Implicit in cubism from the beginning was the tendency of pictures to grow out into the spectator's space, as evidenced, for example, in the early making of both relief constructions and constructions in the round. It seems relatively unimportant which came first, collage or construction, for the basic ideas in either case are involved with concepts of time and space peculiar to this century.

Alfred Barr suggests that the cubists may have employed two different concepts of space: that of early seventeenth-century geometry as reflected by Descartes, and the modern time-space continuum.[1] The modern concept adds a

[1] Barr, Alfred H., Jr., *Picasso, Fifty Years of His Art*. New York, Museum of Modern Art, 1946, pp. 67–68.

time dimension to the three dimensions of the real world. The earlier concept involved the multiple point of view. The Cartesian geometry is exemplified by the mechanical drawing of architects' plans, in which projections from various points of view (e.g., horizontal plan, vertical elevations) are rendered, and can even be superimposed in one drawing together with cross-sectional views. Freely and intuitively, rather than logically and with rigorous system, this is what the cubists did in their pictures. It is, perhaps, gratuitous to point out that the cubists' superimposition of seventeenth- and twentieth-century ideas would itself, in the philosophical sense, constitute a collage activity.

In any event, ideas of space were foremost in the cubists' minds, together with questions of reality. Real space, therefore, and the real objects and materials in it, were bound to try to enter painting, and conversely, the painting was bound to try to enter real space. The one underlying motive so clearly informs all the activity—cutting and pasting paper or its construction into objects, painting of metal and wood, incorporating sand into the paint surface, and all the other processes and materials so foreign to painting tradition—that Max Ernst quite justly summed it up under the collage idea.

This idea, like the activity that stems from it, involves two basic concepts. The one is a new sense of pictorial plasticity that may be called "constructing"; the other is the reversal of the traditional idea of pictorial space.

Traditional painting was not constructed in this sense. It was felt to flow from the artist's vision and intent in semiliquid paint from brush to canvas where it might dry slowly into permanent form. Regardless of the retention of the painting technique, cubist canvases from the very beginning did not "flow" in this way from artist's consciousness to canvas. Real appearances were broken up into parts and then, through an imaginative "constructing," were assembled in the picture. With such thinking, both collage and construction were inevitable. Pasting-up paper fragments is two-dimensional carpentry; objects merely carry it into three dimensions. Implicit in the flattest collage and even before it in the cubist canvas, is the idea of extension outward from the picture plane. Arp's band-sawed wooden reliefs, produced since 1916, are like visual demonstrations of collage's paper laminae thickening out into the spectator's space (Fig. 124).

Cubism's deliberate rejection of perspective is simply another expression of the same idea. For traditional perspective went inward to a vanishing point, not toward but away from the spectator. From the Renaissance through most of the nineteenth century, paintings invited you to "come in." But once cubism had reversed the direction, perspective began rushing into the spectators' world like a motor car at an unwary pedestrian—directly to a new vanishing point out in front of the picture.

While this reversal of direction is clearly related to space concepts, psychologically it is, perhaps, even more significant. As materialism, or at least an increasing preoccupation with the "practical," progressively increased from the beginning of the industrial age, the public became more and more unconcerned with serious art. Exiled in effect, artists

124 Arp: *Formes terrestres* 1916

sought re-entry. It is this psychological urge to get back into society in a useful sense that most modern art expresses. Artists, estranged, seek to involve the disinterested public by shocking its proprieties and sensibilities. They lay snares. Their pictures reach out physically like tentacles of the spirit into the viewer's domain.

In such circumstances, paper's minuscule third dimension of thickness was not even needed: constructions were inevitable, and the growth of the paper collage through thicker excrescences—cardboard, wood, etc.—into the bas-relief was equally inevitable. And, in the future, which is now our time, distinctions between painting and relief, or full three-dimensional construction, would begin to become essentially meaningless.

The picture's outward movement is readily demonstrable in Picasso's work. A selection of eight works from 1911 to 1917 will be used, not forming a strictly chronological cause-and-effect series but, like Picasso himself, darting back and forth, striking outward from a central idea. From this new idea of picture into space so many possibilities loomed that a free play of intuition, rather than a laborious stage-to-stage process, became the artist's better method.

111

1

125   Picasso: *L'Arlésienne*   1910–12

2

126   Picasso: *Man with Arms Crossed . . .   c.* 1915

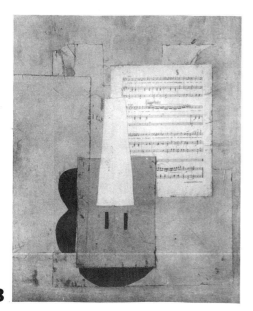

3

127   Picasso: *Guitare et feuille de musique*   1912

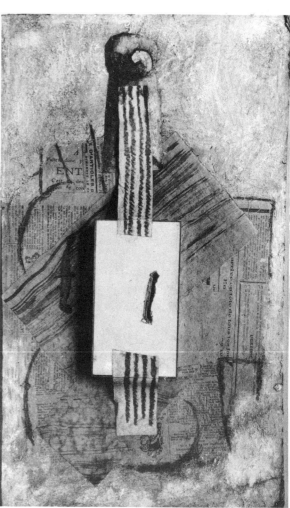

4

128   Picasso: *Collage-Construction*   1913

The Painting . . .

5

129 Picasso: *Construction* 1913

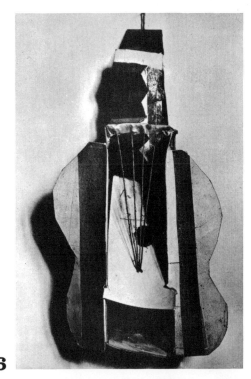

6

130 Picasso: *Construction in Papers . . .* **1912**

7

131 Picasso: *Mandolin* 1914

8

132 Picasso: *Manager* 1917

. . . into Space

Sequence Showing Picture-into-Space

1. *L'Arlésienne* (Fig. 125)

A typical cubist canvas, this shows "constructive" elements as clearly as if Picasso had been painting a realistic picture of an actual construction. So strongly do the facets and planes with their highlights and shadows enforce this illusion that one may conclude that ideas of construction were in the fore of Picasso's mind.

2. *Drawing of a Man* (Fig. 126)

A few years later Picasso made his most explicit demonstration of the organic relation of cubist pictorial construction to the real object. In one of these drawings a seated figure is shown in light lines behind a construction. With this as a working drawing an actual construction could readily be built out of paper, cardboard, tin, or wood.

3. *Guitare et feuille de musique* (Fig. 127)

For intermediate steps we will now turn to certain works depicting stringed musical instruments. We return to the flat picture plane in this 1912 collage. At first glance, the sheet music and the flat, unshadowed, and unmodeled geometric forms seem firmly glued into an uncompromising two-dimensional area. However, the overlapped pieces of pasted paper begin subtly but firmly to suggest projection from the picture plane. Study the picture persistently and the pieces finally will seem to be moving forward as though floating in the air. This, then, is the suggestive power of paper's minuscule third dimension.

4. *Collage-Construction* (Fig. 128)

Now the implied construction begins to become actual. In this 1913 study, while part of the violin body remains behind with its F-hole, a rectangular piece of cardboard bearing the other F-hole actually projects out into space, secured top and bottom by strips of pasted paper representing fingerboard, tailpiece, and strings. The actual date of this picture is not crucial: it shows the collage becoming construction, as the pieces of paper become, in effect, unglued and, one by one, float out into space.

5. *Construction* (Fig. 129)

The ancient idea of the picture nevertheless still has power. So the idea of a leap into space must be consolidated in relief constructions that still adhere to the rectangular picture area and are hung from the wall. However, materials suitable to construction begin to be employed. This 1913 relief construction of wood with still life of ale bottle, drinking glass, and fragmented guitar, is just such a consolidation of the idea of picture growing out of relief into freestanding construction in space.

6. *Construction in Papers* (Fig. 130)

An important step in this progression occurs when the relief object frees itself from the rectangular confines of the picture shape with its limiting implication of the immobility of two-dimensional picture plane. The guitar in this paper construction has made this flight. Though it hangs by a string against the wall it could just as readily hang in space. Flight is imminent.

7. *Mandolin* (Fig. 131)

The realized object, the picture in space, will be apt to employ constructed components more durable, if not more architectonic, than pasted paper and string. This mandolin construction of 1914 is made mainly of wood. Here, then, is the object built to stand the disintegrating forces it now must meet, since it is to exist wholly in the real world.

Nevertheless, the possibilities of metamorphosis remain undiminished. This construction could readily be translated back into pasted paper collage, and still further back to its genesis, the oil painting. From this it appears that construction is primarily a **creative idea** and that categories—like painting and sculpture—are apt to prove more limiting than descriptive. For example: the construction moves from idea into concrete form, say a flat paper collage. Next, the artist translates it unchanged into a three-dimensional object constructed from paper. Finally, he makes a replica in metal. The metal may be tin, aluminum, iron, or bronze. He may assemble it by welding or have the object cast in a mold. So here we face the question: at what precise stage did picture end and sculpture begin? The answer may seem easy, but one may end up calling a flimsy paper thing, sculpture. New terms, obviously, are needed to describe art in our time.

8. *Manager* (Fig. 132)

Perhaps the first collages or sculptures, or even the first cubist paintings ever to walk around in real space came in 1917 with some fantastic theatrical costumes designed by Picasso. These were for the ballet *Parade* which Barr described as an

avant-garde demonstration [that] combined the revolutionary theatrical ideas of Cocteau, the music of the most advanced composer of France, Erik Satie, the painting of Picasso and, rather subordinately, the choreography of Massine and the dancing of Diaghilev's Russian Ballet. . . . There were only four dancers: a Chinese conjurer (danced by Massine), a little American girl and two acrobats. In addition there were three managers [and] Satie's unassuming music "like an inspired village band" was . . . accompanied by noises, a dynamo, a siren, a telegraph key, an airplane propeller, a typewriter—"ear deceivers" Cocteau called them, employed with the same object as the "eye deceiving" newspapers, facsimile wood graining and moldings which the cubist painters had used.

The gigantic cubist managers like moving sections of scenery were intended by Picasso to dwarf and flatten out the dancers, turning them into unreal puppets. Thus cubist reality—the agglomeration of pipes, hats, split faces, architecture and angular dissections which made up the inhuman managers—triumphed over the traditional reality of the characters, human in shape and scale.[2]

[2] Barr, *op. cit.*

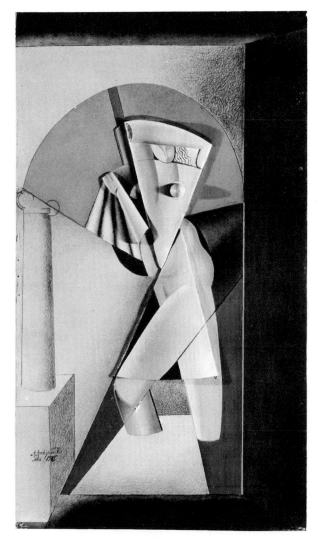

133 Archipenko: *The Bather* 1915

These ten-foot apparitions of panoplied cardboard looked like cubist collages come to life. Indeed, they symbolized the artist's dilemma even more than his picture, as, having wrenched themselves free of their pictorial prison, they strode out into life and action.

Cubist collage and construction modified sculptural tradition in hybrid, or rather, transitional, works unified by the central idea. Even amid cubist unorthodoxy a work like Archipenko's *The Bather* (Fig. 133), combining drawing with curling, projecting sculptural planes, is startling and upsetting except

115

against the historical background of collage.

Painting's slow reflex into space occurred not only in cubism but in a number of art movements. By 1913 similar ideas were fermenting in czarist Russia, where important concepts developed independently until the notoriously reactionary Communist esthetic policy brought it all to a halt in the early 1920's. The construction idea was implicit in the beginnings of both suprematism and constructivism. Malevich, Rodchenko and El Lissitzky based their suprematist theory on Cézanne's famous dictum: "You must see in nature, the cylinder, the sphere, and the cone." These three-dimensional entities are represented pictorially (that is, two-dimensionally) respectively by square or rectangle, circle, and triangle. As the suprematists used these in painting and collage the planar shapes symbolized the solid entities. In his *Proun* series (Fig.

134), Lissitzky explicitly indicated fin-like planes projecting as in relief constructions. He did this by employing the architect's device of isometry which—as in Chinese painting—is a stylistic indication of perspective through angular delineation without vanishing points. And in at least one suprematist collage there is the emergence into real space. This is Malevich's 1914 *Le civil de la 3e division* (Fig. 135), with its glued-on thermometer.

The constructivists' work is Russian, not Gallic: severe and serious rather than witty; derived from geometry's cold genera rather than the table paraphernalia of warm cafés; monumental rather than floriate. True to their name, the constructivists thought in terms of actual construction. As early as 1913, Vladimir Tatlin was making relief constructions in Moscow of the type shown in the illustration (Fig. 136). Within a year Tatlin's reliefs had moved out of

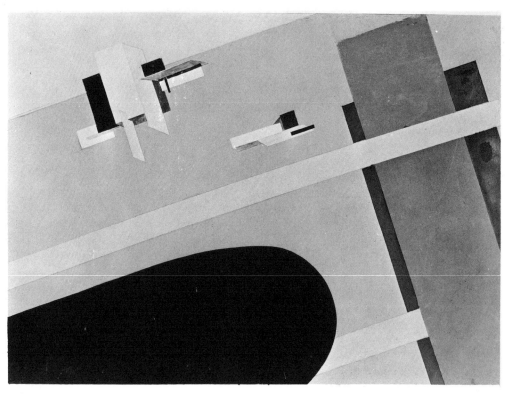

134   El Lissitzky: *Proun III*   1926

135 Malevich: *Le civil de la 3e division* 1914

the picture into three-dimensional counterreliefs which, held by guy wires, floated in room corners. In 1920, shortly before the demise of Russian modernism, Tatlin constructed a gigantic model for a Monument to the Third International. This was an ascending spiral—a leaning ziggurat—of openwork scantlings rather startlingly prophetic of the scaffoldings around the giant rockets of today.

Nahum Gabo's constructions began in 1915 with a head that is described as having been of cardboard, built up of intersecting planes. This was probably made in neutral Norway where Gabo and his brother Antoine Pevsner worked during the war years 1914 to 1917. A head of thin plywood sheets followed immediately. One year later Gabo pioneered the use of welding, a technique that has revolutionized modern sculpture. Barr relates that the cardboard head was followed by torsos in iron. The head motive now appears in iron (Fig. 137). Gabo writes: "This piece was made of iron sheets and is *welded*."[3]

[3] In a letter, December 17, 1960, to Rudi Blesh.

Gabo and Pevsner returned to Moscow in 1917 after the Revolution. When esthetic repression began, Tatlin, Rodchenko, and others elected to stay and were lost to modern art. The brothers Pevsner, however, when the state police closed their studios, made their escape to Berlin where they joined forces with the German modernists. By 1925 they were active in Paris. At the present time Gabo lives in the United States, and Pevsner is in England where, due basically to his inspiration, a fresh constructivist movement is under way.

Architecture was the background of the Dutch De Stijl movement organized in Leyden in 1917 by painters Theo van Doesburg and Piet Mondrian, sculptor Georges Vantongerloo, poet Kok, and modern architects J. J. P. Oud, Wils, and Van't Hoff. Yet the impulse toward pictorializing out into space, in re-

136 Tatlin: *Relief-Construction* 1913–14

117

137   Gabo: *Constructed Head No. 2*   1916

liefs and constructions, did not operate obsessively with De Stijl as with other groups. Perhaps the volumetric realization foretold in architectural drawing was sufficient to satisfy the architectural mind, as merely scanning a musical score may satisfy a musician. Collage is at least implied in certain Mondrian paintings, like his 1917 *Composition* (Fig. 140), with its squares and rectangles so similar to Arp's collages (Fig. 141). Yet De Stijl ideas might as easily interpret these shapes as those of buildings in a municipal plan. It was not until some years later that De Stijlist Domela (Nieuwenhuis) made relief constructions similar to the Mondrian and Van Doesburg pictorial conceptions, with the linear grids free-standing in front of the picture plane (Fig. 142).

A Uruguayan, Torrés-Garcia, studied art in Barcelona just ahead of Picasso, then was associated with the extraordinary architect Gaudi. Torrés-Garcia combined remarkable influences—*L'Art Nouveau*, Uruguay Indian pictography, Catalan folk art, and Gaudi's floriate neo-Gothic—into an intensely personal constructivism. His constructions (Figs. 145, 146) of rough wood employ primitive symbols in one of the earliest uses in modern art of the cubicle idea. In 1936, he founded the Taller Torrés-Garcia in Montevideo. The school, with an international student body, continues to work in Torrés-Garcia's tradition of wood constructions (Figs. 147, 148).

Torrés-Garcia's primitivism by no means typified twentieth-century constructionism. The construction idea, on the contrary, naturally gravitates toward a union with machine symbolism, materials, and techniques. Mechanical precision and control enter drawing in the early 1920's in De Stijl drawings like Van Doesburg's isometric drawing-board renderings of architectural projects and Lissitzky's drawings called "Constructions" which utilized ruler, T-square, and compass. Gabo and Pevsner pio-

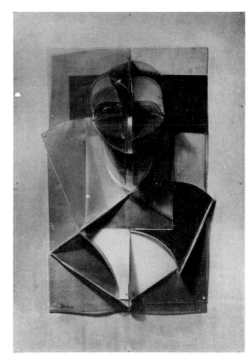

138   Pevsner: *Portrait of Marcel Duchamp*   1922

139   Pevsner: *Bust*   1923–24

140 Mondrian: *Composition, 1917*

141 Arp: *Construction élémentaire . . .* 1916

neered in the use of metals and industrial synthetics such as plexiglass.

De Stijl and constructivist influences merged in the "machinism" of the Bauhaus, founded by architect Gropius at Weimar in 1919, moved to Dessau in 1925, and finally terminated by the Nazis. With the Bauhaus in industrial Germany the machine, which had haunted art, became its ally. Its position ever since has been so central that the following chapter will be devoted to the many ramifications of machinism as an esthetic idea.

Among the many Bauhaus achievements in its planned art-for-use, there is one, however, which—though carefully reasoned and programmed—can be traced far back in history to poetic intuition and whimsy. This is the characteristic Bauhaus typography in book, poster, and advertising that, through emphatic asymmetry and visual impact, has helped to transform the modern world. Its origins trace back to ancient Greek poems shaped like eggs, altars, and other objects, a curious custom that had a Renaissance revival. In the late nineteenth century the "shaped poem" reappeared with Mallarmé and a poem like *Un Coup de Dés (A Throw of the Dice),* a free spatial typographical arrangement worthy of the twentieth century. Cubist poet Guillaume Apollinaire wrote verses shaped like hearts, crowns, mirrors, and cravats. Yet Apollinaire was being quaint, not modern, for cubism had already dispersed the alphabet and pied the type in painting and collage, while futurism was pasting random letters in its manifestoes. Then dada made fun of typography altogether with outrageous misfits of letters in all styles and sizes. At this point—tradition and clichés utterly destroyed—De Stijl, followed by Bauhaus, was free to develop modern typography.

Despite all this, the letter's ancient power remained unexorcised and was, if anything, increased. The cubists, in-

142 Domela: *Construction* 1929

143 Schwitters: *Breite Schnurchel* 1923

144 Seligmann: *The Hurdy-gurdy* *c.* 1924

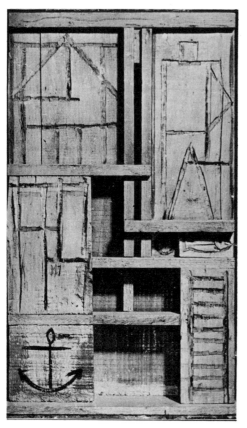

145 Torrés-Garcia: *Untitled* 1929

146 Torrés-Garcia: *Untitled* 1928

122

147 Fonseca: *Structure*

deed, had already sensed the potency
of a word or even a single letter, both
as symbol of idea and as pictograph,
which is to say, vestigial image. Using
this hypnotic magic De Stijl architects
fused gigantic letters into the structure
of buildings.

In 1927, a revived futurism had, probably, the last word in this typographical
giantism when Fortunato Depero designed an editorial office building that
looked like Brobdingnagian alphabet
blocks. (For the entire sequence from
300 B.C. to A.D. 1927 see Figs. 149 to
160).

148 Fernandez: *Structure*

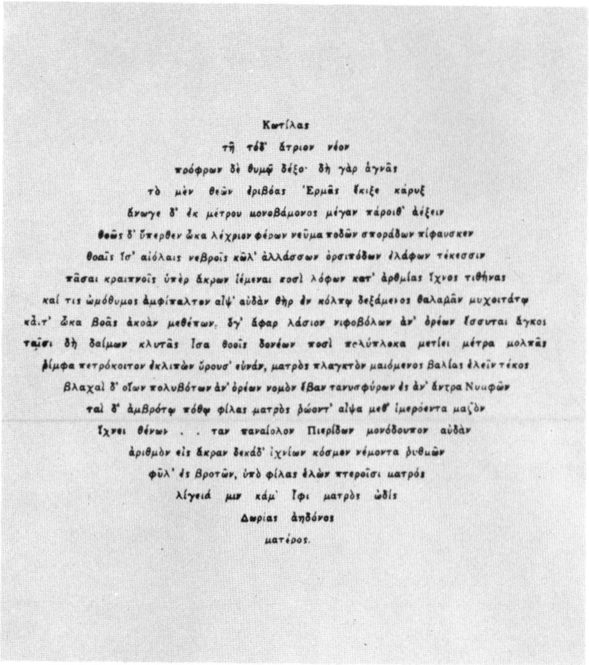
Κωτίλας
τῆ τόδ' ἄτριον νέον
πρόφρων δὲ θυμῷ δέξο· δὴ γὰρ ἁγνᾶς
τὸ μὲν θεῶν ἐριβόας Ἑρμᾶς ἔκιξε κάρυξ
ἄνωγε δ' ἐκ μέτρου μονοβάμονος μέγαν πάροιθ' ἀέξειν
θοῶς δ' ὕπερθεν ὦκα λέχριον φέρων νεῦμα ποδῶν σποράδων πίφαυσκεν
θοαῖς ἴσ' αἰόλαις νεβροῖς κῶλ' ἀλλάσσων ὀρσιπόδων ἐλάφων τέκεσσιν
πᾶσαι κραιπνοῖς ὑπὲρ ἄκρων ἱέμεναι ποσὶ λόφων κατ' ἀρθμίας ἴχνος τιθήνας
καί τις ὠμόθυμος ἀμφίπαλτον αἶψ' αὐδὰν θὴρ ἐν κόλπῳ δεξάμενος θαλαμᾶν μυχοιτάτῳ
κἆιτ' ὦκα βοᾶς ἀκοὰν μεθέπων, δγ' ἄφαρ λάσιον νιφοβόλων ἀν' ὀρέων ἔσσυται ἄγκος
ταῖσι δὴ δαίμων κλυτᾶς ἶσα θοοῖς δονέων ποσὶ πολύπλοκα μετίει μέτρα μολπᾶς
ῥίμφα πετρόκοιτον ἐκλιπὼν ὄρουσ' εὐνάν, ματρὸς πλαγκτὸν μαιόμενος βαλίας ἑλεῖν τέκος
βλαχαὶ δ' οἴων πολυβότων ἀν' ὀρέων νομὸν ἔβαν τανυσφύρων ἐς ἀν' ἄντρα Νυμφῶν
ταὶ δ' ἀμβρότῳ πόθῳ φίλας ματρὸς ῥώοντ' αἶψα μεθ' ἱμερόεντα μαζὸν
ἴχνει θένων . . ταν παναίολον Πιερίδων μονόδουπον αὐδὰν
ἀριθμὸν εἰς ἄκραν δεκάδ' ἰχνίων κόσμον νέμοντα ῥυθμῶν
φῦλ' ἐς βροτῶν, ὑπὸ φίλας ἑλὼν πτεροῖσι ματρός
λίγειά μιν κάμ' ἶφι ματρὸς ὠδὶς
Δωρίας ἀηδόνος
ματέρος.

149 Simmias: *Poem in Shape of an Egg* 300 B.C.

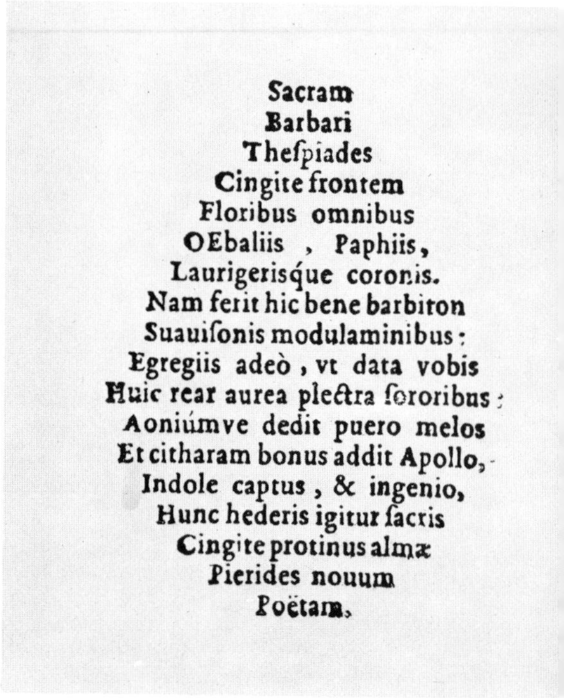
Sacram
Barbari
Thespiades
Cingite frontem
Floribus omnibus
OEbaliis , Paphiis,
Laurigerisque coronis.
Nam ferit hic bene barbiton
Suauisonis modulaminibus:
Egregiis adeò , vt data vobis
Huic rear aurea plectra sororibus:
Aoniúmve dedit puero melos
Et citharam bonus addit Apollo,
Indole captus , & ingenio,
Hunc hederis igitur sacris
Cingite protinus almæ
Pierides nouum
Poëtam.

150 Valeriano: *Poem in Shape of an Egg* A.D. 1550

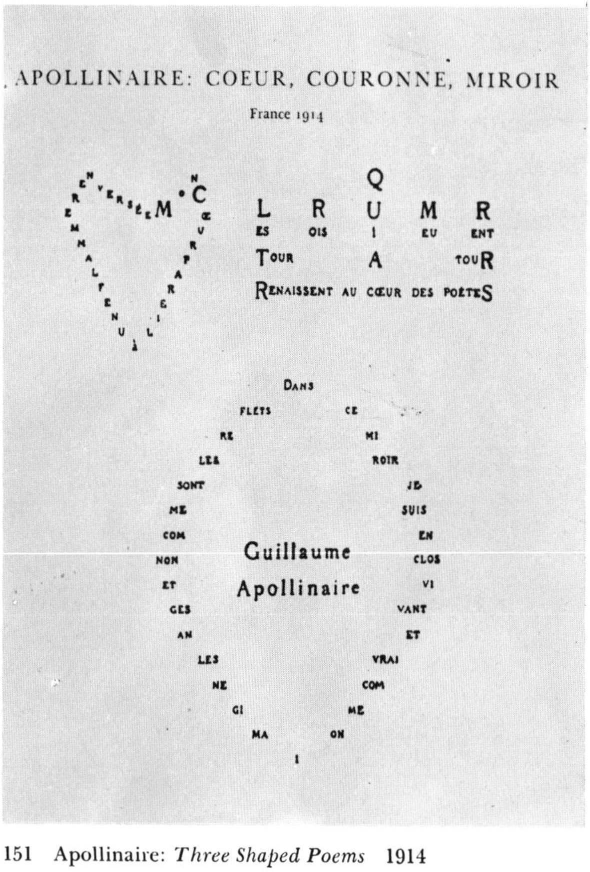
APOLLINAIRE: COEUR, COURONNE, MIROIR
France 1914
MON CŒUR PAREIL À UNE FLAMME RENVERSÉE
Q
L R U M R
ES OIS I EU ENT
TOUR A TOUR
RENAISSENT AU CŒUR DES POËTES
DANS
FLETS CE
RE MI
LES ROIR
SONT JE
ME SUIS
COM EN
NON CLOS
ET VI
GES VANT
AN ET
LES VRAI
NE COM
GI ME
MA ON
I
Guillaume
Apollinaire

151 Apollinaire: *Three Shaped Poems* 1914

152 Apollinaire: *La cravate* 1914

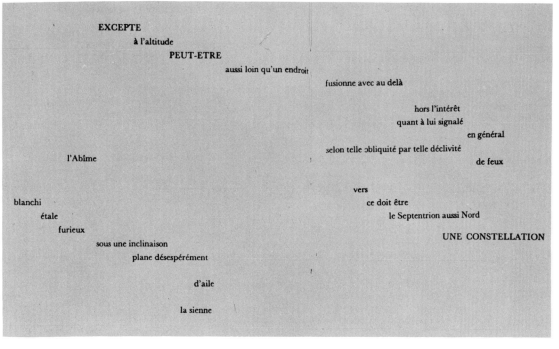

153 Mallarmé: *Constellation and Wing* 1897

154 Futurist "Free Words" 1915–16

155   Baader: *Schrift Montage*   1919

156   Van Doesburg: *Drawing and Typographical Design*

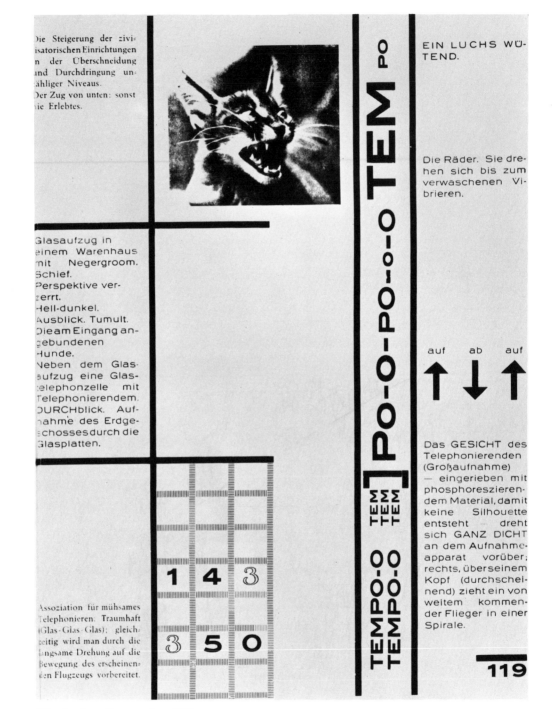

Die Steigerung der zivi-
lisatorischen Einrichtungen
in der Überschneidung
und Durchdringung un-
zähliger Niveaus.
Der Zug von unten: sonst
nie Erlebtes.

Glasaufzug in
einem Warenhaus
mit Negergroom.
Schief.
Perspektive ver-
zerrt.
Hell-dunkel.
Ausblick. Tumult.
Die am Eingang an-
gebundenen
Hunde.
Neben dem Glas-
aufzug eine Glas-
telephonzelle mit
Telephonierendem.
DURCHblick. Auf-
nahme des Erdge-
schosses durch die
Glasplatten.

Assoziation für mühsames
Telephonieren. Traumhaft
(Glas-Glas-Glas); gleich-
zeitig wird man durch die
langsame Drehung auf die
Bewegung des erscheinen-
den Flugzeugs vorbereitet.

1 4 3
3 5 0

TEM PO

PO-O-PO-O-O

TEM TEM TEM

**TEMPO-O
TEMPO-O**

EIN LUCHS WÜ-
TEND.

Die Räder. Sie dre-
hen sich bis zum
verwaschenen Vi-
brieren.

auf   ab   auf
↑   ↓   ↑

Das GESICHT des
Telephonierenden
(Großaufnahme)
— eingerieben mit
phosphoreszieren-
dem Material, damit
keine Silhouette
entsteht — dreht
sich GANZ DICHT
an dem Aufnahme-
apparat vorüber;
rechts, über seinem
Kopf (durchschei-
nend) zieht ein von
weitem kommen-
der Flieger in einer
Spirale.

119

157   Bauhaus Typography   1925

158　Dickenson House, Alloway, N.J.　1754　　　159　Oud: *Café de Unie*　1925

160　Depero: *Architettura Tipografica*

10

THE MACHINE ESTHETIC

The machine esthetic, implicit in cubist practice and futurist theory, was explicit in the pre-dada work of Duchamp and Picabia. In 1911, even before *Bicyle Wheel,* Duchamp painted the first modern picture in which the *deus ex machina* actually sat as artist's model: humble domestic machinery concealing well its inherent diabolism—a coffee mill. Public machinery followed: a chocolate grinder outlined in stretched string glued to a painting. But in between had come one of Duchamp's most cynically frightening paintings, the *Bride.* With Duchamp the philosophical ideas behind mechanism—the slave become master, the materialist Mammon, the blasphemous creation, etc.—were racing with astonishing celerity to the final denouement of the uncompleted *Large Glass,* 1915–23. Already in the *Bride* of 1912 Duchamp was painting the machine that, he felt, would inherit the earth:

The Bride is not a woman at all, even in outward appearance, but a machine built for voluptuous enjoyment and for a terrible metallic insemination. She predicts the machine state of machine men, the strength of steel through the joy of steel.[1]

Duchamp's masterpiece and swan song, the *Large Glass* (Fig. 161), is an elaborate and excessively recondite summing up of his extraordinary, ambivalent pro-anti-machine attitude. To give the *Glass* its correct title, *La mariée mise à nu par ces célibataires, même (The Bride Stripped Bare by Her Bachelors, Even)* this is the classic example of picture-collage-construction as well as the picture-invading-space. Duchamp painted his famous earlier objects and drawings like *Chocolate Grinder, Glider With Water Mill,* and *Uniforms and Liveries,* on clear glass, outlined with glued wire and silhouetted precisely as though affixed by collage. Actually it was Duchamp's intention, by using glass, to glue these forms, as it were, upon the air. Long since broken and laboriously reassembled, the *Large Glass* is a collage-in-space of pictures that have escaped the pictorial prison, marched out into the world, and assembled there. In this one great, shattered, enigmatic masterpiece the whole struggle of painting and painter to invade our world flashes in an ultimate gesture. As the two disparate space continuities interpenetrate, dada's great negation becomes affirmation.

Yet for Duchamp the *Large Glass* marked his renunciation forever of art's formal practice. Memories, recapitula-

[1] Blesh, Rudi, *Modern Art USA.* New York, Alfred A. Knopf, Inc., 1956.

161 Duchamp: *The Bride Stripped Bare by Her Bachelors, Even* 1915–23

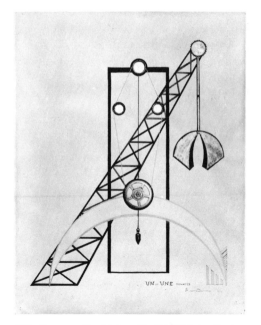

162 Suzanne Duchamp: *Multiplication: Broken and Repaired* 1916

163 Moholy-Nagy: *Collage*

164 Schwitters: *Kleines Seemansheim* 1926

tions, final statements throng silently across its great transparencies. He had planned his last formal work; found a medium both more durable than canvas and more imminently destructible; then wrote his valedictory not on sand but on a symbol of the void. And soon the glass was shattered.

No other artists, in fact hardly any other men, have seen the meaning of the machine in terms as final as those of Marcel Duchamp. Nevertheless the machine haunts our century; hypnotizes and obsesses our artists; constitutes major theme, psychological overtone, medium, or motivation of a large part of the serious art of our time. Machinism has become an integral part of modern art in the following ways:

1. Use of Machine-Made Objects, Parts, or Materials

Beginning with collage, this use of technological material had an early climax in Duchamp's ready-mades as works of art by virtue of the esthetic judgment exercised in selection. The principle continues in the use of machine parts, especially discarded ones, in welded sculpture. In the present-day sense, to be discarded by an obsolescence-motivated society is equated with selection by the artist.

2. Machine or Machine Parts as Design Motive or Subject Matter

This is the machine not as actual material but used in representational form. Although it was a basic part of futurist theory, here again Duchamp was probably first with a concrete realization in his *Coffee Mill*. The idea spread, both specifically, e.g., Max Ernst's collage clips of mechanical illustrations, and allegorically, e.g., Léger's human figures constructed from cones and cylinders, and the American Morton Schamberg's abstract compositions of mechanical parts.

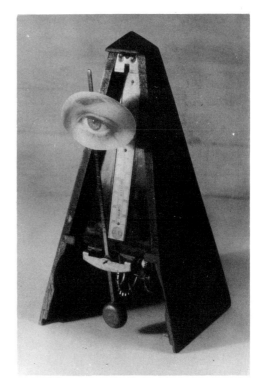

165   Man Ray: *Object of Destruction*   1932

3. The Non-utile Machine or Machine Products in Art

On the popular side the fantastic, complicated, and nonsensical machinery in the Rube Goldberg cartoons exemplifies this tendency, which is explicit in Man Ray's dada *Object of Destruction* (Fig. 165) and in Duchamp's demonstration of pure abstract plasticism, *Roto-reliefs* of 1934–35. These comprise a set of cardboard disks that rotate on a phonograph turntable at a speed of $33\frac{1}{3}$ r.p.m., creating spatial optical illusions—contracting and expanding, rising and falling—which derive from designs of spirals, counterspirals, concentric and eccentric circles, etc. The ideological relation of this unreal plasticism in unreal space to the collaging of forms in space on the transparent foundation of the *Large Glass* seems clear. Duchamp had already explored similar false-space-motion possibilities in the film *Anemic Cinema* made with Man Ray in 1924, and had

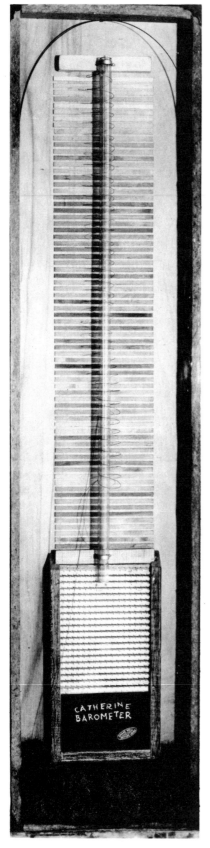

also produced a complete non-utile machine to operate in real space. This was the *Rotary Demi-sphere* of 1925 (Fig. 167) with a painted multiple spiral that seemed to move out in space and then recede in rhythmed sequences of illusion. Marcel Jean observes that

machines which age and die in a few years [are] real only as long as they are useful. But Duchamp's machines, real beyond utility, begin to live on their own account; they are about to make love.[2]

Other artists worked less from philosophy and a regnant, haunted sense of fate and more from art's customary concern with pure plasticism. Within modern art's broad machine mythos, some invoked exactitudes of mechanics and physical laws; others committed their creation to the laws of chance—although generally, it is true, in the sense of Hume's definition of chance as the

[2] Jean, Marcel, with Arpad Mezei, *The History of Surrealist Painting.* Translated by Simon Watson Taylor. New York, Grove Press, Inc., 1960.

167   Duchamp: *Rotary Demi-sphere*   1925

166   Man Ray: *Catharine Barometer*
1921

168 Westermann: *About a Black Magic Maker* 1959

169 Crotti: *Le clown* 1916

170 Cornell: *Blériot*

135

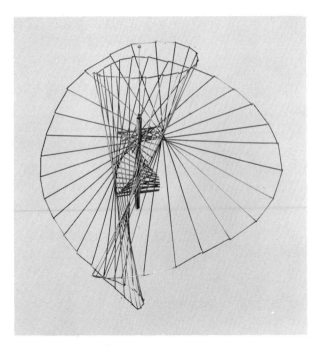

171   Kenneth Martin: *Screw*   1959

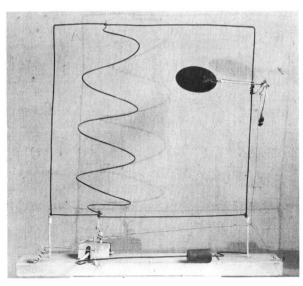

172   Calder: *Construction*   1931

"equivalent of the ignorance in which we find ourselves in relation to the real causes of events."

The Russian constructivists' exact minds led to precise non-utile machines qua sculpture, like Gabo's *Kinetic Plastic* of 1922, a columnar ribbon of clear plastic that when twisted by a clock spring whirled with great speed in the opposite direction. Similar in intent are Calder's mobile reliefs (Fig. 172) and both better known and more dramatic are his famous mobile sculptures, which he began constructing about 1930 (Fig. 173). Calder's mobiles are enclosed systems: when set in motion, part activates part in almost infinite combinations of movement. Gabo's machines are like mathematical truths expressed in visualized equations; Calder's mobiles, like small universes or galaxies of orbiting forms.

4. The Work of Art as Utile Machine

Here the work of art performs esthetic tasks. The art machine can be real mobile apparatus, or only a symbolic machine or assemblage of mechanistic shapes. Architect Frederick Kiesler's stage setting for *Emperor Jones,* built in Vienna in 1923, was a mobile three-dimensional abstraction timed to follow the O'Neill text, changing the aspect of the jungle to keep pace with Jones's frantic and lost wanderings. The complex tangle of shapes opened slowly, inviting escape, and then as slowly closed into hermetic doom.

Like deserted factory or mechanized world was the fantastic mechanical clutter of the stage set for Diaghilev's 1926 ballet *La Chatte* (Fig. 174). Designed by Gabo in transparent plastics, the setting was executed on stage at Monte Carlo by Gabo and Pevsner. The great stage-wide machine had genuine esthetic function, yet the constructivists believed just as stubbornly in the reality of art as the cubists did. If Picasso's gigantic collage managers in *Parade* were more

173   Calder: *Stabile-Mobile*

real than the dancers, in Gabo's *La Chatte* the dancers were only phantom interlopers in a frozen mechanistic universe.

5. The Machine that Produces Art

This cybernetic myth is part of our machine preoccupation, the calculating machine that rules man and will fulfil a new concept of life, the mechanistic, eventually including reproduction and perpetuation of its kind. Picabia and Duchamp had employed concepts of this kind. Archipenko actually designed, constructed, and patented such a machine. He built his *Archipentura* (Fig. 175) in New York in 1924. A motor moved 110 painted canvases so that narrow strips of each were visible between parallel slats like those of Venetian blinds. By this means an almost astronomical number of combinations became visible as pictorial wholes, pictures continually changing or motionless at option. Archipenko observes: "The left side of the apparatus shows one picture; the right side an entirely different subject, complete with its title 'Miracle.'"

6. The Machine that Is Alive, or Is Substituent for Reality

Only esthetic value or conceptual scope separate this idea from eighteenth-century automatons like Maelzel's famous chess player. It reached a culmination as symbol for civilization or world in Tinguely's suicidal machine in the Museum of Modern Art garden.

7. Machine Technologies

In a broad, diffused sense, the machine's effect on art is felt in the adoption of machine techniques and the employment of machines in painting processes, etc. As we have seen, Max Ernst pioneered a number of these mechanical and semimechanical procedures. Machines are used in a number of ways, e.g., airbrush painting, and the spot-welding of metal in sculpture. Among such technologies are photographic techniques independently developed by a number of artists. In general these consist in placing objects at random or by design on photographic paper, exposing it to light until the shapes are

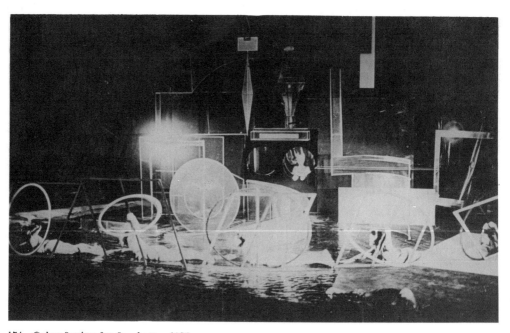

174   Gabo: Setting for *La chatte*   1926

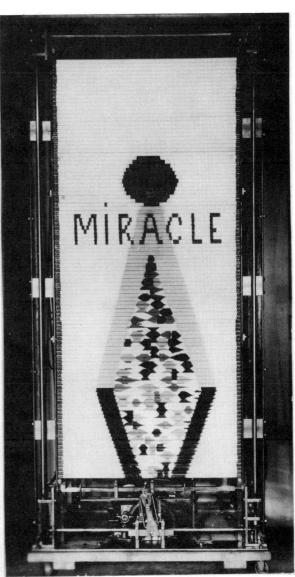

175 Archipenko: *Archipentura* 1924

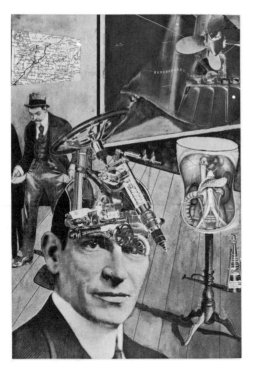

176   Hausmann: *Tatlin at Home*   1920

177   Man Ray: *Rayograph*   1922

printed, and then fixing the picture. The results of this abstract photography are so personal that the Zurich dada Christian Schad called his pictures "Schadographs," Man Ray calls his "Rayographs" (Fig. 177) while "Photograms" is the term used by the late Bauhaus professor Moholy-Nagy and still in use by artist-professor Gyorgy Kepes of the Massachusetts Institute of Technology (Fig. 178). During the 1940's the American sculptor David Hare invented a method of printing caloric reactions photographically, a method that he called "Heatages" (Fig. 179).

These techniques of printing abstractions directly on light-sensitized paper are kinds of monotype not to be confused either with collage made by pasting up fragments of photographs, or photomontage, a technical process in which parts of negatives are assembled before printing.

In this same category of techniques based upon light was an art machine of the 1920's, the Clavilux or color organ of Thomas Wilfred. With the inventor at the console the Clavilux projected changing abstract compositions of colored light called "color music." John Hoppe recently revived the idea in New York with his Mobilux, which allows interpolated visual improvisation.

The camera is one of the earliest art-producing machines, as contrasted with still earlier artist's aids like those that indicate and measure aerial perspective, or the pantograph, which is a mechanical means to reduce or enlarge pictures. Many artists have used the camera as art-producing machine to aid their own art work. Degas did intensive photography which is credited, together with Japanese prints, in his development of the tilted horizontal plane (e.g., floor or stage), the unposed or candid camera pose, and the decentralized composition with objects or figures partially cut off at picture's edge. In America Thomas Eakins made similar use of the camera, and in our century it serves the painter Charles Sheeler in much the same way. In all these cases it must be emphasized that the artist uses photographs not to copy but to clarify his vision and to explore pictorial possibilities. As independent art-producing machine, however, the camera has in some cases—as with Edward Steichen—come to replace painting altogether.

The use of machine-made parts, objects, and materials is a broad concept actually including any manufacture in its fullest sense as "goods or wares made by manual labor or by machinery." Schwitters chose such materials, not on the basis of machine versus manual technologies but on the basis of the discarded or lost. Similarly his concept of *Merz* does not seem to have made any particular distinction between two-dimensional paper collages, relief constructions, actual three-dimensional constructions, and the collage become environment or architecture, as in the *Merzbau* (Figs. 63, 64, 413). The term manufacture in its wider sense thus includes handicraft like the old wood panel with antique wrought iron hinges used by Miró in his 1927 collage-construction *Shutter* (Fig. 180).

With the surrealists the machinism concept was chiefly important in contexts wherein any artifact, machine-made or handmade, was made to seem unreal and dreamlike. The house and hinged gate in Ernst's famous painting-collage-relief, *Two Children Are Threatened by a Nightingale* (Fig. 181), may have been made by Ernst or found as ready-mades —it makes no essential difference because they are parts of the landscape of a dream. Similar considerations apply to materials included in other surrealist works, as for example André Breton's *Poème objet,* with its hand-carved torso and faceless head, boxing gloves bursting through the picture surface, and ancient lantern (Fig. 182).

No such ambiguities are harbored in

178 Kepes: *Collage* 1938

179 Hare: *Heatage* 1944

180 Miró: *Shutter* 1927

Archipenko called this work an "assemblage," and it could have been described with equal fairness as construction, sculpture, or three-dimensional collage. Made of metal, wood, mirrored glass, and painting, it created actual reflections of head and torso, which Archipenko says were indistinguishable from a *trompe-l'oeil* painting of still life objects on part of the mirror's surface.

Illusionism, one side of modern art's dual approach to the thorny epistemological question of reality, is a characteristic Archipenko method. Since 1912 his abstract concave sculptures of female figures have employed hollow modeling, or intaglio, to represent solid form through the lights and shadows of sculptural voids. The empty spaces leap forward into space by the familiar optical illusion through which the lettering of an incised inscription often seems raised.

A far more baffling and basic illusionism, however, is that which is inherent in so much art today: is a specific work a picture, object, construction, or sculpture? The ambivalence of collage material has introduced shifts in space, sub-

the work of a Russian constructivist like Gabo or the Russian-American sculptor Alexander Archipenko. Gabo's 1930 *Construction in a Niche* (Fig. 183) is a good example of the constructivists' adoption and frank use of technological materials like vinyl plastics as soon as they were developed for industrial use.

Alexander Archipenko, who went to Paris in 1908, became one of the first cubist sculptors. Though he made papiers collés in 1913 he had already used the collage idea in sculpture in experimental works of 1912. Then in 1914 he gave full treatment to the play of reality versus illusion in a life-size sculpture, *Woman before Mirror,* which was soon destroyed in a German bombing.

181 Ernst: *Two Children Threatened by a Nightingale* 1924

142

stance, identity, and meaning; traditional terminology compounds the confusion. Now that we come to the last two decades when collage and its manifold derivatives engage the majority of modern artists, these quicksands of interpretation become a matter of concern lest through applying outworn criteria we omit some activity that has become operable through the workings of the collage philosophy Max Ernst prophetically formulated more than a generation ago.

For a prime example: much of today's sculpture would, not so long ago, have been totally inadmissible as such even from a technical point of view. Assemblies of rusty iron junk, or scraps and tatters of metal, old or new, glued together by welding and modern synthetic adhesives, or abstract vanes of sheet metal swinging in the air, or even taut, drawn wires defining complex esthetic geometries in space—all of these now ask to be called sculpture. So too do crazy-quilt arrangements nailed up from old boards. Today all of this is accepted as art, and it seems unimportant whether it be called sculpture or object. The court of last appeal is the basic collage idea: the assemblage of disparate, even hostile, objects snared from the real world and creatively fused into new esthetic unities.

We need a flexible set of standards corresponding to the procedures of collage making as they now have expanded into the hybrids, derivatives, and extensions of today. These procedures are three: (1) choice of materials; (2) shaping the materials; (3) assembling the materials. In any collage-oriented activity, 1 and 3 are essential; 2 may be omitted, that is to say, materials may be used as found. It will be discovered that in any resultant work these steps are indispensable to esthetic significance and value.

Several following chapters will examine the nature and meaning of the wide

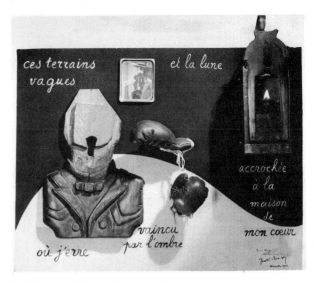

182   Breton: *Poème objet*   1941

183   Gabo: *Construction in a Niche*   1930

range of materials which collage has introduced to art. Let us here discuss the procedures of shaping and assembling, beginning with the making of pure collages, that is, papiers collés.

Cutting (*découpage*) was the original method; scissors, razor blades, or any cutting edge, the tool. Tearing (*déchirage*) came next, to give the expressive qualities (vagueness, haste, accident, etc.) inherent in the irregular deckle edge. Nowadays paper is often shaped by burning the edges (*brûlage*). It makes no essential difference if materials be used as found: man, machine, or nature has already shaped them for the artist.

The pieces of paper traditionally are assembled by pasting or gluing. Even in the cubist days the basic idea of "fastening" was extended through use of tacks, pins, etc. Extensions and broadenings of concept have continued ever since. In materials, cloth followed paper,

185 Weinrib: *Untitled* 1960

wood followed cloth—and the door was open. Similar progressions have happened with shaping and assembling. In this historical perspective it is not surprising to find broad parallels to scissoring and gluing in today's sculpture. Metal is found ready-shaped or else the gross pieces are cut to shape by the artist. Whether he cuts the metal by laborious hacksaw or scissors it with the flame of acetylene torch, it is the sculptor's equivalent of *découpage*. Or if the work is in wood, then sawing, breaking, chopping, or burning planks and fragments into shape, are equivalent to the collagist's scissors. Spot-welding, soldering, or brazing the metal, or gluing with modern adhesives—all of these parallel pasting and gluing. So do the wood sculptor's nails, screws, and dowels, and ply laminations. All such sculpture is part of the collage idea permeating our esthetics.

This leaves the sculpture made by traditional methods of carving, modeling, and casting. Even here ambiguities and uncertainties arise. A sculptor, for example, may model or carve a work with

184 Gonzales: *Woman Combing Her Hair* 1936

forms derived from, influenced by, or imitative of the forms of welded sculpture. In another case (as Picasso did with his 1959 group *The Bathers*) he may nail up constructions of wood from which molds are made to cast the final sculptures in bronze.

The acceptance of these new standards, at once broader, more specific, and related to the new space concepts, will help in judging some of the baffling hybrids now coming into existence. For example, there are the "combine–paintings" of the American Robert Rauschenberg, with their startling combinations of beverage bottles, old curtains, parts of garments, radio sets, stuffed birds and animals. It is not merely that Rauschenberg extends Schwitters' poetic selection of the lost to a resigned, encyclopedic acceptance of our whole heedless harvest. This is only a difference of degree. But Rauschenberg is determined to make us realize that he is giving us documents concerning ourselves. Collages or constructions will not suffice.

His "combine-paintings" flow out into the room and onto the floor—a determined encroachment, a shocking aggressiveness, an armed invasion of our living space.

With no great straining, collage concepts—significance of real materials, constructionism, the picture-into-space—explain and justify a Rauschenberg. If collage, however, is really the central expanding idea in the art of this century, it must meet harder tests of interpretation and justification. There are developments today more drastically revolutionary than Rauschenberg's—by artists who are even abandoning works of art in any concrete, formal, permanent sense. Not only is their art externalized but, no longer even pictures of concrete objects, it is ephemeral action in space. These are the Environment and the Happening, which we will discuss in the last chapter. It is our belief that the new criteria will clarify the meaning of such esthetic phenomena and help in their evaluation.

11

PAPER

THE CLASSIC COLLAGE MATERIAL

Material is important in collage as in no previous art medium, because it *is,* it does not pretend to be. Formerly material always tended to become a convention, hence invisible like the emperor's clothes. An arm, whether clay or bronze or marble, was first and last an arm. All pretensional material moved toward anonymity: even gold if its use became common, or in cultures that did not ennoble it. Even the Greeks' chryselephantine could have been dulled by common use.

In collage, materials have not only presence but highly complex presence, retaining memories of a previous existence that overlays their present use like images in a double-exposed photograph. They guard their identity so stubbornly that it is doubtful whether they will ever wholly lose it. The bus ticket and the label in a *Merzbild* are still bus ticket and label, not willed into anonymity but living in the picture, as it were, by Schwitters' invitation. It is equally so in the arts born of collage: in a Stankiewicz welded construction the rusty machine

fragments are unforgetting—mutely yet eloquently they speak of honorable service and then the oblivion of disuse. It is this simultaneous existence in two worlds—art and reality—that creates such powerful expression. Examining a collage we must look in two directions and think and feel as it were from two different centers of our being.

Choice of materials, then, is a process closely akin to the realistic painter's choice of subject. By choosing still life, quiet landscape, or battle scene, and by the way he portrayed them, he told us about himself while making statements about life. Choosing his artifacts of actuality, the collagist's task is just as basic: bright new paper or soiled flurries from the street—polished teakwood or grayed, weather-beaten clapboard—shining sheet steel or broken anatomies of machine—piece of silken lace or torn and dark-stained burlap—he too makes revelations and statements. Material and its memory have become the subject in direct statements from the real world.

Take paper: Marcel Duchamp defined its outworn intimacy, imminent sadness, and defenseless fragility when so long ago he hung his geometry book in the winter snow and rain. The core of classic collage, paper, is one of the commonest, most trivial things in our world. Its nature is evanescence—water can dissolve it, flames consume it, fingers tear it, light darken and light fade it, wind blow it as perversely out of reach as Mark Twain's famous million-pound note. Disappearing in the gusts around the corners of the world each bit of paper could as well be an important document—a will, the pardon of a condemned murderer, a treaty of peace—as a discarded newspaper.

Even new, unused paper cannot lose this poignant vulnerability. A cut or torn edge, mutely referring to frangibility, is like a wound. In papers used, soiled, torn, and aged in human commerce, then framed into pictures, all this weighty, unknown history comes sadly, intimately into focus. They never cease referring to two different existences. No wonder Schwitters found paint so unsuited to his complexities of feeling and purpose. Paint is inert—used paper, strangely alive and, even used, still subject matter: fragments mutely whispering history.

Old wood is also a living chronicle. Weather-beaten, gray, it speaks to human beings in intimate ways: the great trees of vanishing forests, the fire and shelter that preserved the race over uncounted precarious centuries, or perhaps only sad fragments of childhood histories, bits of lost and broken toys.

No collage material is more evocative than cloth. It is intensely, personally intimate: material we wear from swaddling clothes on, to protect and shelter the physical constituents of our lives. Even used abstractly, as Marca-Relli uses painter's canvas in his collages, it still refers as artist's material, to the artist's life. Bits of lovely silk, brocade, or woven tissues, as Ann Ryan uses them in her most abstract collages, retain the echoes they so variously sing for each beholder, just as an elderly woman's patchwork quilt might always remind her of beautiful dresses she wore when young, of parties, of friends, of love, of weddings and births and deaths. Plain sail canvas, as Arthur B. Dove used it in the collage called *Huntington Harbor*

(Fig. 261) to form the literal outline of a sail, combined with an area of glued-on sand—means more than representation could mean. Oil paint might better have *represented* sail and beach; canvas and sand actually live the parts, and yet by very literalness enclose poetry.

Man Ray dates an early patchwork cloth composition of his own as early as 1911. In 1912 Boccioni included cloth in a list of sculptor's materials. By 1914 Picasso incorporated bits of cloth into collage. Yet Degas had long since utilized the idea. His little wax ballet girl, later cast in bronze, still wears the *tutu* of real tarlatan with which Degas first clothed her in 1881.[1] It has remained for very recent tendencies developing from collage to explain the enigmatic, powerful emotions that this strange juxtaposition of bronze and lace have always evoked. Faintly, the emotion is partly horror. The macabre assemblages of Rauschenberg point the way to this explanation; Bruce Conner's gruesome *Child* (Figs. 334, 335) makes it explicit. It is death that lurks in this Degas sculpture, faintly but nevertheless there, a Victorian premonition of Freudian nightmare. Such is the emotional power of clothing (and hence of cloth) that swaddling clothes can suggest the winding cerements waiting at life's other end.

The range and depth of human feelings evoked by clothing are suggested by a consideration of shoes in different contexts. Strong differences exist in the emotional responses to a baby shoe, a child's shoe, or an adult's shoe; to a woman's shoe or a man's. A shoe with holes evokes pity, particularly for children or the extremely old and poor. Consider the degrees of feeling called forth by the following: a new shoe in a display window or a used one on the floor of a clothes closet; one lying enigmatically in the street, its origin un-

---

[1] *Petite danseuse de quatorze ans* in the Havemeyer Bequest at the Metropolitan Museum of Art.

known, or one lying in the highway amid broken glass.

These degrees of involuntary emotional involvement that shoes can command, from nostalgic pleasure or pity to horror, can be caused by mere cloth if selected and used by a perceptive artist. From the nearly pure esthetic response to Marca-Relli's clean forms of canvas we leap to the macabre and tragic in Burri's bandage-like burlap with its burned holes and its gaping wounds of paint.

With collage, art materials become an inventory of our time. Each bit and scrap with its indelible memories is subject to the selection, shaping, and intent of the artist. No longer wrestling with stubborn, obdurate, anonymous materials, he orchestrates rich new resources. His counterpoint tells its story and his, while setting each beholder's memories echoing, willingly or not.

Today's artist has the intoxicating feeling of working with living entities. It is no wonder that Louise Nevelson speaks of her great, compartmented, sculptural walls as "living communities"; or that Rauschenberg's studio is inhabited impartially by stuffed animals and birds and the living marmoset and kinkajou which he daily feeds; or that Stankiewicz's studio, stacked high with

187   Huzsar: *Figure composition pour une théatre*

broken machinery, is so palpably thronging with presences.

Still, with the ever-widening choice of materials, paper has remained the classic material through five decades of collage. Cubists, futurists, constructivists, dadas, surrealists—even Kurt Schwitters and Max Ernst—have not exhausted its flexible adaptability and expressiveness. New uses, new techniques or variations of techniques are still being developed, and meanwhile there is constant search for untouched possibilities in the older, classic methods.

Paper responds to imagination and the shaping touch. Its infinite adaptability is suggested by the possibilities in edging it, i.e., cutting, tearing, and burning. Each type of edge monitors our space perceptions differently; each sounds its own affective overtones.

Fresh, sharply edged, plain paper

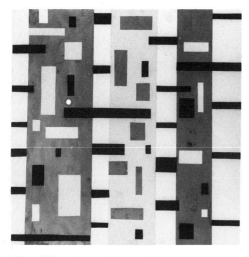

186   Diller: *Composition* 1950

188 Pasmore: *Square Motif in Brown and White*
1951

forms convey a sense of precision. Arp knew this from the start, deliberately chose the severe edge or the torn edge to express reality and presence or an amorphous becoming. Universally those collagists who seek precision employ the sheared edge for clear statement, as—to name a few veterans—the American Burgoyne Diller, the Hungarian De Stijlist Vilmos Huszar, and the English artist Victor Pasmore (Figs. 186, 187, 188). Within their stable geometric world to introduce imprecise or romantic materials (e.g., wallpaper) is as startling a step as to disturb the calm right angles with diagonals.

The value of papier collé's potential chiseled sharpness is not confined to geometric abstractions of the De Stijl order: some concepts involving freer forms and rhythms benefit from the sharply cut edge. This is shown by the 1939 collages of the English artist Ben Nicholson (Fig. 191) and the American A. D. F. Reinhardt (Fig. 192). Today, Will Barnet is among those employing cameo-sharp cutting together with limited primary color or monotone in free but precise collages. His *Big Black* (Fig. 193) is typically executed in black and gray papers, aided by ink, on a white ground.

Edge declares form, however, and

forms can in themselves be hard or soft, definite or amorphous, as shown in Arp's wide range of morphology. Arp employs these paradoxes as wit in his white marble sculptures of amoebic forms. The paradoxes operate in either direction: soft nature in hard material or granitic form in soft material, dissolving as in mist. Or similar material can speak in different ways. Rectangular cards, for example: computer cards in a Vera Spencer collage (Fig. 194) have clear presence; subway tickets in Walter Gaudnek's *Metro* (Fig. 195) are pre-

189 Von Wiegand: *Persian Court*

149

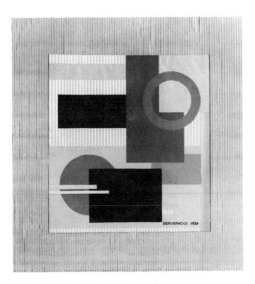

190   Servranckx: *Opus 20*   1924

191   Nicholson: *Composition*

192   Reinhardt: *Collage*   1939

193 Barnet: *Big Black* 1960

cisionism lost in the darkness. Paint swirls over the tickets like tunnel dimness as the signal lights flash by.

The torn or *déchire* edge has its own advantages. Like crayon or pencil it can convey a sense of hasty inspiration, especially if the artist only partially pastes each piece of paper, leaving the edges unattached. The French artist Jeanne Coppel (Fig. 198) uses this effect to advantage, enforcing it with hastily painted crumpled paper visibly emended in new form after new form on top of old ones.

Miró made effective use of partial pasting, as in the large 1929 *Collage* (Fig. 94). In a similar Miró collage in the historic Paris exhibition of 1930, *La peinture au défi,* this deliberate hastiness was interpreted by the critics as a cynical built-in impermanence in a work of art. They were right: Miró was merely agreeing with industrial merchandising.

Torn paper hastily slapped into collages can actually express the artist's haste and, more, his dissatisfaction and even anger. Arp has created successful collages out of fragments of "failures." Franz Kline, American abstract-expressionist painter noted for his gigantic abstract black calligraphy, has followed Arp's example (Figs. 199, 200). Kline has stated that this is a deliberate effort on his part to break up patterns that threaten to solidify in his mind and block invention. A younger American, Michael Goldberg, sometimes cuts up

151

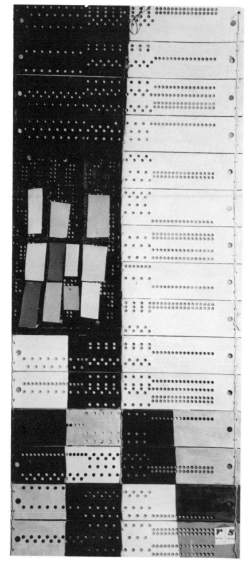

194 Spencer: *Collage*

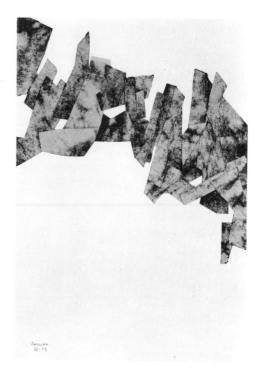

196 Chillida: *Collage No. 1* 1959

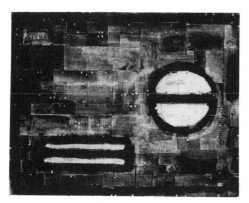

195 Gaudnek: *Metro* 1953

197 Johnson: *Overhang* 1958

oil paintings and re-combines the parts with cut papers (Fig. 201).

Among its many other allusions, the torn edge can be made to suggest thickness, weight, and solidity. Pieces torn from painted paper and used with this intent cluster together like fragments of slate in a De Staël collage of 1954 (Fig. 202).

All of these are contemporary meanings that have become attached to ancient methods. In the Far East collage, like paper, has a long history. By A.D. 700 the Chinese were mounting scroll paintings on backgrounds of many-layered paper collage. Designed to secure the utmost elasticity in the scrolls, the technique became traditional. Papers made from rice stalks, cotton, bamboo, mulberry bark and hemp, as well as silk, were superimposed in prescribed orders and secured by adhesives which were guild secrets. The method required time and limitless patience.

A Chinese-American collagist, Tseng

199 Kline: *Black and White* 1957

Yu-Ho, learned this ancient technique in Peking. Moving to Hawaii, she combined the old method with painting.

She selects a variety of irregular shapes and sizes among the oriental papers available, applies them to the permanent background, and paints each layer before superimposing another, sometimes using as many as a hundred sheets in one composition to attain the effect of opacity, translucency or transparency she desires.[2]

Traditional Chinese representation—itself so abstract—combines with modern abstraction in Tseng Yu-Ho's personal style. In *Forest* (Fig. 203) tree forms in scroll-painting style fill abstract forms of translucent *déchire* paper, while the torn edges themselves, branching outward with the fibrous constituents of the paper, define a forest of their own.

The chaste sumptuousness of Japanese screens develops into modern collage-painting in the work of the Japanese

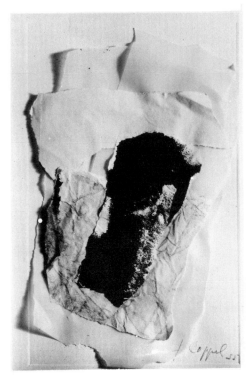

198 Coppel: *Collage* 1955

[2] Arnason, H. H., Foreword to catalogue, Tseng Yu-Ho exhibition, Downtown Gallery. New York, 1960.

153

200 Kline: *Wall Collage* 1960

201 Goldberg: *Murder, Inc.* 1960

202 De Staël: *Collage in Color* 1954

Yutaka Ohashi, born in Hiroshima in 1923. His large works approximate the traditional height of a folding screen. In a typical example, *Mashiko* No. 5 (Fig. 204), modern forms of torn paper float on a sea of gold leaf under a painted sky.

Oriental influences are at work in the collages of the Toronto artist, Harold Town, as evidenced in an extremely large collage, *Monument to C. T. Currelly, No. 2* (Fig. 205). The artist writes:

> As a print maker I cut up prints that don't please me . . . and [also] print many proofs to use as collage material. In this way I live on my creative self and in the end, like a meat packing plant, I waste nothing. I use found material too . . . any substance that seems suitable. . . . This collage is in honour of C. T. Currelly who created the Royal Ontario Museum which has one of the finest Chinese collections in the world.
>
> Forgive me if I say something about collage that appeals to me more than any considerations of . . . edges, contrasts in texture, etc. etc. It seems to me the one medium most suited to the age of conspicuous waste, and it's marvelous to think of the garbage of our age becoming the art of our time.[3]

Let us briefly survey the contemporary international use of paper in collage. Among Spanish artists, the Barcelonan, Francisco Farreras, uses soft handmade oriental papers to create mysterious semitranslucent forms against dark backgrounds. Some of these are pasted on in even masses, others seem to have been soaked in adhesive and flung on the canvas. In the one case we feel immobility, in the other, rapid motion, a drama of kinetics and antikinetics that evokes hallucinatory wraiths: a bull's head or skull (Fig. 207), or more haunting metamorphoses (Fig. 208). Fellow Barcelonan Antonio Tapies evokes topographies rather than specters, drawing veils of glue-softened paper like wrinkled earth

[3] In a letter to Harriet Janis, January 11, 1961.

203 Tseng Yu-Ho: *Forest* 1956

204 Yutaka Ohashi: *Mashiko No. 5* 1959

155

206   Alcopley: *Peinture-collage*   1954

205   Town: *Monument to C. T. Currelly, No. 2*   1958

156

207   Farreras: *Collage*   1960

157

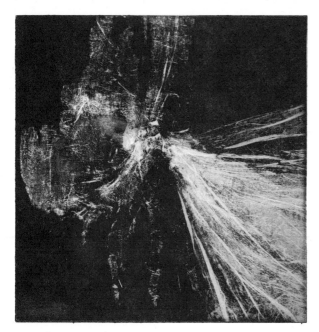

208   Farreras: *Collage*   1960

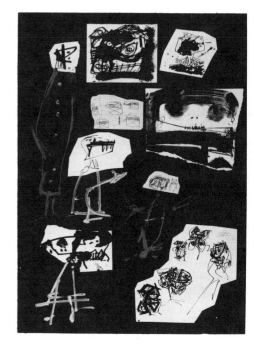

209   Saura: *Collage*   1959

210   Paolozzi: *Head*   1960

211   Tapies: *Number 16*   1959

212   Vicente: *Collage No. 5*   1957

159

213   Vicente: *Collage*   1957

214   Baziotes: *The Drugged Balloonist*   1943

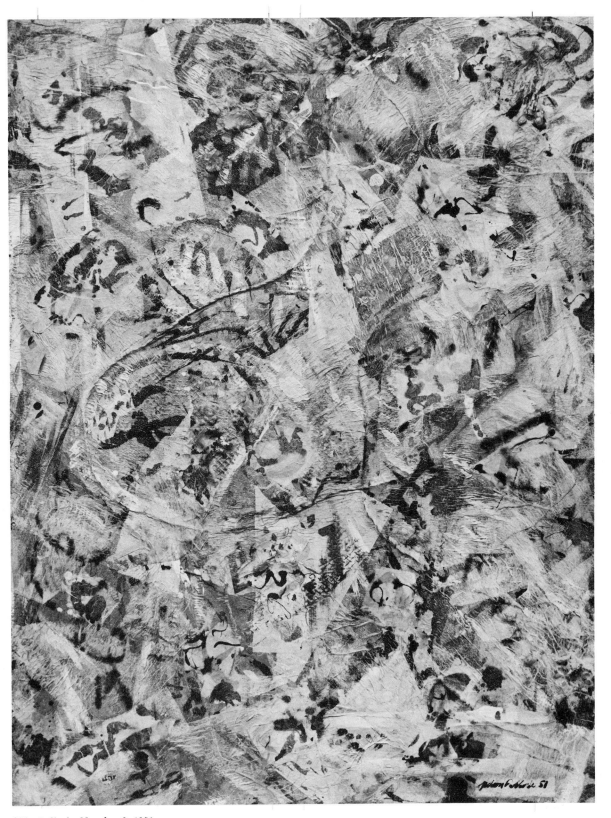

215   Pollock: *Number 2, 1951*

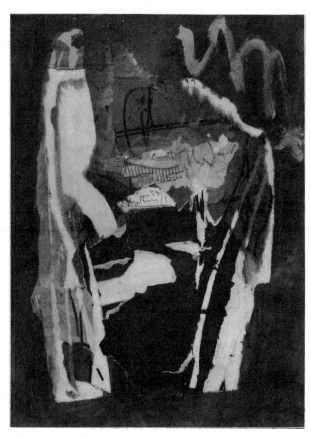

216   Motherwell: *The Joy of Living*   1943   217   Motherwell: *The Tearingness of Collaging*   1957

218   Motherwell: *Collage with Ochre and Black*
1958

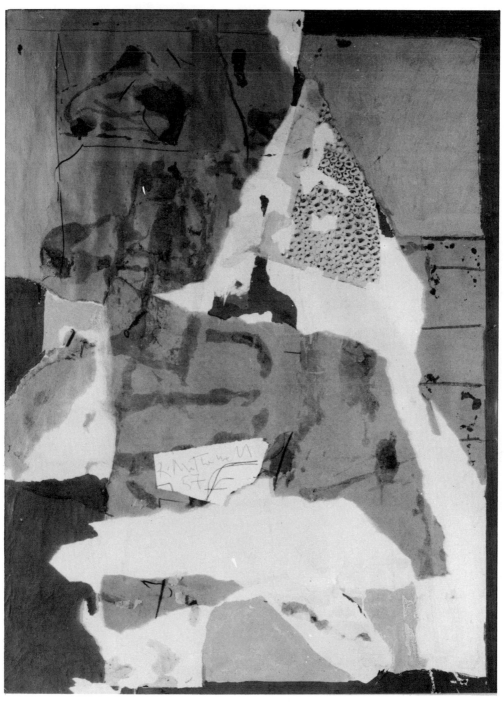

219   Motherwell: *The End of Dover Beach*   1953–57

220   Motherwell: *Reversible Collage*   1960

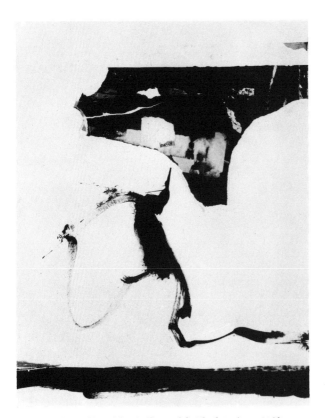

221   Motherwell: *White Collage with Black Stripe*   1960

222   Sugarman: *Two Forms on Black*   1957

223   Stamos: *Stirling VII*   1959

224   Stella: *Collage*   *c.* 1922

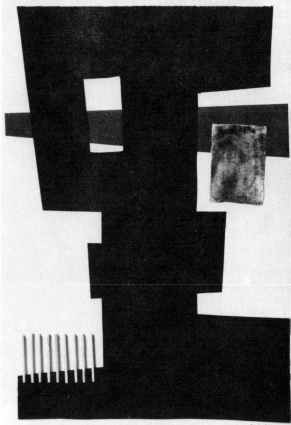

225   Gisiger: *Sphinx*   1955

226 Tryggvadottir: *Island* 1955

227 Seuphor: *Coryphée rouge* 1959

167

228 Longobardi: *Collage* 1956

229 Jimmy Ernst: *Collage and Counter-collage* 1952

230 Plunkett: *Cubanola Glide c. 1913* 1960

230A Pousette-Dart: *Untitled Collage* 1948

231 Lurie: *Les lions* (detail) 1960

232   Roh: *Umfruchtet*   1929

across and into his collage-paintings (Fig. 211). In certain pictures Tapies employs the same technique with muslin rather than paper.

The American painter Esteban Vicente, using papier collé as a "holiday from painting," has developed personal techniques of painting the paper both before and after pasting. He tints large sheets of handmade paper with lacquer, then tears and cuts out the shapes he wants, and pins them over a charcoal drawing. At this stage he does further coloring with oil paint or pastel, and shifts, removes, or adds pieces. When finally satisfied Vicente pastes the layers into place, having removed the pins.

Vicente's abstract collages are handsome without lapsing into the decorative. Working with colors that have a Spanish flavor—white, gray, yellow, etc. —he alternates cut and torn edges. The unpasted edges are precarious, almost floating. Sensitive and quivering, the shapes lie on the canvas like leaves about to be whisked away on the wind (Figs. 212, 213).

Collage-making in the United States was given impetus by a 1943 exhibition at Peggy Guggenheim's Art of This Century. The young artists she was sponsoring, Baziotes, Motherwell, and Pollock, made papiers collés expressly for this showing. Their work showed strong surrealist influence. Breton, Ernst, Masson, Duchamp, Tanguy, and others were war exiles in New York; the surrealists had just put on an international exhibition in the same city; the surrealist ideas, particularly automatism, had strong fascination for the younger Americans.

William Baziotes has made no more collages since then (Fig. 214); Jackson Pollock only a very few (Fig. 215); Robert Motherwell went on to alternate between collage and oil painting as his two main techniques. For him as for so many others, collage is endlessly pleasurable, fascinating, relaxing, and evocative. The title of a *papier déchiré* of

233 Lewitin: *The Wizard* 1940–42

1957, *The Tearingness of Collaging* (Fig. 217), indicates this pleasure.

All of Motherwell's collages evince his love of materials. Like Schwitters, he treasures paper for itself, consecrates it in his pictures. "I like a large spatial clarity," he says, "and by overlapping the paper forms I am able to work out the ordering of my space." His Mexican period of the 1940's included the collage *Pancho Villa, Dead or Alive* in the Museum of Modern Art collection. "In the late forties the Mexican color changed to something more somber," Motherwell says, referring to his colors in the abstract paintings of social reference termed the "Spanish Prisoner" series. These are grave and earthy, in ocher, black, and startling white.

Motherwell's collages vary from single large island shapes as in *Collage with Ochre and Black* (Fig. 218) to complex, packed compositions as in *The End of Dover Beach* (Fig. 219). His painted areas, with strong expressionist overtones, background or overlap the collage or set it off in contrast, but never dominate. His is a very effective counterpoint of collage with painting.

The spatial ideas inherent in collage are variously interpreted by various artists. One sees bodiless silhouettes while another sees planes tilting and moving in space; one, monolithic corporealities, another, layered, stratified growth. The American sculptor George Sugarman, for example, thinks in terms of layered growth. His vast sculpture-constructions

234 Polak: *Collage* 1955–56

are built up, plywood style, from endless laminations of planks. His *papiers déchirés* are stratified, too, his intent being to express not multiple forms but single forms in a kind of spread out lamination (Fig. 222).

Spatial sense can spur technical invention, as shown in Jimmy Ernst's large *Collage and Counter Collage* (Fig. 229), which involves an original use of *dépouillage* or peeling. Active calligraphic personages move in a broad but extremely shallow world. Some of these forms are painted on the original illustration board surface. An actual third dimension, advancing and receding, is then created by opposite methods: cameo and intaglio—the former in cut-out shapes pasted on; the latter by peeling shapes deeply into the cardboard. The pasted figures advance; the peeled ones retreat into shadow in the dark brown manila core of the illustration

board. The artist's strong spatial sense creates a kind of silent, oscillating drama.

Another striking example of inventiveness involving both form and new technique, is the tatterdemalion paper shapes floating in the collages of Marcel Polak, a Dutch artist now working in France. His method involves certain technical innovations as evidenced in his description of one of his collages (Fig. 234). The materials, he says, included paper and tar, together with *pastel mouillé*, that is, pastel softened in water and used as a kind of "paint in sticks."

Just as the littered sidewalk once riveted Schwitters' gaze, it was inevitable, sooner or later, that that ubiquitous horror the billboard would capture the artist. With its many-layered peeling huckster skins—movie queens and political candidates, patent medicines, food products, beers and whiskeys, hotels, motels and boatels, motor cars and summer resorts—it is auto-collage, the self-portrait of our time.

So all over the world a special kind of collagist peels these wonderful, tawdry documents from walls and billboards and reassembles them, as sentient and as memoried as the *Merzbilder*. The new genre has already had an important exhibition[4] and it has gotten proper designations: in England—"hoardings"; in the United States—"billboardism"; in France—*affiches lacérés*, "torn posters," or *lacérés anonymes,* which might be rendered as "torn, nameless things."

In England Gwyther Irwin assembles hoarding (billboard) strippings into large papiers collés like *Distant Land* (Fig. 242). He writes of his work:

Only the reverse side of the posters is used so that the work is always non-associative. The coloured die of the actual posters seeps through to the back of the paper, the paste used by the bill stickers rusts the paper in contact with the metal hoarding, and the soot and grime of London produce a monochromatic scale of tone. Lorry loads of posters (otherwise destined for the incinerator) are delivered to my studio. The collages are made up of small, thin strips minutely graded as to tone, colour, and texture.[5]

However, the material is not so easily subdued—it hums with a visible babble like radio or television commercials tuned on in a dozen rooms. With Irwin, and with Britisher Austin Cooper (Fig. 243), the effort at "non-association" is not wholly successful—the material is rude, lively, insuppressible, charming—and sad.

In Paris in the early 1950's Raymond Hains began collecting and presenting torn posters as ready-mades. Now a group makes regular exhibitions of *af-*

[4] "Lacéré anonyme," included in the First Paris Biennial: *Manifestation biennale et international des jeunes artistes de Paris,* October 2–25, 1959, Musée de l'Art Moderne, Paris.

[5] Irwin, Gwyther, Statement for Gimpel Fils Gallery, London.

235   Goodnough: *White Intervals*   1960

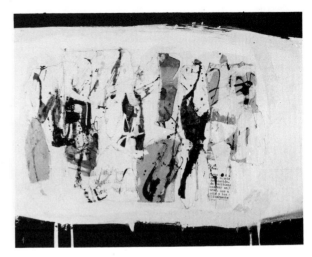

236   Girona: *Collage No. 8*   1960

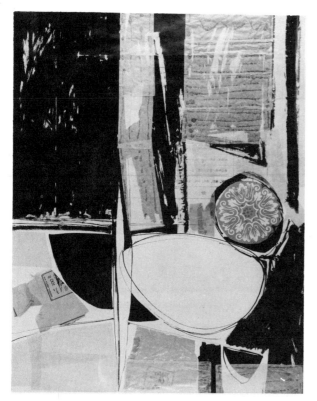

238   Leslie: *Oval*   1959

237   Clinton Hill: *Registrata*   1960

239   Getz: *Spanish Landscape*   1959

fiches lacérés both altered and "as found." Mimo Rotella of Rome exhibits with them, his eyes sharpened in 1951 by the billboards of the Midwest while he was artist-in-residence at a Kansas collage (Figs. 244, 245). Wide diversities of vision characterize the group as shown by examples of their work: Hains—*Il est né le Divin Enfant* (Fig. 247) and *Le 13 Mai* (Fig. 248); François Dufrêne—*L'art, c'est le vol* (Fig. 246); Villeglé—*Fragment de l'affiche* (Fig. 249).

A photograph—when photographer's artist-eye chooses and isolates specific detail from general welter—proves how essentially realistic this type of collage is, even when the artist rearranges the material and the photographer does not. This point is proved by comparing Aaron Siskind's photograph *Guanajuato* (Fig. 252) with one of William Getman's collages made in San Miguel de Allende in the same Mexican state (Fig. 253). The collage seems as much a likeness of a specific postered adobe wall as does the photograph. Yet Siskind employs only camera and selective eye, while Getman, to realize his selection, invokes a skilled and complex technical process.

Getman is an American living in Mexico. His intricate manipulations are probably no more arduous or involved than those of other billboard-collagists. Briefly, he soaks and scrapes the posters from walls, then tears them into usable shapes while they are still wet (*déchirage mouillé*). After drying they are assembled: shuffled and reshuffled, stud-ied and restudied. Meanwhile, cabinet-maker's hide glue which has soaked overnight and is now hot on the stove, is used to fasten everything to a masonite panel. "Over-glue," says Getman, "and let it squeeze out for emphatic portions of your design." Now follows collage-on-collage: patches of semitransparent Japanese paper to "veil" some of the parts.

The glue hardens overnight; then the collage is laid on the floor. Getman brushes a thin amber glaze of glue over the entire surface, and into it, here and there, sprinkles brown-black adobe earth from his garden and, following this, driblets of powdered white zinc "like snow on the earth."

If, after all this effort, a billboard-collage will only look like a billboard, why, one asks, not choose and present actual examples, as Hains and Villeglé do? Take as a case in point another Getman collage (Fig. 254) which represents highly selected elements. Though the arrangement is dynamic and striking it must be admitted that it might have happened by itself. It is, however, the result of a creative effort and to say that sun, rain, wind, and man's neglect might have duplicated it, is merely another way of saying that the poetry of this kind of collage is also completely pertinent to our time and our world. This is surely the highest praise one could give, just as the touching relevance of these works constitutes the highest kind of realism.

240   Ippolito: *Collage No. 10*   1958

241   Vostell: *Décollage*   1960

242   Irwin: *Distant Land*   1959

243   Cooper: *Apache*

244 Rotella: *Auto-portrait* 1960

245   Rotella: *Untitled*   1959

246   Dufrêne: *L'art, c'est le vol*   1961

247   Hains: *Il est né le Divin Enfant*   1950

248   Hains: *Le 13 Mai*

249   Villeglé: *Fragment de l'affiche*   1960

251   Porter: *Collage*   1960

250   Elliott: *Carnival III*   1957

181

252 Siskind: *Guanajuato* 1955

253 Getman: *Collage* 1960

254   Getman: *Collage*   1960

12

OTHER MATERIALS

COLLAGE AS THE ARTIST'S ADJUNCT

Cloth brings to collage an expressive gamut of its own. Far more intimate than paper, less fragile and less the subject of deliberate waste, it bespeaks human histories. Besides its tactile intimacy, cloth has a wider range of intrinsic values, from beggar's rags to lace and brocade.

In the usages of folk art, bits of cloth have always been assembled into patterns. They remain consecrated to use, however, as in the patchwork quilts that are among the glories of folk art, while bits of paper are generally assembled into more frivolous, decorative, or entertaining things.

In modern collage the use of cloth with other materials sets up dialogues, as of man with his environment. A worn scrap of once lustrous and costly silken velvet, placed with imagination next to a soiled bit of cheap newsprint, creates allegories: life's precariousness, the rise and fall of family fortunes, etc.

Cloth's collaged entry into modern art was far from startling. As we have seen, it was a piece of oilcloth simulating

woven cane in Picasso's *Still Life with Chair Caning* (Fig. 7). By 1914, however, Picasso boldly included a floral-striped weave as the shirt front of *The Smoker (Fumeur)* (Fig. 257), a figure prescient of the grotesque *Managers* in *Parade* three years later. Also in 1914 suprematist Casimir Malevich incorporated lace and ornamental braid with paper in his collage *Woman Beside a Kiosk* (Fig. 258). Here the textiles function abstractly as symbols of femininity, where with Picasso the fabric *was* shirt front. These strikingly different functions indicate the potentiality of real yet associational materials such as these.

255 Dove: *Grandmother* 1925

256 Schloss: *Dow Road* 1958

257 Picasso: *Fumeur* 1914

258 Malevich: *Woman Beside a Kiosk* 1914

259 Schwitters: *Merz 149* 1920

Picasso was witty, Malevich precisely intellectual, Schwitters poetic and essentially sad. The tatter of coarse cloth in a collage like his *Merz 149* (Fig. 259) is as stark and as somber as poverty itself, proving once again that collage's retrieved materials are memoried, and, in themselves, subject matter.

Eventually, in the postwar disillusion, Picasso too would discover these sad, tattered, anonymous biographies. The *Guitar* of 1926 (Fig. 260) is no longer the instrument of ballad and serenade but a kind of obituary of youth and romance—as though fashioned from some household drudge's worn-out dishtowel and a bedraggled newspaper with her picture as she once had been.

Women artists are apt to use cloth less pitilessly. In her *Still Life with Bottle and Cup* (Fig. 262), Tour Donas almost sets up housekeeping within the confines of an abstract collage. Though this is a seriously composed picture, the arched chair back, table, and teacup, together with the lace curtain and upholstery fabrics, reflect domesticity. Equally feminine is Natalia Goncharova's collage (Fig. 263) with its painted replicas of decorative fabrics. With her husband Michael Larionov, Mme. Goncharova founded the abstract rayonist movement in Moscow in 1911, and later began designing ballet sets.

Even the late Ann Ryan, a serious American artist who worked almost solely in collage, had a woman's special feeling for textiles. Whether in compact, formal compositions (Fig. 264) or loose, free-form assemblages (Fig. 265), the bits of cloth interwoven with paper bespeak, not sadness, but a kind of warm, intimate wistfulness.

Oriental materials seem to fascinate collagists. For example, Sue Fuller has used Japanese paper labels, and leaves from shrubs and trees, while her *Sonnet* (Fig. 266) is an abstract assembly of lustrous silks. China furnished Ronnie Elliott with far different cloth for far different collages. Mrs. Elliott became a "rag collagist"—her term—in 1944 (Fig. 267). She writes:

The rags [came] from Kunming in Yunnan province, southwest China. In China the poor waste nothing and these rags were sold in the market place to patch the already patched and to make soles of shoes with many layers. The colors reminded my husband—a news correspondent during the war—of the painting I was doing at the time so he sent them to me. I pasted them in the shapes I found them or tore them as I felt the need, used oil paint to heighten or lower colors or to blend edges. I worked freely to achieve poetry and not violate the character of the rags. I still work [1961] with pieces I have left.[1]

In Mrs. Elliott's collages an indwelling sadness only heightens something heroic—the visible honors of age, in

[1] Elliott, Ronnie, written to the authors, 1961.

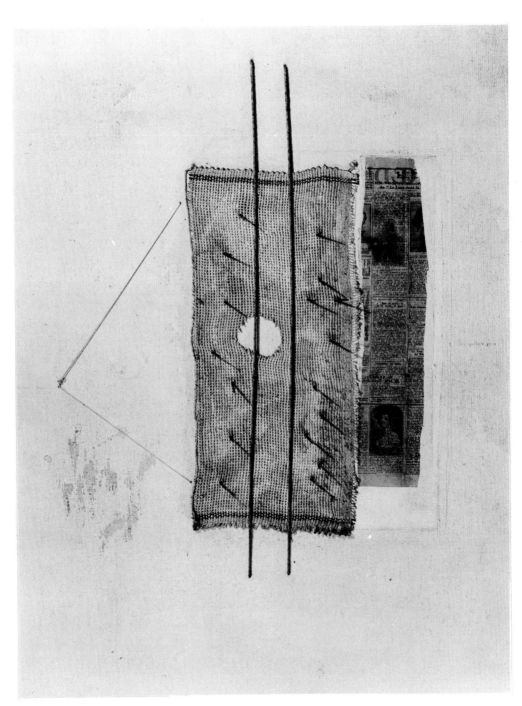

260   Picasso: *Guitar*   1926

261 Dove: *Huntington Harbor* 1926

263 Goncharova: *Collage*

262 Tour Donas: *Still Life with Bottle and Cup* c. 1920

264   Ryan: *Collage*

265   Ryan: *Collage*

266   Fuller: *Sonnet*

267　Elliott: *Rag Collage*　1957

268   Siskind: *Arizona*   1949

these artifacts from China where age was honored and use, not waste, was venerated. "They were so alive," she says. "They had earned the right to be used once more."

Women collagists are not really classifiable as such, of course. Many, in fact, have a strong and forthright sense of plasticity and space that partially de-emphasizes cloth's overtones. Among these artists, Karskaya in France marshals scraps of cloth and chips of wood so that their identities fuse into anonymous deposits (Fig. 269). With the painter Lee Krasner, abstract expressionism activates cloth and paper collage-paintings like *Blue Level* (Fig. 270). Miss Krasner comes close to subduing the individuality of her materials to the plastic needs of her pictures.

The edge qualities of cloth are different from those of paper. Its edges—due to weaving—create other kinds of line and space form. Certain fabrics can also be ripped and raveled into fringed edges, possibilities well demonstrated in the collage by the French painter Jean Deyrolle (Fig. 273).

Man Ray, the veteran American modernist, used cloth in 1911 in a proto-dada anti-art gesture, derisively titling his sewn patchwork of clothing fabric samples *Tapestry* (Fig. 274). He says: "It was one of my first declarations of independence when I got out of art school." Though following the patchwork quilt formula, *Tapestry* is strongly masculine in material and feeling. So, too, is the 1939 collage (Fig. 275) by another American, Jean Xceron, in which suitings are also used, but isolated, begrimed with paint, and eloquent of the deprivations of the long depression of the 1930's.

Two contemporaries, Spaniard Manolo Millares and Britisher Adrian Heath, aptly illustrate opposite poles of cloth's expressiveness. Millares' combinations of paint and old sacking are feverish, disturbed, and nocturnal (Fig. 276) while Heath, using similar mate-

rials (Fig. 277), creates classical structures slightly disarrayed by only the most imperceptible commotions.

Another veteran American painter, Lee Gatch, makes collages with painter's canvas as a utilitarian material nearly devoid of emotional connotations and therefore able to function as abstract form and texture. Gatch incorporates collaged canvas into oil paintings that represent an equilateral fusion of two materials. Gatch paints and stains canvas, shapes it by cutting and tearing, then imbeds it in oil paint. Close-spaced as in slotted tapestry, the edges set up strong tactile tensions, as in *Tapestry to a Square* (Fig. 278). Gatch's distillations from appearances are so remotely abstract that his need for anonymous collage material becomes quite evident. *Kissing the Moon* (Fig. 279) is such a picture; its reference to figures in a boat (it is an adaptation of a well-known Winslow Homer painting) is well aided by the compliant canvas but could have been garbled and sentimentalized by strongly charactered cloth—for example, worn rags or at the other extreme, brocades.

269   Karskaya: *Collage*

270   Krasner: *Blue Level*   1955

271 Leuppi: *Collage* 1950

Conrad Marca-Relli was one of the pioneers in the abstract use of painter's canvas. His earliest collages were composed entirely of unpainted canvas forms. He has continually explored the possibilities of this pure, uncommitted medium. Born in Boston in 1913, Marca-Relli has lived alternately in Europe and in the United States. He began painting at the age of seventeen and, as a member of the abstract-expressionist group, had his first exhibition in 1948. In 1953, during a brief stay in San Miguel de Allende in Mexico, he first assayed collage, has concentrated on the medium ever since. Marca-Relli was attracted to collage by what he calls its "speed." Matisse felt this too, and like him, Marca-Relli cuts directly into the material without patterns or preliminary sketches. "You get a linear quality from collage," he says, "that is more rapid than the swiftest drawn line." He wields the shears in lightning-swift motions, then glues the forms immediately to the stretched canvas. This is the abstract-expressionist speed-action idea otherwise exemplified by De Kooning's slashing brushwork and Jackson Pollock's "drip" paintings. In Marca-Relli's words, "it is speed not for its own sake but to create through free, automatic action, before conscious thought can censor out the creativeness."

Through speed-cutting and speed-pasting Marca-Relli builds up his forms. If a shape looks wrong he does not peel it off, but laminates another shape on top of it. Some of his pictures have as many as twenty layers in certain places. No matter how laminations pile up, Marca-Relli points out that the picture retains its freshness. He welcomes interesting textures that may develop, and as for volume, feels that collage shapes, unlike drawn lines, include form and volume in their very nature.

Marca-Relli's collage work began with the human figure delineated by biomorphic forms cut from plain, sized,

197

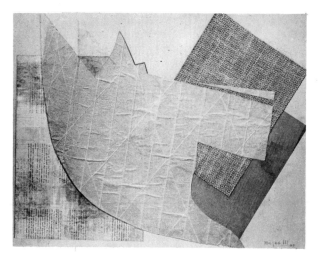

272 Magnelli: *Collage* 1949

white canvas, thickly coated on the back
with black oil paint or tar and then
pressed down until the black squeezed
out around the edges, forming in effect
a line drawing. "But," he observes, "not
drawn lines—lines created by the process." A figurative collage, *The Inhabitant* (Fig. 281), shows pressed-out lines
and drips.

Marca-Relli moved gradually into a
greater degree of abstraction, while adding color in various ways to his original
all-white concepts. His forms sometimes
tumble and sprawl across the canvas
(Fig. 282) and at other times are mar-
shalled in interwoven tiers (Fig. 284).
The background canvas is now frequently painted an even, clean color—
blue, red, yellow, or black. The background remains at the picture plane,
forcing the collage laminae to thrust
out into space.

Marca-Relli calls his collages "paintings" and he has effected, certainly, a
unified synthesis of the two media. His
technical speed enables him to create
collages of vast size as fresh and spontaneous in appearance as his smaller
works.[2]

Wood is another important material,
with wood constructions dating from the

2 *The Trial,* in the collection of the Minneapolis Institute of Arts, is 6′9″x11′0″ (Fig. 285).

beginnings of cubism. Schwitters' *Merzbau* and *Merzbarn* mark the extremes
of size reached so far in this direction.
More recently wood is becoming a material for collage-like assemblages. Along
these lines two American artists use
wood in markedly personal ways. Bernard Langlais, as in *Southern Comfort*
(Fig. 286), assembles flat scraps of cabi-
net woods into packed, jumbled par-
quetries not unlike galleys of pied type.
Sunk into the picture plane, Langlais'
works are plank collages. Some, like
Totem (Fig. 287), are open like grille-
work. Roy de Forest calls his work
"boardism." His wood constructions and
objects show the inspiration of American Indian art in patterns of bold paint
and feathers that stir memories of totem
poles, Kachina dolls, and sand paintings
(Fig. 288). A former carpenter's feeling
for size plus an artist's feeling for spatial
dynamics inform the board collages of
the English painter Joe Tilson (Fig.
289).

String as an over-all collage element
has been utilized by hoarding collagist

273 Deyrolle: *1–2–3–4*

274 Man Ray: *Tapestry* 1911

275 Xceron: *Collage* 1939

199

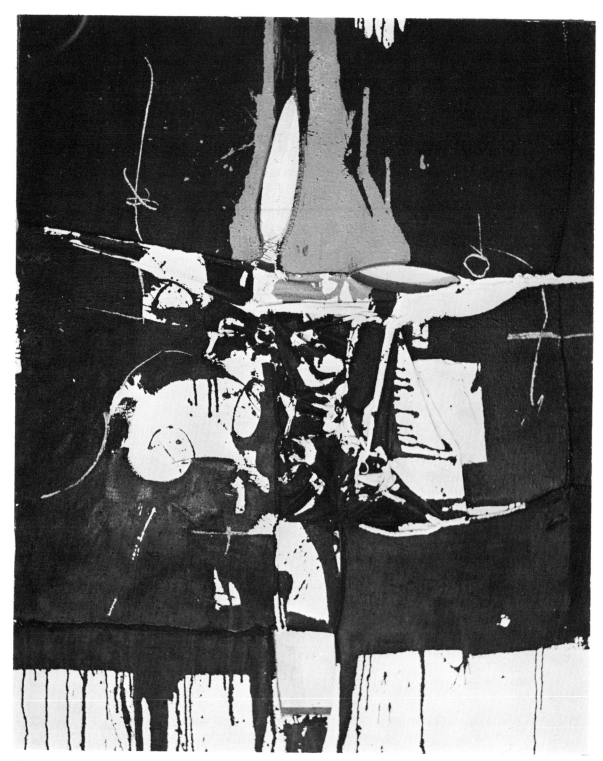

276   Millares: *Cuadro 120*   1960

Gwyther Irwin, as in his large and seriously conceived but playfully titled *A String of Beauty Is a Toy Forever* (Fig. 290).

Wire is variously used in collage and collage-oriented work. As early as 1926–27 Alexander Calder created a group of mobile sculpture-toys, the *Circus*, its animals and performers wittily bent from wire. Spanish modernist Manuel Rivera creates "wire pictures" in relief against plain backgrounds (Fig. 291), and tangled wire is used for abstract linear quality by the German artist Ernst Geitlinger in constructions closely related to collage (Fig. 292). Another use occurs in a construction-painting of 1950 (Fig. 294) by Jackson Pollock, which employs cutouts of wire mesh with string, pebbles, and other extraneous materials, entangled in drip paint on a transparent glass ground. There is a hint of Duchamp's *Large Glass* in the Pollock picture.

Air and space exert strong fascination for twentieth-century artists. Calder's mobiles are collages in the air, space-motion theorems of airborne metal. Similarly conceived in space is David Smith's welded steel sculpture-construction, *Hudson River Landscape* (Fig. 295), pictographs on an aerial tablet. Smith, whose metal work began in the mid-1930's, is one of the pioneer American iron welders whose work stemmed from the iron sculpture of the Barcelonan Julio Gonzales (Fig. 184). Smith's work, in turn, presaged the present-day object-sculptures of welded junk by Stankiewicz and others.

The blue of empty space is the concern of the French artist Yves Klein who, besides utilizing materials like gold leaf, Tunisian sponges, and burning Bengal lights, has personally founded three art movements: "Monochrome," "Immaterial," and "The Void." The relation of the concept of the void—physically present in modern art since Archipenko's earliest cubist sculpture—to the deep galactic space now obsessing scientists, is well indicated in Klein's statement: "I did not like the *nothing*, and it is thus that I met the *empty*, the *deep empty*, the depth of the *blue*." The definition of a physical entity like a "blue" void, that though empty is still not "nothing," would be best supplied by the deep space we are now preparing spaceships to explore—and it actually came to Klein in childhood days on the beach at Nice, as he lay staring up into the Mediterranean sky. Klein has made abstract collages of gold leaf, which he calls "Monogolds," and also creates open-air pyrotechnical paintings, *murs du feu* or "walls of fire." These began with the blue Bengal lights, and now are created by banks of gas jets (Fig. 299). Klein also uses flame to "paint" pictures by swift scorchings (Fig. 300). He is one of the most adventurous of the new theorists of esthetic time-space. His intricate philosophy, which he calls *réalisme mystique*, conceives blue as both Void and Being, with flame at its core.

The Void as metaphysical substance was actually "exhibited" and sold in a

277 Heath: *Oval Theme I* 1956

278 Gatch: *Tapestry to a Square* 1959

279 Gatch: *Kissing the Moon* 1959

now-famous show of Klein's at the Iris Clert Gallery in Paris in 1958. Klein stripped the gallery, painted it pure white, then occupied it for a certain period while mentally "creating" works of art. Then, filled with "art," the show was thrown open to a baffled public which, face to face with Klein's Void, saw only an empty gallery. Nevertheless several prominent collectors actually bought "works," paying in gold about $500 apiece. One even "carried" his to Milan, on his return home.

Klein rapidly explored many of the major contemporary concepts. In the late 1940's, he made monotype prints with his own hands and feet. Then, as a part of his developing theory of maintaining "distance" from his works of art while creating them, he used models as "human brushes" to make action painting in a way also employed in Japan by the Gutai. He mixed colors, instructed his models which to lather themselves with, then directed them to "print themselves" upon blank canvases. As an added experiment Klein airbrushed auras around them as they lay face down. *Suaire* (*The Shroud*) is one of these extraordinary monotypes (Fig. 301).

Quiet and gentle in demeanor, Yves Klein's imagination is wild, ranging, and fertile, but unlike dada it is sanguine, not disillusioned, springing from a "spirit of continuous wonderment." He is called "silent, concentrated and meditative-explosive" by Dr. Paul Wember, who describes Klein's conceptions as more emotional than logical because "he thinks with his soul rather than with his mind."[3] Still, it is a thoroughly contemporary mixture of realism and mysticism. He has made "wind paintings"—freshly painted monochrome canvases exposed to the wind atop his automobile

[3] Wember, Dr. Paul, Director Museum Haus Lange, Krefeld. Article: *Yves Klein—le Monochrome*, in *Art International*. Zurich, Vol. V/2, March, 1961.

280 Varda: *Cosmopolis* 1942

281 Marca-Relli: *The Inhabitant* 1955

282 Marca-Relli: *El Passo* 1959

283 Marca-Relli at work

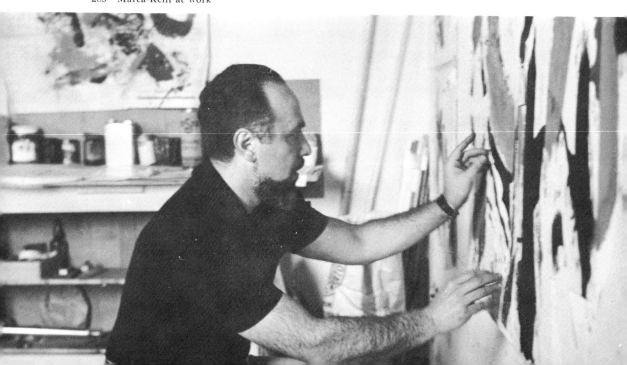

on swift trips between Paris and Nice (Fig. 302). His "rain paintings," the *Cosmogonies de la pluie* (Fig. 303), are equally factual, equally poetic: canvases covered with tinted gouache dissolved in alcohol and set out for the rain to write its patterns on, then taken indoors, dried, and permanently fixed. This is not Duchamp's cruel icy rain dissolving his childhood book but the gentle canticles of natural change—an event in Yves Klein's "great theater, which is Eden."

Klein has composed Silent Symphonies, proposed a Theater of the Void, and envisioned and sketched a Space Architecture—cities walled and warmed with columns of fire and roofed and air-conditioned by horizontal jets of water. Recently, he actualized a series of huge murals collaged entirely from sponges dyed blue and "stratified in polyester resins." The *murals éponges* are in the new opera in Gelsenkirchen, West Germany. The good burghers of Gelsenkirchen did not buy a Void: they got 280,000 choice Tunisian sponges and Yves Klein is the hero of the sponge divers of Djerba (Fig. 304).

284   Marca-Relli: *3 December* 1959

Klein's action ideas influenced Japan, while judo attracted Klein, eventually luring him to Japan in 1952 to study it firsthand. Klein, in fact, had a Japanese spiritual forebear in one of the most wildly inventive and individualistic artists who ever lived. Hokusai, who was born in 1760 and died in 1849, was indeed a kind of artistic progenitor of all the reckless revolutionisms and wild individualisms of modern Western art. In

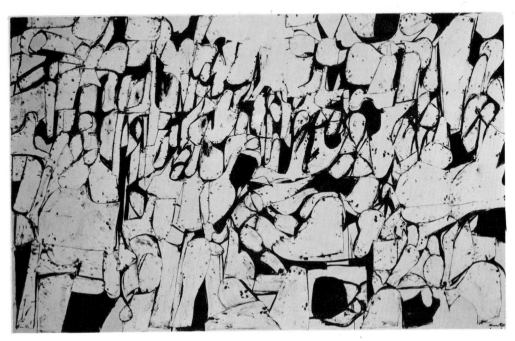

285   Marca-Relli: *The Trial* 1956

205

286 Langlais: *Southern Comfort*

287 Langlais: *Totem* 1960

his book on Japanese prints, James Michener has told the fantastic Hokusai story:

In 1817 an impoverished artist already in his mid-forties and lacking fame concluded that some dramatic gesture must be used to attract attention. Accordingly he lined off an area before a temple in Nagoya and prevailed upon a group of loafers to help him paint the largest picture so far seen in Japan.

With rocks he weighted down a pasted-up sheet of heavy paper containing 2,250 square feet, an area larger than ten average-sized Japanese rooms. One end he lashed to a huge oak beam to which ropes had been fastened so that when completed the monster picture could be hauled aloft. Then, with big vats of ink and tubs of color, with brooms and swabs of cloth tied to sticks he went to work.

Tucking his kimono up about his waist and kicking off his sandals, he ran back and forth across the huge paper, outlining a portrait of Japan's best-loved saint, Daruma, who once sat so long in one position contemplating the nature of world and man that his arms withered away. Of Hokusai's portrait it is recorded that a horse could have walked into the mouth of the gigantic saint.

Soon the temple court was filled with people of Nagoya marveling at their mad painter as he sped about with his brooms, slapping color down in tremendous and apparently unplanned strokes. By dusk the portrait had taken form and when men at the ropes hauled the oaken beam into position, the vast expanse of paper rose into the air and disclosed Hokusai's miracle, a portrait of Daruma nearly sixty feet high.

The artist had accomplished his purpose. He was talked about. He became known as Hokusai, who painted pictures so big that a horse could pass into the mouth of the subject. Not content, Hokusai soon painted with an ordinary brush the picture of two sparrows so small they could be seen only with a magnifying glass. These exploits were reported at court and Hokusai was summoned to exhibit his unusual powers, which he did by ripping down a paper door, smearing it with indigo ink and catching a rooster, whose five-pointed feet he dipped

288   De Forest: *Moe Journeys East*   1960

289 Tilson: *Wooden Relief No. 9* 1960

Collage technique has had varied uses as the artist's tool or adjunct in which it serves as sketch, cartoon, or model, and is then discarded. There is small doubt that collage greatly assisted Picasso and Braque in developing certain phases of cubism. There is some indication—if only in the character of certain paintings—that both artists may have made collage-like constructions from paper, cardboard, tin, and the like, and then painted representations of these, just as though the constructions were still lifes. Later on, papier collé character reappeared in the work of both, in painted patches of color over which linear designs or painted forms are irregularly fitted, so that the patches—too wide here, too narrow there—only approximate the areas of the superimpositions. The French term—*couleur en d'hors:* color on the outside—rather exactly expresses this technique, which is one of the early methods of indicating the rapid flow of inspiration, as though the artist had slapped large areas of colored paper on the canvas and had as swiftly developed forms from them. *Couleur en*

in red ink. Shooing the bird onto the flat door, where his tracks produced an impression of red maple leaves, Hokusai cried, "Leaves in autumn on the blue Tatsuta River."

No kind of personal exploitation was beneath his dignity. He gave public demonstrations during which he drew from bottom to top, from right to left and painted with a finger, an egg, a bottle or a wine stoup, yet he was one of the most careful and dedicated artists. In his great sketch books, published in voluminous editions for students, his work seems thrown down in confusion and contempt, yet we have discovered as many as four meticulous experimental studies which he worked out in detail before daring to put down in final form what appears to be a casual sketch. He had profound belief in his work and charged a high price for it, yet he lived his entire life in abject poverty because he held money in contempt: he paid his bills by tossing uncounted packets of yen at tradesmen. He became one of the most famous and popular artists in Japan, yet he lived for years in obscurity, hiding from bill collectors.

He was a prodigious man. He lived in ninety-three different houses, abandoning them in turn when they became either too dirty to clean or too burdened by back rent. He used more than fifty aliases, abandoning them too whenever he discovered some new artistic principle meriting a new name.[4]

[4] Michener, James A., *The Floating World.* New York, Random House, 1954.

290 Irwin: *A String of Beauty is a Toy Forever* 1960

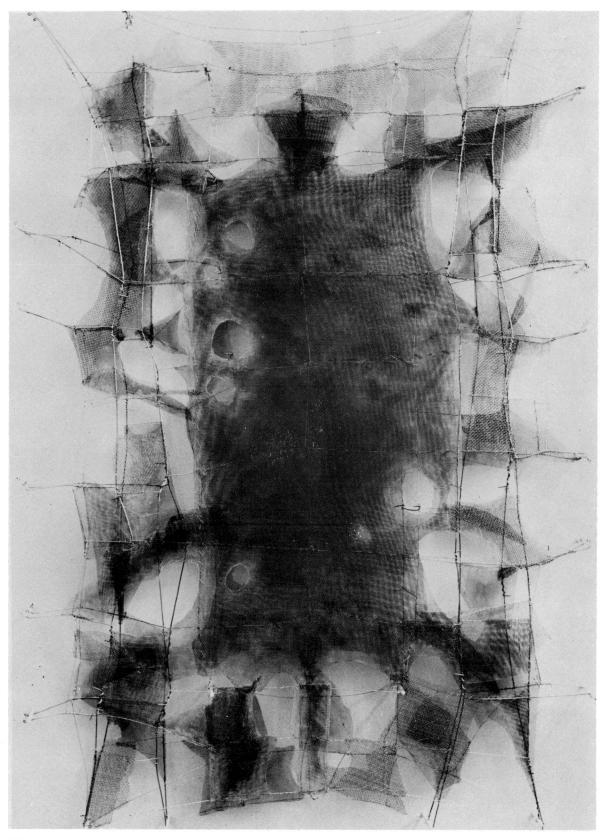

291   Rivera: *Metamorfosis Heraldica*   1960

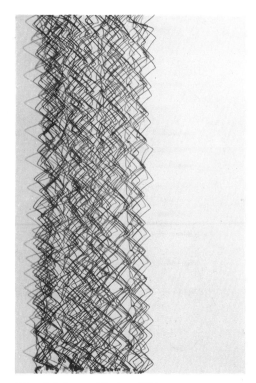

292   Geitlinger: *Black on White*   1958

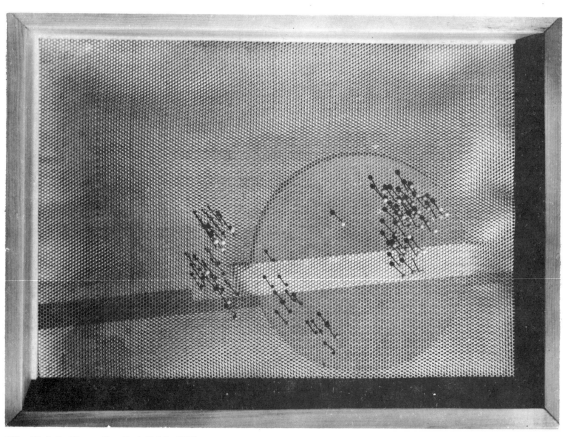

293   Moholy-Nagy: *Das Nadelbild*   1935

294   Pollock: *No. 29, 1950*

d'hors also figured strongly in the work of Léger. The patches function and look like the pasted paper in the very earliest collages.

Probably the largest papier collé ever made—nearly fifteen feet wide—was pasted up by Picasso as a full-size cartoon for the weaving of a tapestry. He made this collage, *La Toilette* (Fig. 305), in 1937 after the completion of the great *Guernica* painting. Though the tapestry was never executed the collage-cartoon, made principally of patterned wallpapers, survived to be shown in 1950 at the Galerie Maeght in Paris.

Matisse's first use of *papier découpé* technique seems to have been in the early 1930's as an adjunct to painting. He had held aloof from the cubist experiments of Braque and Picasso that led to collage. While they battled deep-space thinking by detaining the eye at the picture plane with bits of clipped paper, Matisse achieved depthlessness by unmodulated paint areas and silhouetted forms. He did not need collage as guide to spatial thinking, nor did he seem attracted by the anti-art qualities of mundane materials like newspaper.

Matisse was in his sixties when he at last turned to *papier découpé* for the cartoons of the Barnes Foundation murals at Merion, Pennsylvania. Like an actor's late entry, however, he swept in with grandeur, first drawing with a long crayon-tipped pole, and then fitting single cut-paper shapes into figures ten feet tall. Following this, the Matisse collages shrank to a more normal size. In 1935, he pinned pieces of paper to a painting, *Pink Nude*, to study revisions, and in 1937 included *papier découpé* in the cover design of the first issue of the magazine *Verve*. An entire picture, *Dance,*

211

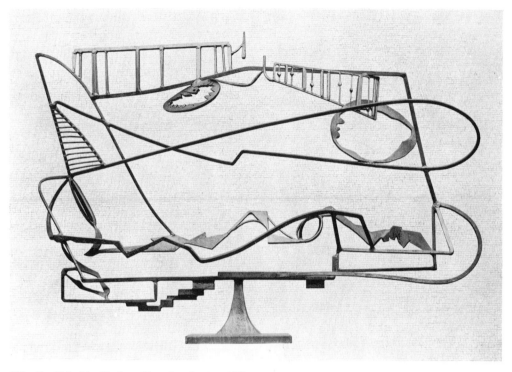

295   David Smith: *Hudson River Landscape*   1951

296   Narez: *Structure*

was made in the spring of 1938 from cut and pasted colored papers. Another important project of that period was the costume and scenic designs for the ballet *Rouge et Noir* by the Ballet Russe de Monte Carlo. These were all executed from Matisse collages.

Still he remained a painter. In 1941, however, a series of major operations confined him to his bed in Lyon. When able to sit up, he began making *découpages*, using unpatterned papers of brilliant, prismatic hues. In delighted fascination he began a flood of individual works and, finally, a book. Soon he was cutting and pasting papers to design a chapel at Vence, the major work that crowns his career and that he could not have accomplished without scissors, paste pot, and paper.

The book of *découpages*, which he titled *Jazz* and began during the war, was not published until 1947. Nearly 150 pages bear colored plates of his collages with text in a facsimile reproduction of his handwriting. Jacques Lassaigne describes it as an "extraordinary portfolio of chromatic and rhythmic improvisations."[5] In the text Matisse called the *découpage* technique "designing with scissors" and "cutting to the quick in color," adding that it "reminds me of direct cutting in sculpture." He marveled at the element of control inherent in so seemingly facile an operation: "My curves do not run wild."

Matisse started the chapel designs in the mid-1940's, working out the plans with Fr. L. B. Rayssiguier who supplied architectural data and liturgical details. However, as Barr points out,[6] it was Matisse who supplied the creative vision of the whole chapel as a work of art, down to the last detail of furniture and

[5] Lassaigne, Jacques, *Introduction to Matisse.* Editions d'Art, Albert Skira, 1959.

[6] Barr, Alfred H., Jr., *Matisse: His Art and His Public.* New York, Museum of Modern Art, 1951.

297 Reynal: *Cardinal*

298 Schwitters: *Stone Collage* 1947

299   Yves Klein with *Wall of Fire*   1961

300   Klein painting with fire

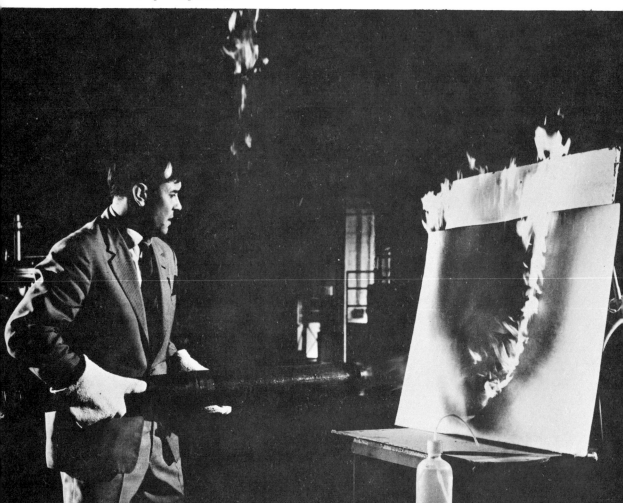

decoration—a project ranging from fifteen stained-glass windows and five murals on glazed tiles to crucifix, candle-
sticks, and vestments (Fig. 306), with
even a design for the floor. A good share
of these designs were realized by Matisse in *papier découpé*.

The flood of work that Matisse poured
out after illness struck him shows how
the new technique freed his imagination,
leading into a fruitful final period. During 1950–54 he developed a method of
prepainting collage papers in flat
gouache colors prepared to his own samples. Technical innovations, however,
seem unimportant compared with the
way that the perennial joyousness of
Matisse's work seemed, in those final
years, to burst into a late sunset glow.

Max Ernst, master collagist, employed
the medium in designing the stage set-
tings for the posthumous première of
Alfred Jarry's play, *Ubu Enchaîné,* produced at the Comédie des Champs-
Elysées of Paris in 1937. Among other
stage designs made from collages was
surrealist Kurt Seligmann's project for
a backdrop for Hanya Holm's *The
Golden Fleece* (Fig. 308).

In his last years, Mondrian used a
collage variant to develop his classically
severe, rectilinear abstractions. He
placed color tapes on plain canvases, as
shown in the painting *New York City,
No. 3* (Fig. 309), left unfinished at his
death. Mondrian studied the space re-
lations, rhythms, and precise equilibrium
set up by the tapes, constantly shifting
and rearranging them for weeks, even
months. When finally satisfied he
painted actual lines in place of the
tapes. It must be emphasized that he did
not use the tapes as commercial painters
use masking tape, that is, as a guide
against which to paint. His idea of skill
and careful, meticulous craftsmanship
would not have permitted the use of a
crutch of this kind. He made true collages with removable tape, then removed
the tape before the final painting.

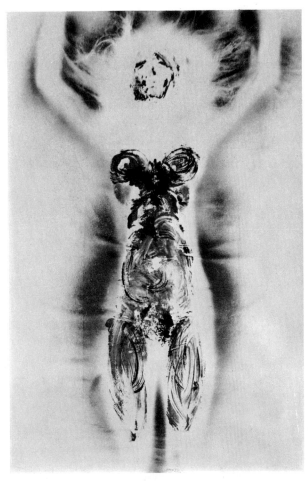

301 Klein: *Suaire I* 1960

The late Sophie Taeuber-Arp made
a series of collage maquettes in 1927
as designs for a dada rendezvous, the
Aubette in Zurich. In lieu of working
drawings, Mme. Arp made maquettes
to scale by collaging cardboard to a
commercial pressed board (Fig. 310).
Collaged cardboard is ideal for creating
low reliefs to be painted. It is a favorite
method of Arp (Fig. 311), as well as
the Swiss precisionist Gottfried Honegger (Fig. 312).

The American abstract-expressionist
leader Willem de Kooning has used removable collage in painting, particularly in shuffling and assembling the biomorphic forms of his famous series, *The
Woman.* These paintings, dating from
the early 1950's, all of which are now

in museum and major private collections, created perhaps the most severe public shock since the debut of fauvism in 1905. The key work of the series is *Woman I* in the collection of the Museum of Modern Art in New York. To create its psychological and visual distortions, De Kooning made scores of charcoal drawings of anatomical parts on tracing paper. Scissoring these apart, he pasted them to the canvas, right side up or wrong side up, in the proper place or in the wrong place (e.g., a hand at the end of a leg), and then studied the increasing wildness, dislocation, and angry frenzy of the whole. At one stage, the rouged lips of a "glamour" advertisement were pasted to the face. Thus, through collage's quick, suggestive adaptability and easily removable traces, De Kooning created a masterpiece of twentieth-century art. Fortunately, a photograph exists of *Woman I* in an early stage with collage scraps attached (Fig. 314). An earlier painting also survives in an incomplete state with collage adjuncts still in place where De Kooning hurriedly affixed them with homemade paste and thumbtacks (Fig. 315). One says "incomplete" advisedly. Considered as collage and not as oil painting, this is an outstanding work.

It is evident that collage as a tool or adjunct has left its mark upon other media and other arts. In addition, collage functions as a pedagogical tool. At the Bauhaus, students were encouraged to make collages and constructions, not as permanent "works of art," but as études to help them grasp concepts of space and material basic to Bauhaus theory. The late Moholy-Nagy continued to use collage in this way in the School of Design he set up in Chicago in the early 1940's. Joseph Albers, also of the Bauhaus faculty, consistently employed collage in teaching in the United States, at Black Mountain College and later at Yale, until his recent retirement.

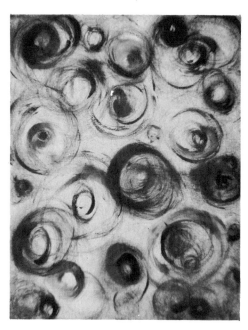

302   Klein: *Le vent du voyage*   1960

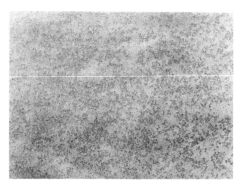

303   Klein: *Cosmogonie de la pluie*   1960

216

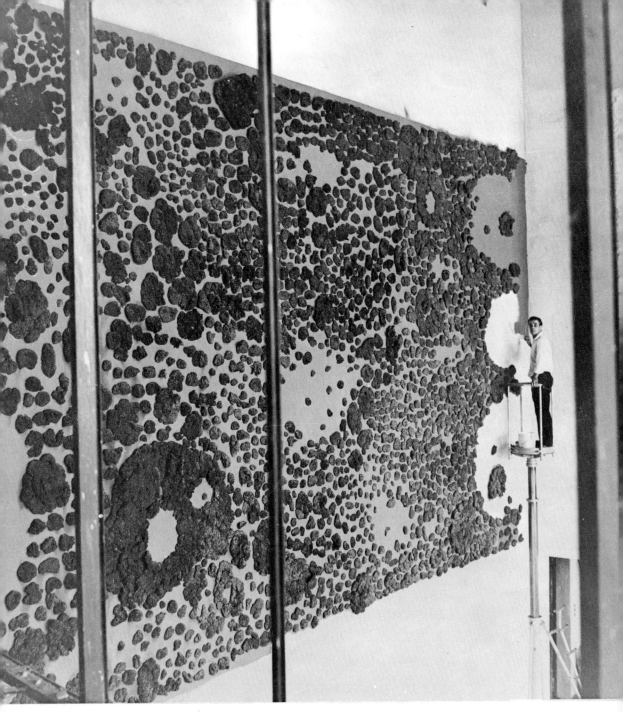

304   Klein working on the *Mural d'éponges*   1959

305   Picasso: *La toilette,* 1937

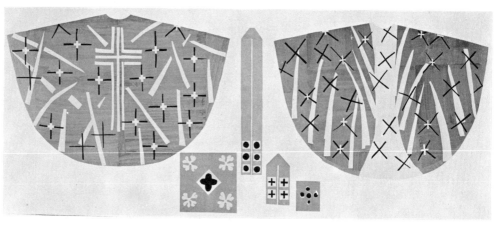

306   Matisse: *Design for Red and Yellow Chasuble*   *c.* 1950

218

307   Matisse: *Maquette for Nuit de Noël*   1952

308   Seligmann: Cartoon for Backdrop for *The Golden Fleece*   1940–42

309   Mondrian: *New York City No. 3*   *c.*1942

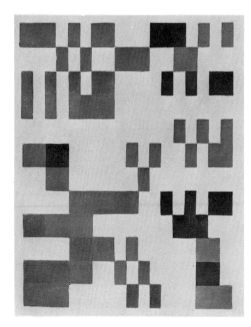

310 Taeuber-Arp: *Maquette No. 16 for Aubette* 1927

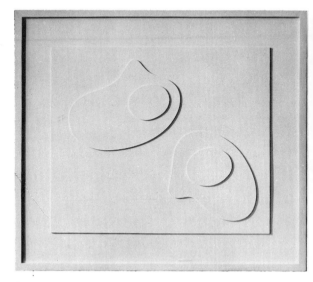

311 Arp: *Deux profils* 1959

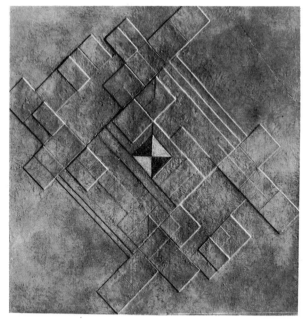

312 Honegger: *Cayuga* 1959

313 Stazewski: *Hommage à Jean Arp*

314   Willem de Kooning: *Woman I* (early state)   *c.* 1950

315 Willem de Kooning: *Asheville Collage* 1949

316 Kamys: *Untitled No. 3* 1959

13

THE IMAGE:

MAN, MACHINE, MATHEMATICS

In this century of the machine and the atom, we have three different images, built up from three different kinds of material: man, machine, and mathematics. Since art—even the most rigorously abstract—consists in and of images, one or another of the three is both crux and core of any modern work of art.

Each beckons; each deceives; each is incomplete; each repels—the human image can be warm and close as kin, or mad and cruel; the machine can be slave or destroyer; blank-faced mathematics is pure but empty, just but cold, with the madness of too much reason. The devotees of the one accuse the devotees of the others of escapism, yet, since no one can embrace all, to embrace any one is to escape the others. Pluralistic products of a split age, they signal and foster the disunity of the species, forcing some kind of alienation upon everyone, leaving everyone in some way homeless or without identity. All three are haunting images.

Surrealism redirected attention to the haunting anthropomorphic image. In the decades since then, as man through alienation or faceless conformity gropes for his own fading image, the image of man in art becomes more and more strongly charged with emotion.

The surrealists, through their found objects and through paranoiac double-imagery, exploited the hallucinatory likenesses inherent in metamorphosis and the isomorphic relation of disparate things. Everyone at some time or another has experienced the morphogenesis of a strange, sudden, disquieting presence out of the familiar seen under special conditions, either subjective or objective. The kind of collage that uses strange, and, especially, natural materials is a fertile breeding place for such images. Fully aware of this, Max Ernst in *Beyond Painting,* called collage the noble conquest of the irrational and defined it as "the coupling of two realities, irreconcilable in appearance, upon a plane which apparently does not suit them."

Da Vinci observed long ago that natural textures like weathered rock and rough bark are almost literally haunted by the images we imagine into them. Simply arranged and presented they can form a collage, into which the spectator can read his own interpretations. Such a work is Jean Dubuffet's *assemblage* titled *L'Esprit du bois* (Fig. 317) . A pattern of dried leaves, it is the inchoate image. Dubuffet's imagery is found in

317 Dubuffet: *L'esprit du bois* 1959

agave leaf patterns, terrain, and land-scape. He reconstructs moor, lawn, des-ert, and thicket in the *éléments bota-niques* he collages from various dried leaves. Then animal life enters: a wild dog, or a lost, wandering donkey (Fig. 319). These animals, so alive, so sen-tient, are created from the same dried herbals: agave, artichoke, and burdock; camomile, coltsfoot, and hart's-tongue; lotus and plantain; medalar, mullein, sorrel, and many more. Scanning these fragile Druid tablets we meet a myth.

When Dubuffet's pictures were first seen in the mid-1940's they elicited the name *art brut,* which connotes a class of brutally primitive or self-taught art existing in many cultures. His early work showed awkward, ungainly people starkly painted in disagreeable colors or monotones, the paint clotted and gravelly, full of dirt, pebbles, and bits of coal. The people were simply being people; they were not models. They did what they needed to do, working or

sleeping, walking or talking, riding in carts or streetcars, or like the naked woman in one famously shocking paint-ing, quietly bearing her child.[1] The image was man; the material, however, only seemed to be oil paint. By intro-ducing dirt and minerals into his *haute pâte,* Dubuffet made us remember that paint is made from minerals, and that minerals come from the earth.

From 1943 to the present, Dubuffet has been restlessly exploring materials, inventing and adapting techniques in-volved with the collage idea. With him, as with Max Ernst, the ceaseless inven-tion is never for itself but is integral with the image. He insists on the name of "assemblages" for all his works:

The name collage is a critic's term, a pre-established category for stereotyped art forms and trite and conventional ideas. My assemblages are a whole cycle of pic-tures pasted, cemented, or sewn, and of little statues—made from butterfly wings, fragments of torn newspaper, bits printed with Chinese ink, paper or canvas bits painted in oils; cinders, clinkers, sand, soil, stones, sponges; dried leaves and other bo-tanical elements; crumpled, painted metal-lic paper . . . you can see that, even if the name collage pleased me (which it does not) still it could not embrace all these works, all these materials.[2]

Sometime during those years Dubuf-fet looked past man at the asphalt of New York pavement and a far memory revived. He saw the earth. He painted it, over and over, and called the paint-ings *concrétions terreuses.* Back in Eu-rope, he looked at his garden in Vence and saw the earth. He gathered its leaves and flowers, dried them, assembled them on canvas. It was a picture but Dubuffet did not think so: he had cre-ated a patch of earth from living sub-stance.

[1] *Childbirth,* 1944. Collection Mr. and Mrs. Pierre Matisse, New York.
[2] Dubuffet, Jean, in a letter to Harriet Janis. Vence, December 16, 1959.

It was then that Dubuffet's mythology became complete, as if Creation had been reversed and the Earth made from Adam. His discovery was a return to something lost, for Western man, as Dubuffet says, has "a great contempt for trees and rivers, and hates to be like them."[3]

With the soil, Dubuffet discovered trees and rivers, not in books or laboratory but by going to them: "If there is a tree in the country, I don't bring it into my laboratory to look at it under my microscope, because I think the wind which blows through its leaves is absolutely necessary for the knowledge of the tree and cannot be separated from it. Also the birds which are in the branches, and even the song of these birds."[4]

Dubuffet rejected intellect and analysis in order to embrace intuition and synthesis. Having always believed in living man, he had discovered man's whole image. Beyond man, beast, insect, foliage, it is the terrain. It is the substance of earth, cognate with conscious life and incarnate with a collective personality. A score of pictures, a dozen titles, confirm the discovery: "language of the soil," "the nude soil," "the soul of the subsoil," "the ancient skin of the esplanade," the kind of pictures he calls *topographies*, and the *sols et terrains*. It is the Earth Image, haunting us with awe of the everlasting primeval.

Dubuffet the mythologist is essentially a realist. He deals with truth, not with data. The grandeur of his view is that he sees life as all-pervasive, and feels its realities through all its cycles of birth and seeming death. The Sahara Desert that he loves is as alive as the garden in Southern France and both are places where, as Lawrence Alloway has

[3] In a lecture, "Anticultural Positions," given by Dubuffet in December 1951, at the Arts Club of Chicago.
[4] *Ibid.*

318 Dubuffet: *La forêt* 1959

319 Dubuffet: *L'âne égaré* 1959

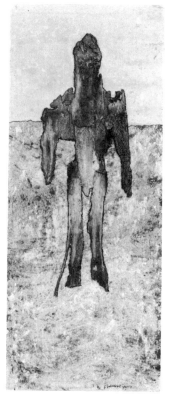

320 Dubuffet: *Travesti minable*
1959

321 Dubuffet: *Le hanteur des
landes* 1959

322 Dubuffet: *Barbe des dynas-
ties régnantes* 1959

323 Dubuffet: *L'africain* 1959

324   Dubuffet: *Compagnonnage*   1956

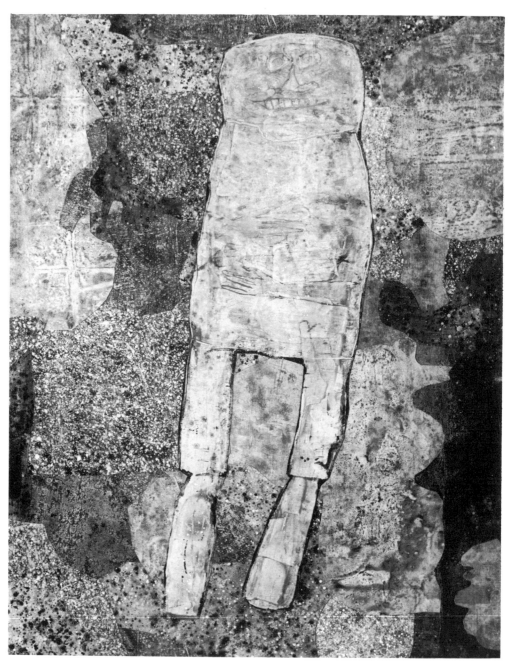

325   Dubuffet: *Partie liée au sol*   1958

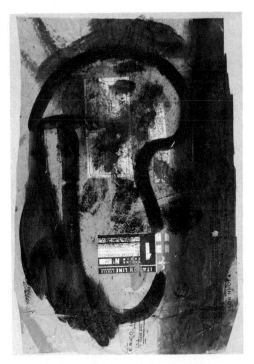

326   Frankenthaler: *Cabin No. 118*   1959

327   Carmassi: *Untitled*   1951

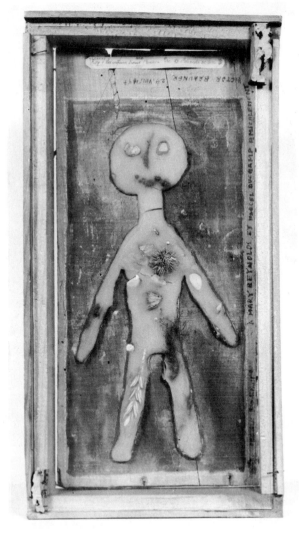

328   Brauner: *Les contraires . . .*   1947

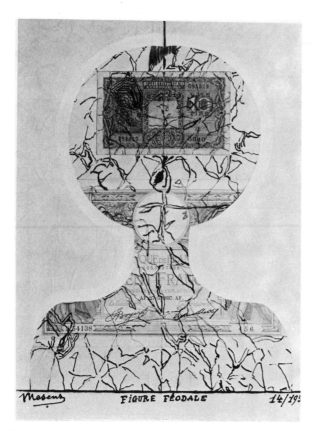

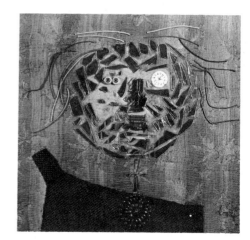

329 Mesens: *Feudal Figure* 1957

330 Baj: *La belle Alice*

331 Picard: *Pacific People* 1960

332   Cohen: *Game of Chance*   1954

333   Conner: *Mirror Collage*   1960

334 Conner: *Child* (detail) 1959

observed, "Dubuffet can confirm his intimate vigil of nature . . ."[5]

Dubuffet's *assemblages* of paint, paper, or leaves, are places where all of us might confirm our own private vigils. Still, even if Dubuffet views a living whole greater than the sum of its parts, his panoramic insight is not possible to many people, even artists. And it is precisely in the phases separate from the whole cycle that we find sadness and even tragedy. Childhood, once past, becomes a memory that however magical is shadowy with loss. The sad little puppet dolls in Hans Bellmer's surrealist constructions (Fig. 107) are naked ghosts trapped in a limbo of grief. Dolls, childhood games, toys—all of these are parts of the terrain of childhood, motionless in the stare of memory.

So it is with death, in these partial human views of parts of life separate from the whole. And here the image becomes a phantom. Bruce Conner's *Mirror Collage* (Fig. 333) is the phantom image—the mirror that reflects death. Conner, absorbed with his own *memento mori,* has made collages and constructions that are among the most macabre in recent art. Completely gruesome is the wax *Child* (Figs. 334, 335),

smothered in its cerements of torn nylon stockings.

However, these materials of sickness, wounds, and death can be made to transcend morbidity to compassion, anger, and concern with society. Edward Kienholz's work is frightening with a purpose. The portraits of *John Doe* and *Jane Doe* (Figs. 336, 337) are a view of American life that is both pitiless and pitying. American "social-consciousness painting" of the 1930's pales into insignificance beside documents like these and the grim construction that describes California's controversial execution of Caryl Chessman. Kienholz built a wooden case which is the proverbial "open and shut case." Closed, it bears the official Seal of Approval of California. Open, it shows at the left a space empty except for the national and state flags, and at the right the gas chamber, its chair wrapped in a heavy shroud. The references of the name, *Psycho-Vendetta Case* (Figs. 338, 339), are quite clear.

In 1951, Dubuffet had a studio in an

335 Conner: *Child* (full view)

[5] Alloway, Lawrence, Foreword to exhibition of Dubuffet's *Eléménts Botaniques* at gallery of Arthur Tooth & Sons, Ltd. London, May 31–June 18, 1960.

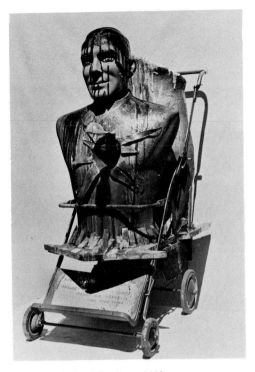

336 Kienholz: *John Doe* 1960

337 Kienholz: *Jane Doe* 1960

338 Kienholz: *Psycho-Vendetta Case* 1960

339 Kienholz: *Psycho-Vendetta Case*
(closed)

340 Elaine de Kooning: *Condemned Man* 1960

old Manhattan loft building. On the floor below was the studio of a young American sculptor who had studied with Léger and Ossip Zadkine in Paris. Now he was struggling with tradition and training—his sculpture would not come alive. Spring came. Dubuffet departed without the two artists ever making an acquaintance. They have not met in their art either, though the art of both is strongly imaged. The image of Richard Stankiewicz is born not in man and soil but in the machine.

Stankiewicz looked into the barren courtyard and decided to make a garden. He cleared out the debris: tin cans, old cartons, newspapers, and all the rest of the anthropo-geologic sediments forever stratifying on New York. He began digging.

All of a sudden I struck a brick wall, then a brick walk. I dug faster. The spade began hitting old hunks of metal which I tossed against the building. Soon I discovered that the brickwork outlined the beds and paths of a hundred-and-fifty-year-old garden. I thought: why not recreate the garden as it was?

I sat down to catch my breath and my glance happened to fall on the rusty iron things lying where I had thrown them, in the slanting sunlight at the base of the wall. I felt, with a real shock—not of fear but of recognition—that they were staring at me. Their sense of presence, of life, was almost overpowering.

I knew instantly what I had to do. I bought a welding outfit, mask and gloves, and a do-it-yourself book—How to Become a Welder in Your Spare Time. My first sculpture was finished in a day.[6]

Stankiewicz will not use new materials; they must be rusty and thrown away. Yet from them he builds the personages of an animate art. Collages in space, their wheel, cog, lever parts fuse identity with organic and animal being. There is wit here—sometimes sardonic—but the meaning transcends the wit. Like Dubuffet, Stankiewicz has made contact with an affirmative, spiraling cycle. His dead machinery is as intrinsic to his cycle as falling leaves and winter rot are to the sprouting of the herbs in Dubuffet's garden. In the Stankiewicz myth human life begins with the death of the machine (Figs. 341 to 348, incl.).

Even farther from the living man than the machine is the empty purity of mathematics. So, nowhere is the artist's search for identity and reality more intense yet less apparent than in the mathematical rigors of precisionist art of all kinds. For here if anywhere will be found the master image and the unchanging reality behind appearance. And yet what human image can exist in mathematics' abstract visage? For Mondrian, nevertheless, the quest was warm and ardent with reality at its end.

So it is also with today's precisionists and constructivists. In England, for example, where Pevsner and Ben Nicholson live and an active constructivist group works, there is direct talk of reality and the image in connection with a flow of purely mathematical work and

[6] From an interview with the authors.

exhibitions with titles like "Artist versus Machine." One of the English leaders, Kenneth Martin, states that "mathematics . . . is part of the nature of man" and "the constructive work is . . . an image of space." His artist wife Mary Martin says, "I moved into the third dimension because I wanted to use real space and real materials," and adds, "a constructive work can have a life of its own . . . it may be an image."[7]

Abstract-expressionist or neoconstructivist, the talk is of image of space or image in itself. Beyond this—and perhaps beyond artist's purview and intent—the image is human, autobiographical of both artist and the race.

The English group, which also includes Anthony Hill and American John Ernest, is typical of a general move toward mathematics that has paralleled the abstract-expressionist move toward automatist intuition. Significantly, both moves sprang from a growing feeling of unreality and loss of identity. The English group, typically, were engrossed with realistic still-life and landscape painting before almost simultaneously turning to extreme abstraction.

Both abstract-expressionism and this neoconstructivist art moves into real space, either to externalize physically the creative act or to "use real space and real materials." Both are moves toward a reintegration with reality. Thus mathematics grasped in need becomes tool and artifact, and this intense need for expression and identification stamps even the most abstract works with the human image.

[7] From answers to a questionnaire by Lawrence Alloway, published in the catalogue, *Statements*. London, Institute of Contemporary Arts, 1956.

341 Stankiewicz: *Europa on a Cycle* 1953

342 Stankiewicz: *Personage* 1960

343 Stankiewicz: *Soldier* 1955

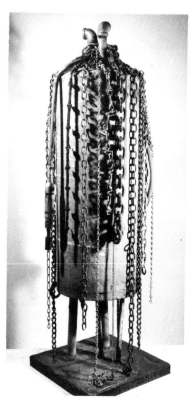

344 Stankiewicz: *Female* 1954

345 Stankiewicz: *Untitled* 1960

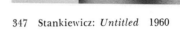

347 Stankiewicz: *Untitled* 1960

346 Stankiewicz: *The Travels of the Pussycat King* 1956

348 Stankiewicz: *Untitled Wall Panel* 1955

349 Pasmore: *White, Black, and Biscuit* 1960–61

350 Kenneth Martin: *Collage in Red and Grey*
1950

238

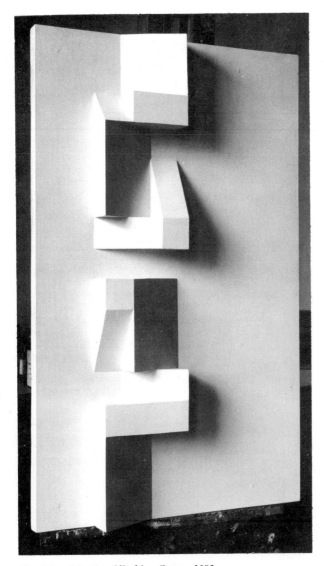

351   Mary Martin: *Climbing Form*   1953

352   Mary Martin: *Black Relief*   1957

353 Anthony Hill: *Relief Construction* 1959

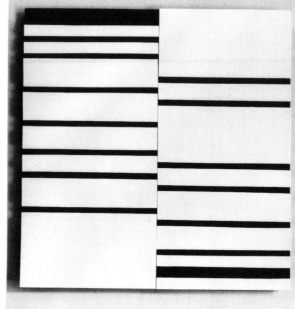

354 Anthony Hill: *Relief Construction* 1959–60

355 John Ernest: *Relief* 1958

356 John Ernest: *Triangular Motif* 1958

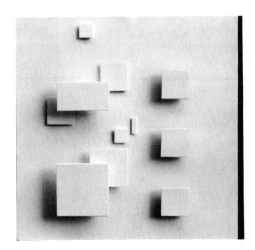

357 Tomasello: *Reflection No. 26* 1959

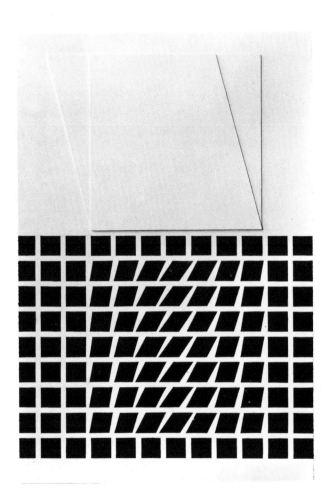

358 Vasarely: *Likka* 1956–59

359 Geitlinger: *Black Ledges* 1960

14

FACTUALISM OR NEO-DADA

The modern artist's recourse to primitive art has been a strong factor in leading modern art to different concepts of realism. It restored the true idea of the image as both the most real expression of identity and the most unequivocal way to express thought. It opened the way for the object itself to become image. It severed the semantic knot by boldly reaffirming (after many centuries) the supremacy of art over language. Dubuffet made this idea specific: "I believe (and here I am in accord with the so-called primitive civilizations) that painting is more concrete than the written word, and is a much more rich instrument than it for the expression and elaboration of thought."[1] Similarly he defined the essential realism of contemporary art—even the most abstract. Whatever exists, he says, is the subject matter of art. He summarily rejects as unrealistic the ideals of beauty we inherited from the Greeks:

I find this idea of beauty a meager and not very ingenious invention, and especially not very encouraging for man. It is distressing to think about people deprived of beauty because they have not a straight nose, or are too corpulent, or too old. I find even this idea that the world we live in is made up of ninety percent ugly things and ugly places, while things and places endowed with beauty are very rare and difficult to meet, I must say, I find this idea not very exciting. It seems that the Western man will not suffer a great loss if he loses this idea. On the contrary, if he becomes aware that the world is able to become for any man a way of fascination and illumination, he will have made a good catch. I think such an idea will enrich life more than the Greek idea of beauty.[2]

The function of art, then, to Dubuffet and to a large part of the artists of today, is to deal with the essential realities of the world. Beyond any doubt this is a time of perpetual crisis, very real dilemmas, and—to thinking people—hobbling frustrations. It is scarcely a time for unqualified optimism. How does a Dubuffet—making pictures from dried leaves and flowers—express this climate and even arrive at an affirmative view? His perishable materials are parts of a cycle that he sees as immortal and from them he constructs an allegory. He sees the confusions and the negativisms of our time in their most final terms: death; and his answer is: life. His escapism is the universal saving reflex of the race: self-preservation. Our

[1] Dubuffet lecture, *op. cit.*

[2] *Ibid.*

360 César in his studio

situation has so developed that no profounder or more realistic statement is possible, in language or in art.

The "realities" of yesterday—the cow in dreamed-up meadow, the imaginary nymph in a Corot sunset—would be impertinent, shocking irrelevancies today. Our artists—in grim document, horrifying image, wild dadaesque play—all according to their means and their view, confront a profoundly unsettling reality. This is a new art, more unorthodox even than Dubuffet's; some of it not art at all by any traditional standards; all of it baffling and disturbing. But then, so are our times. If nineteenth-century political philosophies are failing to solve our real difficulties, then, equally, even the last generation's esthetic criteria are inapropos and futile today.

The newest art is being called neodada. The term is inappropriate and resented by the artists. Dada's world and their world, they say, are two different worlds, at least in terms of degree as widely apart as the incomplete and the final. 1916 was 1916; 1961 is 1961, several wars and The Bomb later. This present movement includes surrealist elements—automatism, psychological overtone, the object; and abstract-expressionist ones—creative time and action, personal space, direct involvement with the work of art (art as environment).

We suggest the name "factualism." No movement in Western art has been so directly involved with facts: the fact of the material entity or object, not represented, but in itself; the irrational as well as the rational fact; the emotional overtone as fact, not as artistic atmosphere; the facts of our real, not imagined or idealized environment; the facts of the human predicament today.

The factualists are complex personalities facing a complex and charged environment. Their work, however simply formed and stated, carries implications, overtones, references to many levels of reality. The future may well see this present art as more directly concerned with the complete texture and meaning of the world than any other art of this century. Dilemma, crisis, disaster, and the search for solutions, all blend and merge both in the reality and the art.

243

Through his own sense of predicament, each artist expresses phases of the general condition. The greater artists add to the personal a more general view. If alienated, unable to communicate, and faceless with loss of identity, he may give us the symbol without meaning, the ritual of the empty gesture. If he feels trapped in claustrophobic and seemingly unalterable situations, he may give us pictures and sculptures of the chessboard, the grid, the compartment. If crushed under the weight of too many and too great pressures, he may give us works of deadly, compressing strata upon strata, or sculptures of flattened and crushed metal. Other artists, particularly those with war experience, feel the sense of crisis and disaster that is our prevailing climate. They, too, give us universal symbols of our time: wounds, fire, and death.

Finally, there are those who go beyond the crisis, personal or universal, to seek escape. Some give us games or neo-romantic imaginings. Others are more venturesome, seek new circumstances offering safer, freer, more fruitful and satisfying lives. These men seek a new environment, a new world—even the outer galaxies that beckon to our time, as escape and as fresh start.

Certain artists typify the main contemporary aims, trends, and expressions. Louise Nevelson sums up the compartment idea, with its general implications of claustrophobic dilemma. Jasper Johns invokes the symbol without meaning and the empty ritual. César and Mallary portray the crushing weight of today's circumstances. Alberto Burri is the prophet of crisis, the poet and healer of disaster. Robert Rauschenberg would resolve all dilemma and overcome all crisis by open-eyed acceptance of the world as it is. Allan Kaprow is an originator and a leader of the newest art movement, one that proposes to do away with picture and sculpture and in fact *all* concrete works of art, to substitute for them The Environment and The Happening—picture's marriage with space; art's marriage with reality.

With all the American emphasis on machine technologies, like brazing and welding in metal sculpture constructions, it remained for a Frenchman to see the esthetic possibilities in the gigantic American compressors used to crush automobile bodies into scrap-metal pancakes. César Baldaccini, known simply as César, was born in Marseilles in 1921, lives and works in Paris. A formally trained Beaux-Arts student, he developed an eye for tattered metal like Schwitters' for paper. He creates mangled steel personages with a presence as strong as those by Stankiewicz but more spectral and disquieting, and without humor. César discovered the dead automobile in a crumpled bale of tortured shapes. It was his revelation; he gave up welded sculpture and now chooses the metal for the monstrous maw, arranges it, and directs the vast compression. Pierre Restany writes, ". . . in the suburbs of Paris I saw César in front of one of the latest American compressors, supervising the movements of the cranes,

361 César: *Governed Compression I* 1960

362　César: *Viens ici que j' t' esquiche*　1961

363　César: *La maison de Roël*　1961

364　César: *On est 3*　1961

365　César: *Château magique*　1960

proportioning the heterogeneous loads, eagerly awaiting the result of each operation."[3] This is machine technique to the highest degree so far.

But the artist's role though narrowed is still crucial: César has an extraordinary feel for metals, eye for form, and responsiveness to overtones of meaning. His term, Governed Compressions, accurately defines the respective role of sculptor and machine in his work. In the end not impersonal destruction but sad and crushing dilemma are the expression of these lifeless bales still tortured with memories of life. As with Stankiewicz, the machine metamorphoses into human form, but with César it is phantom, corpse, or mere habiliments, as in *Governed Compression I* (Fig. 361), where crushed copper looks like a soldier's uniform—muddy, ragged, perhaps bloodstained—crushed beneath tank treads or files of marching feet.

[3] Restany, Pierre, Foreword to catalogue of César exhibition. London, Hanover Gallery, October 6–November 8, 1960.

Despair, not tragedy, fill Robert Mallary's assemblages of the horrible decaying magma of Manhattan streets, or his compressions of stonelike strata. Mallary was born in 1917 in Toledo, Ohio. He began using plastics and other experimental media in 1938 while studying with Siqueiros in Mexico. He pioneered the use of polyester resin in 1948. With this agent he stiffens, reinforces, and makes permanent the grimy, decayed perishables like flattened corrugated cartons, in his portraits of a partial death. The resin preserves impartially, welding paper and cardboard, grime and soot, muck and dead insects, into stone mummies of the modern world (Figs. 367 to 371 incl.).

It is the sense of crisis and disaster that separates the work of men like César and Mallary from the "junk sculpture" being done everywhere. John Chamberlain belongs with these more serious men. His shapes of crushed automobile bodies and fenders, exhaust pipes, grilles, etc., are unrusted and retain their

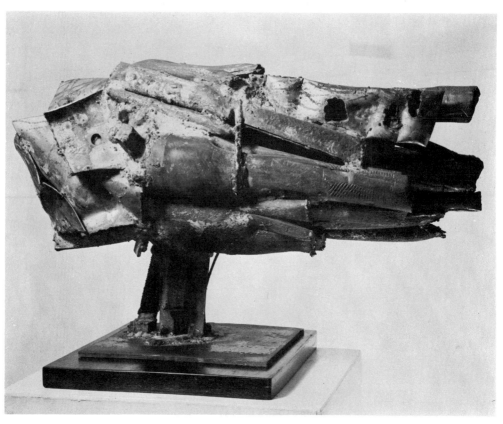

366 César: *Moteur No. 3*

original bright lacquer colors—red, blue, green. Now he is interested in "taxi" colors: garish yellow and orange. After Mallary, the first impression of a Chamberlain is almost gay, as if he were using fragments of toys. This *Motor Merz,* however, has a deadly realism: in any American garage one can see masses (read "sculpture") exactly like these, just brought in from the nearest superhighway by the towing truck that followed the ambulance (Fig. 372).

Polyester resin enables the German artist Wilhelm Wessel to stratify crusty sediments of shells and pebbles, wood, metal, and glass into high-relief collages (Fig. 373). Another German artist, Bernard Schultze, makes veritable grotto walls of canvases collaged with almost incredible collections of material (Fig. 374). The American Bruce Gilchrist imbeds more mechanistic sediments—tin cans, sheet metal, iron fragments,

burned-out electric bulbs—in cement (Fig. 375).

Jasper Johns' personal symbols express deadening facelessness and conformity. His chief themes are the target, the numeral, and the American flag, presented with a deliberately childlike simplicity. Working in encaustic on newspaper pasted to canvas, Johns paints the flag, from full color on to faded monotones, as if the rituals it commands were fading into meaningless repeated gestures. His bull's-eye targets are unmarked by arrow or bullet. It is faceless man himself, butt of all society's slings. In some pictures Johns lays out a chessboard—the field of a game, trivial, obsessive or deadly—and in the squares imprints numerals—no more. In this game the pawn is man with only a number, not even a name. The characterless block stencil type implies the stereotype in place of personality; altogether

367 Robert Mallary with *Casanova* 1961

368   Mallary: *Lafcadio*   1960   369   Mallary: *Assassin*   1960   370   Mallary: *King Canute*   1960

371   Mallary: *Pueblo*   1960

the numerals lie within their squares like stored printing type—stupid blocks without volition that yet, if allowed to work together, could spell out life and reason.

Each splinter of type has a face that is only a partial face: an *A*, a *B*, a *C*, or a single numerical digit. They are the great works of the human spirit —poetry and mathematics—pied and tossed back into the font. Sometimes, with a painted target, Johns makes the mutilation pitilessly explicit, by including actual compartments with hinged doors. When we open the doors we come face to face with horror: man's face and body cut up into parts and cast in livid plaster—nose, ear, hand, genitals, and one dreadful, empty, despoiled compartment. These are the compartments of mutilation into which the whole man has disappeared.

A certain class of Jasper Johns objects consists of mundane trivia—ale cans, electric globes, paint brushes—cast in exact replica in sculptural bronze. The bronze is the equivalent of Madison Avenue advertising giving "value and importance" to the trashy ephemerae of commerce (Figs. 376 to 381 incl.).

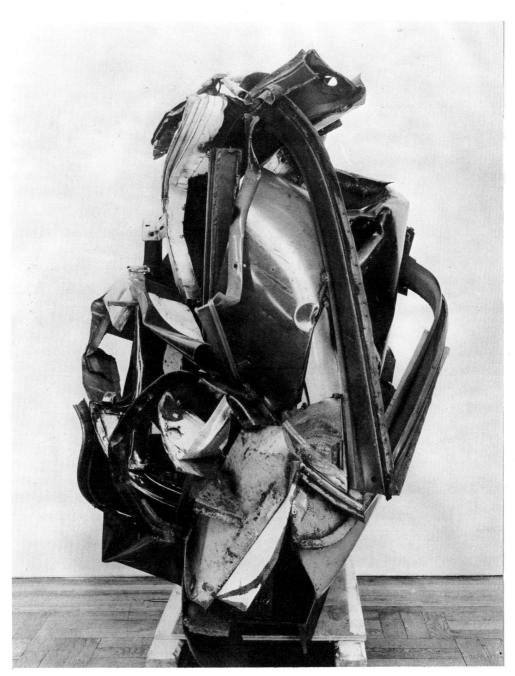

572 Chamberlain: *Nutcracker* 1960

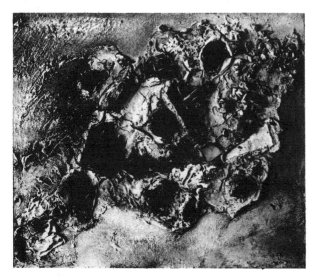

373   Wessel: *Relief*   1956

374   Schultze: *Zlorrib*   1959

375   Gilchrist: *The Walk*   1957

250

376 Jasper Johns with *Target with Plaster Casts* 1955

377   Johns: *Flag Above White with Collage*   1954–55

378   Johns: *0 to 9*   1958

The chessboard-grid-compartment idea, so disturbingly applicable to the human dilemma, appears in the work of many artists. John Hultberg, for example, sees the compartmented grid as an empty or ruined city of doorless houses, without connecting streets or, sometimes, a building façade with certain windows blank and others revealing shadowy human silhouettes or disturbing, unidentifiable objects (Fig. 384). Other artists paint obsessive colored checkerboards, or mazes of lines in which man long ago disappeared forever. Sometimes it becomes an inhuman rectangular geometry, the Mondrianesque nobility lost. Rage and fury can fling the geometry about, tangling it in patterns of frustration, to end in the melee of Jackson Pollock's forests of dripped paint (Fig. 294). At the other extreme, the compartments can become the magical cloistered cells of Joseph Cornell's chambers full of toys and heedless games and assuaging memories. Yet even with Cornell the time comes when the compartments hold only caged birds that no longer sing, and finally the tiny magic rooms turn into bare cells filled with faceless lumps (Fig. 383).

In all of this wilderness of negation and loss, to find affirmation, life, or hope, requires something very much like religious conversion—an acceptance of answers th ough faith alone. For the situation the artist feels is real—even if the average man is numb to it. Even a century ago, Thoreau estimated it as such; even then, average men, he observed, lived lives of quiet desperation.

Louise Nevelson, through an act of both faith and despair, creates some of the most extraordinary objects being made today: vast black columbaria (as for the human ashes of an entire city). To her, nevertheless, they are living communities, cities of living cells, growing and expanding like coral reefs.

Louise Nevelson was born in Kiev, Russia, in 1900, and came to the United

379   Johns: *Light Bulb No. 2*   1958

380   Johns: *Paint Brushes*   1960

381   Johns: *Painted Bronze*   1960–61

253

382 Ortman: *A Sweet Woman* 1957

383 Cornell: *Compartmented Cubes*

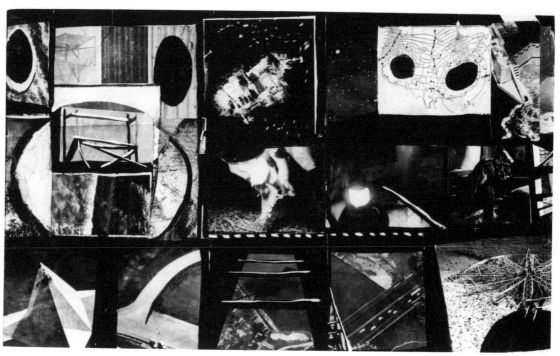

384 Hultberg: *Collage I* 1952

States in 1905. Her art training went from academic to modern (with Hans Hofmann in Munich) and included archaeological studies in Mexico and Central America. Her solo exhibitions began in 1940, extended to 1946, then began again in 1955. During that break of a decade, Miss Nevelson found her extraordinary image, which is so personal yet so universal. Louise Nevelson's effort is to create a safe, friendly, surrogate universe for the race.

Though we are the sum total of the consciousness of the total past, space and time open out in front of us. We no longer want to say the last word—rather, we project a landscape that has never been seen into the future. What I want is a beyondness. *I am not an artist: I am not "in taste." I am in creation.*[4]

So in the late 1950's were suddenly seen the great, potentially endless cellular walls and the towering, animate totems that she calls Sky-Columns-Presences (Figs. 386 to 389 incl.). Like Dubuffet, Louise Nevelson thinks in terms of life: "each niche lives and encloses its own life"—of community: "colonies in which each cell strengthens and supports its neighbors"—of growth: "creation does not have to stop"—and of perpetual change: "place the cells wherever you wish, you are restructuring, not destroying, because life is both in the parts and in the whole."[5]

The great niched walls are almost indescribable—solid black, white, or gold (the "gold" is brass sprayed on)—their hundreds of cells filled with boards and blocks; spindles, turnings, carvings; scrolls, dumbbells and Indian clubs; bedposts and newel posts. Imagine one of these walls as an upended ocean floor, and its bewildering sediment of relics might be artifacts of Atlantis.

Rubens may have had a dozen students to paint the flood of gigantic canvases to which he added the final mas-

4 From an interview with the authors.
5 *Ibid.*

385 Higgins: *Dinghy* 1960

ter's touches: Louise Nevelson does it all herself. On short notice she created rooms full of walls and totems at the Museum of Modern Art. She even has three studios, one each for working in the three colors she uses: "When I'm thinking 'black' or thinking 'white,' I don't want to be confused."

Factualism seems to be sweeping the world, its adherents deserting formal painting to embrace the castoff junk of a culture that produces junk at the most rapid rate in history. Schwitters moved from dada to a prophecy of this generation's leap from anti-art's social and esthetic protest to the calm acceptance of our harvest of junk as material for a truly contemporary art—and let the chips of meaning fall where they may. They use junk as an act of moral and esthetic integrity, as the only realistic course. Their intellectual god is Marcel Duchamp who preceded dada, then transcended its negative limitations; their guide is Schwitters who heard the mute eloquence of our waste. The factualists probe for meanings. They find a wrecked car more real than a new Cadillac.

The wrecked car is wounded or dead; discarded paper and machinery—all discards—are wounded in use and in rejection. A succession of wars, each more

386   Nevelson: *Sky Cathedral*   1958

terrible, has left a human harvest of physical and spiritual wounds. Man's historic inhumanity to man seems never to lessen. So for years some artists have been concerned with wounds and the wounded. Schwitters lavished affection on the lost and unwanted, giving it a home in the *Merzbilder.* Duchamp was pitilessly Socratic. Pointing to the wound he asks humanity, why? In 1945, Duchamp made a collage as a cover for the Fourth of July issue of a popular American magazine, which promptly rejected it. Subsequently it saw publicacation as an illustration in the fourth issue of *VVV,* the magazine edited by André Breton that was sporadically published in New York during the war years. In this picture, which Duchamp named *Allégorie de Genre* (Fig. 390), bandage gauze was used for perhaps the first time—at least in its specific sense—as a collage element. Crumpled, spangled with stars, and bearing its stripes in the form of blood-red stains, it forms a triple primary image: the profile of George Washington, the American flag, and (turned sidewise) the map of the United States. The surreal image is one of horror, as though this gigantic, continent-sized bandage-flag were covering all the wounds of every war, just or unjust, in man's history. It shouts the question: Why?

Among today's artists concerned with wounds, Alberto Burri is leader. His interest is not morbid; his concern is healing and his life explains the positive aspects of his art. Burri's ancestors were Etruscan farmers and he was reared in the agrarian, pastoral atmosphere of plant and animal husbandry. Trained as a surgeon, Burri was practicing at the outbreak of World War II. His war experience was traumatic: the mass spectacle of wounded unreachable for healing.

He began painting as a war prisoner in a Texas prison camp. Returning to Rome, he seems to have made no at-tempt to resume medical practice. A thorough Roman, strong and fiery—yet gently unpretentious—Burri is an extremely sensitive man even for an artist. Though painting perhaps healed his own wounds there were still left, he knew, the many wounded everywhere. So he soon turned from painting to the extraordinary kinds of collage ever since connected with his name. The first of these were the famous *Sacchi,* or "sacks," which consist of ragged burlap collaged on a background of black mourning cloth and sometimes splotched with gouts of sanguine red paint. *But patched:* this is the clue to Burri's intention, which is to stanch the blood and suture the wounds. So clear is this intention that Sir Herbert Read exclaimed: ". . . how expressive . . . of where pain had been, where miraculous healing had taken place . . ."[6]

[6] Read, Sir Herbert, Hanover Gallery exhibition catalogue. London, March 29–April 29, 1960.

387 Nevelson: *Totems* 1959

388   Nevelson: *Dawn's Wedding Feast*   1959

389   Louise Nevelson

James Johnson Sweeney felt it too: "Burri is the Saint Januarius of the collage: one can imagine on his feast day every red gash in his compositions liquefying and streaming blood." But immediately came the sense of healing: "He is an artist with a scalpel—the surgeon conscious of what lies within the flesh of his composition . . ."[7]

The *sacchi* are the collages of a Schwitters turned surgeon, their sad, torn burlap stretched back together with Aesculapian concern. Their horror is unmorbid, their strongest overtones those of pity (Figs. 392, 393, 394). Burri has recently invented several more collage-oriented media likewise concerned with healing. Two are involved with fire: the *combustioni* and the *grandi combustioni legni*. The other, in a remarkable leap of imagination, applies wound-binding to sheet metal.

A *grande combustione legno* consists of thin strips of wood scarred with holes burned by blowtorch then "healed" by being fitted back together in a manner suggesting the sewing of wounds and splints for bones (Fig. 395).

The collages of burned paper called *combustioni* must be considered one of the most original technical concepts evolved in modern art. Holding a sheet of paper, Burri ignites it at one corner and then, as it bursts into flame, allows it to fall upon the surface that will form the background. This surface has been prepared by heavy coating with a slow-drying, noninflammable vinyl plastic. Settling into this wet plastic, the paper burns itself out and congeals into the chance arrangements it assumed in fire and fall. The whole is then fixed with more of the colorless, transparent vinyl. Accident, crisis, and healing are perfectly symbolized in abstract pictorial terms in the *combustioni* (Fig. 396).

Burri calls his sheet-iron pictures *ferri*. In them he converts the very nature of

[7] Sweeney, James Johnson, *Burri*. Rome, L'Obelisco, n.d.

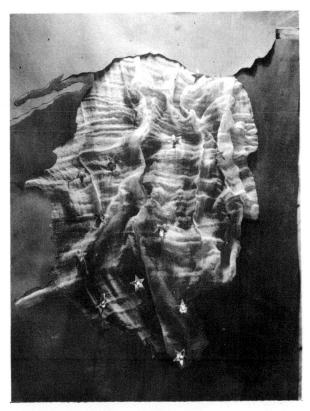

390 Duchamp: *Allégorie de genre* 1945

391 Alberto Burri working on a *ferro* 1959

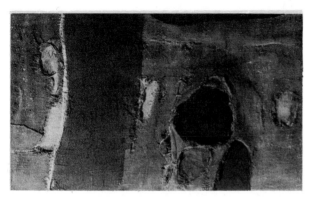

392 Burri: *Rag Composition* 1952

fire, intrinsically destructive, into a "miraculous healing." The sheets of iron or rolled steel, often in the chance shapes of industrial waste, are assembled into patterns and "stitched" by welding. Under the intense heat of the welding torch, the metal shades into permanent tones of blue and fiery red as if forever incandescent in a miracle of purifying flame (Fig. 397). The Roman soil, soil of the martyrs and ground of miracles once thronging with saints in the flesh, is Burri's native soil, too. Perhaps this may help to explain his renunciation of medicine and the profound power of his art.

Though Salvatore Scarpitta and Burri fought on opposite sides, their war experiences in some ways ran parallel. Scarpitta is American, born of Italian parentage in New York in 1919. At seventeen he went as an art student to Italy, and was forty before he saw the United States again. Caught by the war and interned, he escaped and joined the anti-Fascist partisans. With the American invasion he joined the Navy and at war's end helped in locating art treasures buried by the Nazis.

Having married a girl partisan he met in prison camp, he stayed in Italy, had his first painting exhibition in 1944, and several more including participation in the Venice Biennale, before his first American exhibition. This was at the Leo Castelli gallery in 1959. It was then that he came back to his native country after nearly a quarter-century. "I have found my home," he said, greatly moved and excited.

Only a few years earlier he had found his medium: elastic bandages interwoven and stretched over three-dimensional pictures. No wounds intrude in these formal constructions, yet the dyeing with coffee or iodine, or the dull black in which some are sprayed, convey the sense of wounds now healed through the invocation of order. Very recently Scarpitta has found the courage to make more direct allusions, as in his inclusions of war mementos like his own naval insignia (Figs. 398, 399).

Without the urge to heal, trauma and crisis emerge in works of horror and morbidity or in formalisms that ignore or deny the crisis. The encompassing compassion of a Burri gives way to the personal, and universal validity is lessened. The Swiss artist Eric Beynon, for example, uses burlap and other materials typical of Burri but the collage-constructions he calls "paintings" (Fig. 400), with their menacing, monstrous vampiric shapes, convey an unmitigated sense of horror. Lee Bontecou's remarkably structured relief pictures of discolored canvas, with their black, yawning, empty craters, convey the feeling of hypnotic fixation, almost self-extinction (Fig. 401). Looking at Miss Bontecou's pictures, it is difficult to reach past apparent personal dilemma to their more general aspect: the otherworldly landscape of gaping volcanos, bare hills, and hostile inhuman valleys.

Robert Rauschenberg's combine-paintings are dialogues between the old and the new esthetics: pictorial space and real space, art and anti-art, the permanent and the perishable, easel picture and junk. They are painting-collage-construction-object-sculpture, hybrids with a unity that confounds traditional criticism.

260

393   Burri: *Airflight*   1954

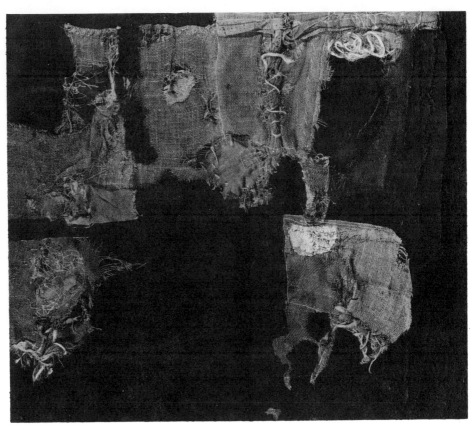

394   Burri: *New York*   1955

395   Burri: *Grande Combustione Legno*   1958

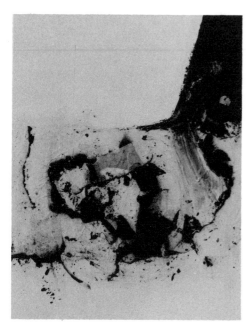

396   Burri: *Combustione M59 No. 1*   1959

397   Burri: *Ferro P. 59*   1959

If I said "paintings" people said "sculpture"; if I said "sculpture" they said "paintings." I found I could limit neither material nor format, and it became impossible to hold them to the wall.

Concerning materials Rauschenberg once wrote:

A pair of socks is no less suitable to make a painting with than wood, nails, turpentine, oil and fabric.[8]

Socks, actually, are a comparatively mild Rauschenberg ingredient, as witness the authors' notes made at his 1960 exhibition:

INLET: collage + paint on canvas—half a pair of khaki trousers, lettering, open zipper, paint-can lid, bent wire, stuffed bird in wooden niche, electric outlet, corkscrew, boy scout's compass . . . (Fig. 404).

HAWK: collage + paint—blue denim, sport shirt fragment, scraps of posters . . . (Fig. 405).

ALLEGORY: collage + paint—more of same trousers, flattened-out red umbrella, mirror panel, crumpled tin . . . (Fig. 402).

BROADCAST: collage + paint—fragment of pocket comb stuck in a dirty glob of white paint, knobs to turn on concealed radios tuned to different stations, news photos (cops beating up a victim, steeple jack at work, finish of a horse race) . . . (Fig. 406).

CANYON: collage + paint—baby photograph, corrugated tin, frayed shirt cuff, stuffed eagle perching on empty carton (is this America?) a puffed-out (but empty) pillow hanging in front of a coverlet (the unrewarding bed?) . . .

GIFT FOR APOLLO: paint-splattered door on perambulator wheels, collaged with St. Patrick's Day necktie, poster bits, print of New York skyline, *the rest of the trousers,* and on the floor a battered bucket half-full of hardened cement . . . (Fig. 407).

398   Scarpitta: *Out of Step*   1960

399   Scarpitta: *Gunner's Mate*   1961

[8] Rauschenberg, Robert, Catalogue of the exhibition *Sixteen Americans.* Museum of Modern Art, New York, 1959. All other quotations are from personal interviews.

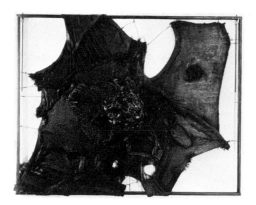

400   Beynon: *Painting No. 2*

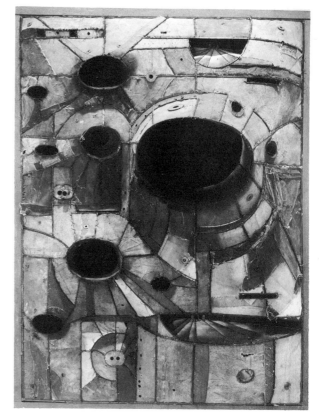

401   Bontecou: *The 1960 Construction*

402   Rauschenberg: *Allegory*   1959–60

Robert Rauschenberg was born in Port Arthur, Texas, in 1925. He joined the U.S. Navy in World War II. While stationed in Southern California in 1944 he saw Gainsborough's *Blue Boy* at the Huntington Library in San Marino.

I had never seen a real oil painting before. In high school I drew all the time, but did not study art. The height of my ambition had been to be a magazine illustrator, doing "handmade" pictures.

Seeing no combat, Rauschenberg saw its results: the war psychotics he tended as neuropsychiatric technician in a service hospital.

Don't be sympathetic, be realistic, were my orders. But you can't help it—and there wasn't enough of me to go around.

Then the war was over, followed by G.I. study at Académie Julian in Paris, then with Albers at Black Mountain College, and at the Art Students League in New York. A professional by 1950, Rauschenberg quickly moved into unconventional work, and by 1953 had conceived his combine-painting idea.

My friends were sending me wonderful junk from all over the world. It was so *real* that it shocked me that it shocked people—but it *made* them look at what was in front of them. It didn't shock children, but then children *like* art: they don't have to forget or remember.

Fleeting images astonished him with their reality; paintings seemed alive.

. . . the shadow of a person cast for a moment on an unpainted canvas was as real a painting as any. One spring I made a painting out of earth and flower seeds. It sprouted. I watered it every day.

But then this picture died. Still, there had to be reality of some kind in art. He made a collage of toilet paper, then its exact duplicate in pure gold leaf. The illusion offended him. He threw the gold collage away, kept the paper one. Then he saw a wrecked automobile.

403 Rauschenberg: *Double Feature* 1959

It looked dead, but it wasn't dead: it had been someplace and done something and had become real—it had *experienced*. Suddenly I wanted to make manifestos: *Rauschenberg was asleep—Rauschenberg is now awake*.

Robert Rauschenberg found his identity and his art in the physical reality of things.

Kerouac had written that he drank a sad cup of coffee. Damn it, a cup of coffee is a cup of coffee—if it is anything it is *happy* simply because it is coffee and knows it is. It was like a miracle: at last I could use *red* paint, by knowing that paint is only itself.

But it is factualism on many levels, nevertheless, just as the red paint is paint and something more. As with Burri it is the blood of war, healed here not by

404 Rauschenberg: *Inlet* 1959

405 Rauschenberg: *Hawk* 1960

406 Rauschenberg: *Broadcast* 1959

407 Rauschenberg: *Gift for Apollo* 1959

408 Rauschenberg: *Monogram* 1959

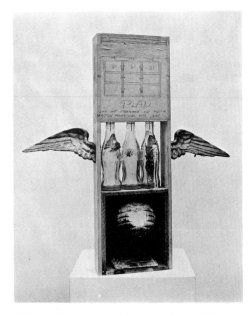

409 Rauschenberg: *Coca-Cola Plan* 1958

surgery but by the obstinate, healing insistence that it is only paint. Like all factualism it is both real and poetic. Rauschenberg wishes it to appear naive and childlike, yet it deals with the reality behind the facts. It is thoroughly contemporary, even to obsolescence.

A collector complained that one of my combine paintings was shedding parts. "After only three years," he said, sore as hell. "Where's the Cadillac you bought that same year?" I asked. Was he surprised! "I traded it in, of course," he said. He stopped beefing. But that's the only picture of mine that's ever needed repair. Something happens to this junk—on the street it's dead; in a picture it lasts forever.

15

ENVIRONMENTS AND HAPPENINGS

The street is the unsylvan landscape of the factual realists. Stony and arid, coursed with machines and people, layered with junk and grime, it haunts our artists. In America, in Europe, they utilize its realities, probe its meanings. Not all can compress this vivid, astonishing, three-dimensional wilderness into flat pictures or even into constructions. No wonder. To appeal to the street as witness is to face the street's reality: it is not a picture, it is not "constructed," it is life. Life is what concerns the latest phase of factualism: the art of Environments and Happenings. These new artists are determined to fuse whole life and whole reality with art. An impossible quest?

Perhaps. But in essence it has been this whole century's quest. Cubism took the first step by rejecting false perspective and photographic illusion in favor of the reality of the picture itself, a two-dimensional autonomy. Collage began: pasted newspaper to hold the viewer's eye at the picture plane. But it was not a halt but a change of direction: the pa-

per scraps pointed to real space, real world. The movement of picture into space had begun.

Almost immediately pictures became happenings in real space in the dada's outrageous anti-art performances, but soon went back into pictorial space with the surrealists' "storytelling" pictures.

In the 1940's the obsessive search for reality led the abstract-expressionists to look for it in the creative act itself. A destructive dichotomy then appeared: the picture is asked to abdicate to the act, but if it does, art's permanent physicality disappears while the act becomes mere ritualistic gesture. Gnawing doubt infected many painters: it halted De Kooning for a while, helped to destroy Jackson Pollock. It seemed to be a dead end.

Two realities, actually, were at war. And that meant two kinds of space, for space of some kind (physical or metaphysical) is the indispensable vessel of reality. The conceptuals of esthetic creation, like the whole drama of individual consciousness, take place in a private space that interpenetrates the public physical space of the real world. The two kinds of space may intermingle forever and yet never fuse into one. It is something analogous to this private space, or perhaps derived from it, that gives each picture its own individual esthetic reality. So while fifty years of endeavor produced a body of extraordinary art, the artist's instinctive attempts to integrate art with modern life had been a long series of failures at the impossible. It is these failures, with the initial impetus more urgent than ever, that young artists inherited at mid-century.

Their answer is the most revolutionary in a revolutionary century: they reject the permanent work of art. Among them artists like Stankiewicz, Rauschenberg, and Mallary are already "old masters" still making "set pieces." This newest generation builds environments and in these bridgeheads of actual space they make happenings take place. They use real space without defining and limiting it in pictorial terms, build real traps, construct dark, cryptic, sometimes terror-filled mazes into which to lure people. They do what the futurists wished to do and the abstract-expressionists talked of doing: they force people to enter the work of art, sit, walk around, live in it.

It is deliberately as ephemeral as passing experience; no collector can own these "works of art" any more than he could preserve unchanged a day of childhood, a spring rain, an October sunset; no museum can embalm these living plasticisms of evanescence. The environments take form and disappear, the happenings happen and are over, and the whole thing is no more to be framed and hung on a wall than those showers of light in which fireworks die. Art finds strange dignity and a new identity in its abnegation: it is at last the seized moment, the naked *thing-in-itself*. It is a gigantic reorientation in esthetic thinking, climax of the convulsive fifty-year movement of picture into collage, into relief, into construction, into object, into space. The real scope and intent of anti-art is at last evident as plastic art becomes action in time-space.

This should be the final insult to a Philistine public long and sorely tried by cubism, futurism, dada, surrealism, abstract-expressionism, and all the rest. But there is no violent anger, no raucous laughter. From the first unveiling of the fauves to the present, no art movement has had audiences like these which willingly, even happily, enter into the environments, sit transfixed by the happenings, unquestioningly accept the idea that art can be action, state of mind or being, and not a *thing* at all.

Variously oriented toward music, drama, or the plastic arts, the environment idea is being manifested in widespread centers as dada once was. There have been environment-happenings in Japan, Cologne, Milan, and Paris; they focus the activity of an artist group in New York. The first environment to appear in New York seems to have been an Allan Kaprow exhibition in 1956. The Japanese manifestations were first publicly seen in a pine forest at Ashiya in 1955. The Cologne and Milan happenings began under the influence of the American pianist David Tudor. All are esthetic events happening in the space-time continuum of the real world. Beyond this, however, strong differences exist between the phenomena in different countries.

One of the earliest manifestations of the Environment began in Munich in the late 1930's—collaborative room-dimension paintings called *Faschings-Dekorationen* or Carnival Decorations. In 1952, a group of young painters led by Walter Gaudnek modernized the concept into abstract environments that, continuing to today, have come to include phantasmagoric floating sculptures —animals, chimeras, demons, etc.—made from paper, wire, and other constructional materials.

The Japanese Gutai are a tight-knit group of modern Hokusais—men and women of daring and unorthodox imagination, led by Jiro Yoshihara, a pioneer Japanese modernist. Though they have produced static pictures, these are apt to result from inventive processes like

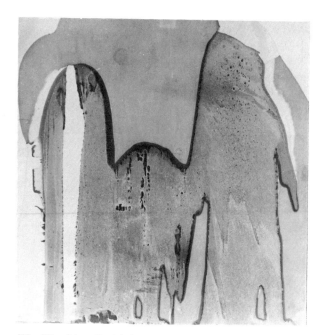

410 Kinoshita: *Untitled* 1958

Toshio Kinoshita's paintings made by the reactions of chemicals on paper (Fig. 410). Other paintings have been made by toy trucks running around canvases dripping paints of different colors, or by paint shot against the canvas by cannon—techniques that point up the strong hold of Jackson Pollock on the Gutai imagination. Sadamasa Motonaga devised apparatus to blow rings and shaped clouds of smoke to be "painted" with colored light, thus reviving or reinventing after half a century the futurist experiment of painting with colored gases. But it is back to Hokusai that the Japanese actionist precedents really go.

The Gutai joined with more conservative artists for their first demonstration. Yozo Ukita writes that midway in the Ashiya pine grove there was a "gigantic pond with the entire bottom filled with paintings."[1] The next year the Gutai Association had its first autonomous show, at the Ohara Hall in Tokyo. Here there appeared elements of violence and revolt less apparent to Western eyes than to Japanese. One major work involved the tearing of paper which in Japan is a symbol of violence, destruction, and danger. The beautiful Japanese houses with their paper walls are so easily destroyed by fire or physical violence that children are sternly forbidden even to touch them. Thus torn paper, for us the sad symbol of rejection and waste, is for the Japanese the shocking symbol of violent revolt.

The work in question was by Saburo Murakami (Fig. 411), a gigantic eight-fold plain paper screen to acquire its design—symbols of violence—by holes to be torn in it. Yoshihara writes that it "made a very big noise when it was torn through. . . . I myself had the honor of hitting myself against it and tearing open the screen. I so to speak substituted for a hammer. . . . But it was a unique experience to find myself standing in another space the instant the paper was torn . . ."[2]

Then a work called *The Bell,* by a girl Gutai, Atsuko Tanaka, was completed and "loud clangs of bells began . . . to run about the hall like living creatures . . . upstairs and downstairs." Tiny Atsuko, who weighs only 85 pounds, made some fantastic costumes (Fig. 412) at the third Gutai exhibition which took place in 1957 and was devoted to stage Happenings. All of the costumes, large and

[2] Jiro Yoshihara in Gutai catalogue No. 4. Translated by Juichi Kuroda. Nishinomiya City, July 1, 1956.

411 Murakami: *Torn Paper Screen* 1956

[1] From Gutai catalogue No. 3. Nishinomiya City, October 20, 1955.

small, some bearing blinking electric bulbs, came out of a single gigantic red garment hung like a curtain across the stage.

The second Gutai exhibition, the year before, had been held outdoors in the Ashiya pine grove. Since many works utilized light and movement the night effect was magical. It was ominous too —as Yoshihara wrote—in good part through Miss Tanaka's seven gigantic figures which, though human, expressed no human feeling. Strings of red light bulbs outlined their skeletons, lighting up in pulsing series like "the circulation of blood." Together with all this was a ready-made submitted by Akiro Kanayama, consisting simply of a railroad signal crossing with red lights and a warning bell that rang all the time, day and night. Kanayama's other entry (Fig. 412-A) was a white vinyl belt 400 feet long with black footprints on it which "meandered through the whole exhibition site and climbed up a pine tree at the end."

The Cologne and Milan happenings—called realizations—stem mainly from music while utilizing acting. A central figure in the Cologne movement is Nam June Paik, a Korean composer-actor who is said to use great physical violence. Advance guard American composer John Cage relates that on one occasion at the Mary Bauermeister Gallery, Paik strode up to him and taking out a knife, cut off Cage's necktie, wrenched off his jacket, ripped his shirt, and then rushed among the audience dashing liquid shampoo on the spectators' heads. The audience's acquiescent involvement is indicated by Cage's remark: "You could almost smell violence in the air, yet people did not cry out, did not get up, did not leave—simply sat there watching it all."

Happenings in Paris retain the dada name: *Manifestations*. They can be static, i.e., Environments like Arman's *Manifestation de Tripaille* (Garbage)

412 Tanaka: *Figure Costumes with Electric Bulbs* 1957

412A Kanayama: *White Vinyl with Footprints* 1956

271

413 Schwitters: *Merzbau*

of 1960 (Fig. 427) which filled the entire Iris Clert Gallery and could be viewed only through the door. Villeglé is an expert at a type of Parisian Happening called *cris* which are simply blood-curdling screams that far transcend the best traditional Grande Guignol efforts. Suddenly exploding after long silence and inaction, they transfix audiences in horror, perhaps the simplest and most cogent symbol yet found for the horror that has stalked our days ever since the last great war.

In New York, German artist Walter Gaudnek, having become a founder of the experimental 10/4 group, has continued to create environments out of oil paintings. His *Unlimited Dimensions* (Fig. 420), made up of twenty-nine floor-to-ceiling panels, is susceptible of a vast variety of arrangements. At the 10/4 Gallery it filled a room, and then later, at the Martha Jackson Gallery, was planned to take on an entirely different arrangement. Gaudnek's work is conceived in painter's terms even while dealing with real space, and he has written almost in futurist terms of the painting engulfing the spectator. Earlier, an Allan Kaprow work called *Wall* was planned more as a toy, or divertimento, for audience participation. Its panels—

414 Early American: The Mercer Museum, Doylestown, Pa.

415 Late American: Automobile Graveyard 1961

416   Richard Stankiewicz in his studio

mirrors, tar and leaves, artificial fruit, etc.—were subject to rearrangement by the gallery goers.

The main New York environment-happening activity, however, involves another group, which has set up its own gallery as an arena for this new kind of plastic creation. The group includes or has included, Red Grooms, George Brecht, Al Hansen, and Edward Higgins, while its steady nucleus is Allan Kaprow, James Dine, Claes Oldenburg, and Robert Whitman, Jr.

Their gallery, The Reuben, now in its third location in the New York lower East Side, shows no pictures, is used only as the small theater for new happenings during one week of each month during the art season. Other Manhattan locations have been used: The Cooper Union for Arts and Sciences, the experimental Living Theater on 14th Street, the Judson Memorial Church gallery on Washington Square, and several of the artists' loft studios. Wherever environments are installed or happenings happen, the same phenomenon occurs of audiences hypnotically fascinated by material-action that is often apparently little more than children's games and impromptu play-acting. One says "apparently" advisedly because depths are quickly to be sensed. The operative magic is reality posed as myth: often horrifying, occasionally deliberately banal, frequently enigmatic, it casts a spell in which thought and feeling become form, action, and sound.

It was in 1956 that Allan Kaprow transformed his own exhibit of collages at the Hansa Gallery into a carnival sideshow, a penny arcade, and the environment had been created. Kaprow is a quiet, bearded, family man and a college professor into the bargain (he has taught art at Rutgers University). As off-campus artist he is relentlessly unorthodox. Collage, by posing a challenge, became his springboard into the unknown.

The environment came out of collage which is the prime mover in a kind of thinking which is "impure"—that is, anti-classical and antitraditional—and which hinges upon accepting not only the accidental *but whatever is there.* Collage inflames the imagination: I began wanting to collage the impossible—to paste-up action, to make collages of people and things in motion.[3]

Kaprow's show was ready to open. He looked around, saw "nothing but pictures on the wall," and something like despair seized him. Hurriedly he nailed brackets to the wall flanking the pictures and from these suspended irregular painted pieces of canvas slashed and pierced with holes. To see the pictures at all, one had to look through these slashed curtains. Then, lest even that be too easy, he placed light bulbs between curtains and pictures and set up automatic circuits to keep them blinking at different speeds and wattages.

[3] From interviews with the authors.

417   Claes Oldenburg carrying part of *The Street*   1960

418 Jean Dubuffet

419 Allan Kaprow in *Garage Happening* (detail)
1960

This was *Penny Arcade;* it captured people, compelled attention; the painting-as-environment was born. With it was born the happening. The realization came to him in the deserted gallery after the opening, when he felt the letdown of life withdrawn and the pictures were left staring at emptiness with the lights senselessly blinking on and off.

The idea was in the air. Soon the name "happening" itself came in an action-score Kaprow created for his students and called *18 Happenings in 6 Parts.* The activity was already the only art activity with which Kaprow could be seriously involved. A group formed and the strange, perishable, impossible "collages of action" began to be seen by the public. The group is highly diversified and personal in the work of its individuals and does not generally indulge in group creation. Kaprow describes them:

Claes Oldenburg—very literary, a social critic using archetypal situations with a warm feeling for people and a strong sense of moral purpose; Jim Dine—an artist of magical, mysterious Gauguinesque symbolism yet using immediate actions; Red Grooms—a Charlie Chaplin forever dreaming about fire; Whitman—the most adventurous and intuitive of all of us; Brecht—his work is an abstract *arcane* suspended in feeling and very pure.[4]

Whitman characterizes Kaprow's work as abstract: "He is not interested in people but in objects," which tallies roughly with Kaprow's own statement: "What I want are archetypal situations with an inchoate, unformed quality."

Among the environments and happenings created by the group have been the following: Kaprow's *Apple Shrine, Penny Arcade, Coca Cola Shirley Cannon Ball?, The Big Laugh,* and *A Spring Happening;* Oldenburg's *Snapshots of the City, Fotodeath,* and *Ironworks;* Dine's *The Shining Bed, Car*

4 *Ibid.*

274

420 Gaudnek: *Unlimited Dimensions* (detail) 1961

Crash, and *A Rainbow Thought;* Whitman's *The Heap,* and *The American Moon;* Grooms' *Burning Building,* and *The Fireman's Dream;* and the Dine-Oldenburg collaboration *Ray Gun.*

Ray Gun was presented in February and March, 1960, at the Judson Church gallery (Figs. 417, 421). It consisted of two parts: *The Street* created by Oldenburg and *The House* created by Dine. Oldenburg says:

> Our desire was to work between painting and sculpture; to invite public action and involvement; to create an altered reality with the full power of reality.[5]

Oldenburg and Dine built the *Ray Gun* environment entirely from waste materials found in a nearby vacant slum lot:

> . . . a wonderful mine of corrugated cardboard, desiccated newspapers, bottles, tinware, beer cans, bedsprings, old clothing . . .

[5] This and all subsequent quotes from members of this group are from interviews with the authors.

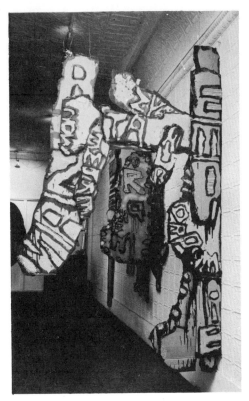

421 Oldenburg-Dine: *Ray Gun* (detail) 1960

Ray Gun reflected and commented upon popular American taste. Its title was taken from a pulp science-fiction comic book, and a mimeograph machine turned out "comic books" written and drawn by various group members who hawked them among the audience at ten cents a copy. The machine also ground out "poems" made up of sign letters in the various forms and shapes to be seen in the streets. After being recited the poems were sold like the song sheets of turn-of-the-century variety houses. *Ray Gun* ended with ad lib performances by Kaprow, Higgins, Dine, Hansen, Whitman, and the others—a concentration of mordant irony concealed in comic book flummery. Through it all ran the hyp-

notic myth-fact of the street as objectified in Oldenburg's maze of grotesque and gigantic cardboard mannikins in their wilderness of signs: *Empire, Orpheum, Romeo, Tarzan* (Fig. 421).

"Those things had become so alive we could not let them die," Oldenburg said. "So we dragged them all home to the lot they came from."

Robert Whitman's *The American Moon* (Fig. 423) was "a strange dark masterpiece," to use Kaprow's description. The audience was seated in six separate wedge-shaped "caves" arranged like spokes radiating from the center of a wheel. After the audience entered through dark narrow tunnels the curtains forming the tunnels were raised and in the central semidarkness a mysterious rustling began; then images of cloth and paper, featureless and shrouded and moving in eerie counterpoint; a pink image (object? person?) arching overhead as if on the irrelevant swing of a summer holiday; paper rustling in the dark and then looming in semihuman shapes out of the shadows . . . it was mysterious out of all proportion, a kind of dream with meanings around its corners.

After a serious automobile accident Jim Dine did the happening called *Car Crash,* "partly for my own sake," he says, "—a kind of psycho-drama." The audience sat at the center surrounded by sounds, sights, and actions—a "speech" and a tape recording of traffic sounds, an endless scroll of cries for help, girls dancing a deathly "sex-tease" of speeding cars on a highway. Here are sample pages from Dine's script book for *Car Crash:*

CAR PARTS: suspended from ceiling. Make a Red Cross from one fender. Bandage gauze to cover all walls.

HEADLIGHT DANCE: constant backing away, elusiveness from one another, a sex-tease with straight-ahead beams—go into audience, encompass them with light.

422 Kaprow: *An Apple Shrine* (detail) 1960

423 Whitman: *The American Moon* (detail) 1960

SLOW DANCE: at geometric angles until two dancers meet head-on.

CRASH OF LIGHTS (hold for 1 minute). Banging on sheet metal with hammers; on last few bangs all lights out except one small globe above audience; horns start blaring from loudspeaker directly above audience.

SPEECH ABOUT CARS AND CRASHES: band-aid mask for girl making speech; Red Cross Nurse—Woman in male clothes, Man is in woman's costume *which is a shroud.*

WORK UP CAR SPEECH INTO A FUGUE FOR TWO VOICES . . .

Everything—speed, crash, tragedy— was frozen into an eerie slow motion, the sense of crisis as drawn out and protracted as the paper scroll being cranked out of a press and imprinted in fresh ink with endless repetitions of the cry "Help! Help!" Even the ending was suspended, leaving the audience to sit in contemplation: "They sat at least ten minutes after it was all over, no one moving, no one making a sound."

Dine's work always has macabre overtones. In *The Shining Bed* he lay on a bed dressed as Santa Claus and encased in cellophane in what he intended to be a "slapstick comedy representation" of a gift-wrapped Santa Claus. In private symbols Dine conceived of the bed as a Christmas tree and placed old-fashioned Christmas candles along the foot of the bed. But the deeper implications inevitably rose to the surface to form the dominant motive. In this case Dine compounded incipient horror by adding a last-minute slapstick effect: Santa Claus struggling to escape from the package. The "funny" scene became ghastly, the audience clearly sensing an allusion to the frequent accidental smothering of children in the plastic food envelopes from supermarkets (Fig. 425).

Happenings are both fable and fact, and their allusions can glance off all the facets of contemporary life. Though Oldenburg's scene is always the street, the street is always life. In *Fotodeath* the pitiless camera lens focuses on harlot

424 Dine: *Car Crash* (detail) 1960

425 Dine: *The Shining Bed* (detail) 1960

and heiress, Insider and Outsider, bum, madman, wastrel, and on the Grand Army of the Respectable, flashing revelation to all and turning them impartially into pillars of salt. In Kaprow's *A Spring Happening* the allegory is as stark as in Melville or Kafka—the audience caged in a dark slotted tunnel, involuntary voyeurs at the strip-tease of a lonely girl, pursuing an elusive spotlight —the whole a symbolism as simple and as fatal as the unchanging human predicament.

Physical danger is often disturbingly close to the audience at the happenings. Crowded into small places with a single narrow exit in the midst of wildernesses of scrap paper and other combustibles, the danger of a flash fire is far from negligible. Risky things happen in the air: people and objects swing above the heads of the audience or participants climb out over shaky scaffolding. But, it must be admitted, danger is as much a part of the reality as it is a part of the myth.

In any event, the happening is unquestionably a new medium in which form and intention merge. When the picture as painting disappears, its long movement into space becomes physical evidence of the artist's overwhelming need to re-establish his art and himself in the general stream of life. He aims to show that art is serious, timely, pertinent, cogent. He is determined to be recognized as being as important as merchant, politician, soldier, and scientist. He intends to force a gigantic reorientation of general thinking.

Pictures, of course, will not be destroyed nor the making of them ended. But the waves of each ism in this century, from cubism and futurism through dada and surrealism to abstract-expressionism, and all the rest, eat away a little more of the stony cliff of materialistic thought. New movements have forced acceptance of earlier ones as lesser evils and the process accelerated rapidly un-

426 Oldenburg: *Ironworks* (detail) 1961

til now the environment and the happening find audiences ready to accept this longest of all the leaps of faith.

The acceleration has become clearly evident: today a new movement lasts little more than seven or eight years as a fresh creative idea that attracts young artists; the obsolescence of artists and art movements is as impressively rapid as that of automobiles and gadgets. Not only are Jackson Pollock and Mark Rothko already old masters even in the public view, but, for the newest generation, so are Nevelson, Stankiewicz, Rauschenberg, and Jasper Johns.

It all began with bits of newspaper pasted to the surfaces of the painting. There and then began the movement of picture into an outer space once postulated as human space but now becoming a dark sea luring us to other planets. Yet with it all, those earliest cubist collages, with their artifacts charged with the magic of reality, remain fresh. The year 1911, Soby has observed, was a long time ago and most things from that

427 Arman: *Manifestation of Garbage* (detail) 1960

279

long-ago time look their age. But he says with justice "The best collages look ours."[6] The half-century-old newspapers are not as out-of-date as yesterday's *Times*. Printed before the first World War they speak with a truth unrelated to dates and undiminished by time. Their continuing currency is that of an ineradicable realism. Once it had been established, this interrelation between artist's world and real world, there began an open-end drama, a dialogue that may have had a beginning but has no surely foreseeable end. New accretions from that real space can come over, trailing their memories, into pictures. Who knows what?—a bit of soil from lunar mountains, an exploded fragment of a ship that landed on Mars . . . leftover relics, otherworldly Environments and Happenings from outer space.

Collage brought the world into art and then art moved into the world. It is evident that art will not end even if pictures should become obsolete. Pictures, somehow, will have to take cognizance of our new expanding space—a vast environment and a strange one in which happenings will become magical with realities yet to be discovered.

[6] Soby, James Thrall, *Modern Art and the New Past*. Norman, The University of Oklahoma Press, 1957.

16

OF MOTION AND TIME
IN SPACE

In 1962, when this book first appeared, certain concepts proved startling. Apart from the idea of collage as germinative in the art of this century, the idea of mere paper laminae as moving the very picture out into assemblage and construction in real space was a novel proposition. So, too, was the idea that these assemblages and constructions had already rendered obsolete the time-honored categories of painting and sculpture. Perhaps even more startling was the concept propounded herein of our contemporary esthetic dialogue between real space and pictorial space—between reality and illusion—between object and image.

Almost immediately, however, these ideas became parts of our current art dialectic. Now even news magazines discuss "Painting into Space" and describe artwork as "somewhere between collage and carpentry," and artists state that they are using "reverse perspective." And, in 1966, the Venice *Biennale,* showing a new awareness of the new facts of art, solemnly asked for less restrictive

applications of the genera, sculpture especially.

Maps of new terrain assist exploration and settlement. So, perhaps, these new guidelines have been a slight factor in the very marked acceleration and proliferation of art in that half decade, 1962–1967. In any event, directions implicit in a few individuals almost overnight became large movements involving many artists.

Shouldering abstract expressionism into the wings, these new movements—or culminations—almost simultaneously filled the stage: Hard Edge painting, shaped paintings, Pop art, Op art, kinetic sculpture and Primary Structures, and a number of new techniques parallel to, or borrowed from, science and technology.

The term "Hard Edge" simply designates current work, like that of the American Ellsworth Kelly, that continues the Purist tradition of sharply edged painted forms. If geometrical, they recall Mondrian's rectangles (Fig. 140) or his lines derived from stretched color tapes (Fig. 309). If free-form, they recall Arp's collages and wood reliefs (Figs. 47, 106, 124, 311) with their prior indebtedness to the sharply sheared shapes of *découpage.*

Shaped paintings let their forms exist independently of the traditional circumscribed pictorial space comprised in the term background. They may, as in Charles Hinman's paintings, float in free

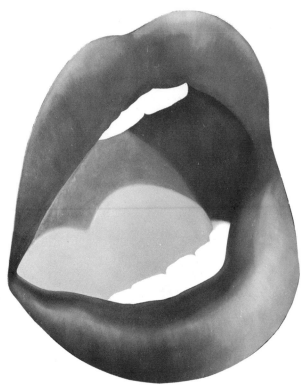

428 Wesselmann: *Mouth No. 7* 1966

had first been painted with background, then cut out by *découpage* and moved out into space, with space (or environment) as background.

The rest of the half decade has been filled with what John Canaday calls the "triumphant blatancy" of Pop, the upsetting coruscations of Op (or Optical), and the many-sided extensions of sculpture, many of which are loosely comprised under the term "kinetic."

Meanwhile, there have been certain developments within the scope of collage proper. Rauschenberg (before he recently deserted pictorial art for a kind of ballet-happening) put together a combine-painting of phenomenal size, almost environmental in its impact. *Barge* is nearly seven feet high and nearly thirty-three feet wide (Fig. 429), thus leaving Picasso's *La Toilette* (Fig. 305) far behind in questions of size.

Among new techniques involving the basic papier collé, Rosalyn Drexler collages—then paints over—paper photostats of news shots, with this technique at the service of a notably stark, documentary vision (Fig. 430).

A young Italian, Pistoletto, has originated a technique of collaging life-size human figures in monochrome on paper, upon sheet steel polished to a mirrorlike brilliance. Hung, these steel sheets reflect whatever is before them, thus placing the collage figures into a potentially in-

space slightly in front of their bounding rectangle—only a step of disengagement beyond the Arp reliefs. Or the very canvases may be shaped to the forms, eliminating background, as in the work of Tom Wesselmann (Fig. 428), the English artist Richard Smith, and the French painter Martial Raysse. Here the end result is exactly the same as if the forms

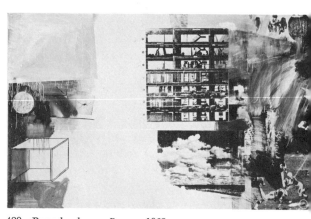

429 Rauschenberg: *Barge* 1962

282

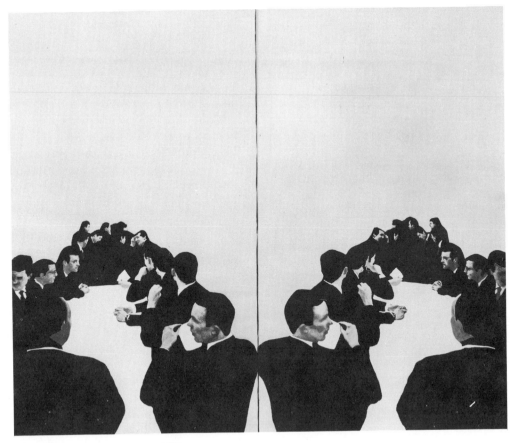

430 Drexler: *The Syndicate* 1964

finite number of environments. In the one illustrated (Fig. 431), a seated woman of collaged paper has visually moved into a library as reflected in the steel background. At the moment she is alone. However, should anyone enter the library and step within this mirror's preview, he will without having willed it simultaneously join her in her pictorial precincts. She is Alice, forever shuttling between the Looking Glass worlds, posing more and more urgently

431 Pistoletto: *Donna seduta vista di tre quarti*
1963

the unanswerable question of *Le vrai et le faux*. On which side of Pistoletto's mirror is reality to be found?

More impersonal, less challenging are certain physical processes now used as pictorial techniques. By embodying a process in a picture, permutation will continue and thereby the picture continue to evolve. Where Duchamp, then dada, embraced the Laws of Chance, some artists today invoke Process which then, in effect, does the creating. The artist in effect kicks himself upstairs.

For example, Ronald Mallory's abstract compositions of mercury contained within an activated area are perpetually evolving through change. Never complete (and designedly so), this by no means negates art, if one will grant substituting "becoming" for "complete," the open-end for the finished form—

flight, as it were, for architecture (Fig. 432).

The young German artist, Hans Haacke, uses natural processes personally and often poetically. Taking two simple, immiscible antagonists, oil and water, he has created pictures (contained areas) within which the two, one neutral and one colored, lock in fresh combat whenever the picture, like an hourglass, is turned end for end. Fluidly continuous once triggered, the process can be properly pictured only by motion picture or television. The six photographs shown of the picture *Scylla and Charybdis* (Fig. 433) are of course only six moments from flux frozen by the still camera.

Group Zero, founded in Germany, in 1958 organized the first Environment in that country. Zero, including Piene, Günther Uecker, Heinz Mack, and, later, Haacke, worked for a time with Yves Klein who communicated his almost pagan, pantheistic feeling for the forces of nature, wind and rain, water, light, and fire (Figs. 299, 300, 302, 303). So, like ancient myth, they underlie much of the work of the Zero artists. Haacke's *The Wave*, for example, is the sea trapped in a picture. Merely water hermetically enclosed between plastic sheets, it is a compressed drama of nature. Push a plastic pane and the water rolls, surges, and crests across its space as if it were as wide as the ocean, a moving image out of myth and history. With such uses of Process, the artist at last touches infinity by unleashing infinite, never-duplicated change (Fig. 434).

Klein, one of the truly germinative artists of mid-century, married Uecker's sister. His ties with Zero lasted until his sudden, tragic death in 1962. His influence also remains on Heinz Mack who, for example, named a flexible aluminum sculpture *Light, Wind, Water* (Fig. 435). Mack constructs steel totems or stelae that, through reflection, veer from substance to void, and from autonomous existence to new, changeling identities (Fig. 436). Assembling hosts of steel and aluminum forms, Mack created an environment-exhibition that he called "Lights of Silver." Almost like an homage to Klein were Mack's two ten-foot "water walls" on the grounds of a hospital in Senegal. Another Mack project is a sixty-foot "Light Tower" on an ocean pier in Scheveningen.

At first in artifact (collaged newspaper clipping) and now in natural process the real world is entering art on today's two-way street of interpenetration. Light and reflection, wind and water, motion, change—all the magic yet real abracadabra of nature—are transforming art into undreamed-of forms. And more vivid, even, than the transformations of the whole genus once called "pictures" are the current transformations of "sculpture."

Sculptural (constructive) modes are being extended today in several directions: one, allied to Pop art, is strongly psychological, stemming basically from surrealism; another, like an apothegm of Mondrian, is the understatement of "minimal" form; a third subjects the sculptor-constructivist's creation to mutative forces: sound (as an attribute), light (as a force), and especially motion. The third category is called in general kinetic sculpture—which read as "construction," "assemblage," or "machine," all prefixed by the adjective "moving." The broadly descriptive term embraces equally each historic stage, from Duchamp's 1913 *Bicycle Wheel* to a 1932 Calder mobile, and from Jimmy Ernst's 1955 *Gizmo*, the kinetic sculpture used as "visual signature" for an NBC television "spectacular," on to a programed electronic construction of today. Kinetic sculptures now are mechanisms and, in some of the robot types, virtually organisms. Their *deus ex machina* is science. They play out their tapes like computers or, like robots, spring into action through the voluntary or involun-

432 Mallory: *Untitled* 1965

tary agency of the human beholder, then ape the movements, and meanings, of man.

But, unlike the ancient marmoreal Venus and Apollo, they all *move*. The medieval public clocks, with Father Time (or Death) and his scythe pursuing mortals every hour on the hour, were one thing—all this is another; this is mortals pursuing Time or his alter ego. It is no mere hunger for novelty or impatience with the inertia of the ancients. It is more than the invoking of science, or tribute to it. For science itself, as a human activity, is *kineticized* by the basic beliefs, obsessions, and dreams of society as a whole. Once, as in Egypt, the dream was of permanence and immortality, and the savants watched the stars obediently wheeling around the motionless earth. Today, the magic image moves; movement is life.

It is movement everywhere: the automobile-encased human tides ebbing and flowing through street and turnpike; the hasty writing of jets across the sky and the busy shadows on television screen; the young, suddenly, impatiently on the

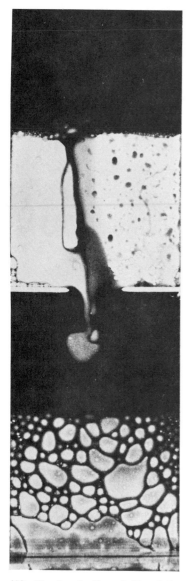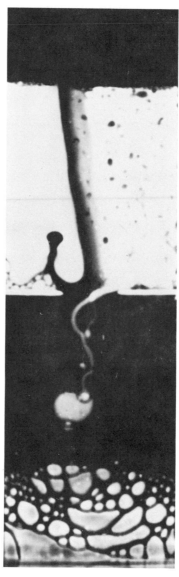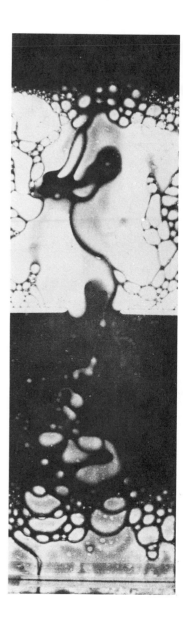

433 Haacke: *Scylla and Charybdis* 1965 (six kinetic stages)

move to the Instant Tomorrow; races and new nations on the move; orbiting space hardware on the move; mankind on the move to Moon and Mars.

Sculpture merely obeys this vast imperative. This century had barely dawned when the futurists, making an idol of the racing car, strove to transliterate speed into paint (Fig. 461). In 1924, when Archipenko motorized painting in his *Archipentura* (Fig. 175), four years had already passed since Naum

Gabo had kineticized sculture with a steel rod called *Standing Wave* that vibrated by means of an electric mechanism (Fig. 437). And, in 1925, Duchamp simultaneously confirmed kineticism and forecast Op art, in the *Rótary Demisphere* (Fig. 167).

For two decades Calder's mobiles virtually preempted the kinetic field. Then in the 1950's more general activity began. Moving sculpture, as a contemporary art, invites a union of universal

286

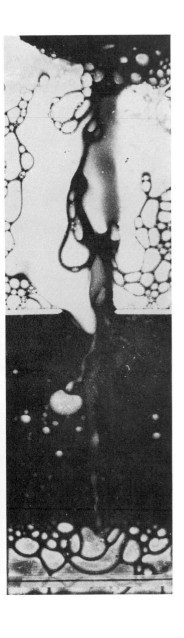 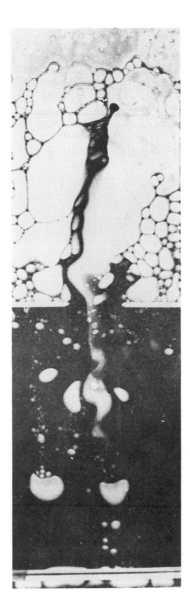 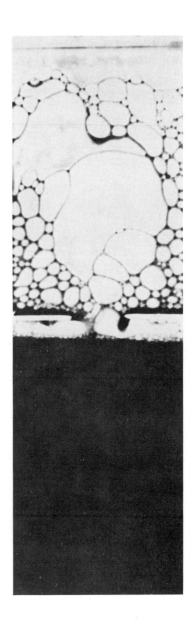

meanings with the personal idiom. Calder's mobiles are innocent lyric analogues of movement in animate nature— Calder is the village blacksmith watching the wind in the leaves of his chestnut tree. Jean Tinguely is the mad scientist turned Isaiah: from maliciously witty to monstrous, to self-destroying, Tinguely's machines are canticles of doom (Figs. 438, 439). Len Lye, as artist, is diabolist: mechanical deviltry infuses his kinetics. Motorized and electronically programed,

a Lye exhibition is a condominium of demons as, unpredictably, sporadically leaping into action, the prim, exquisite surgical steel constructions whip, gyrate, writhe, and shudder in deafening bursts of clangor (Figs. 440–442). And, in complete contrast, Mark di Suvero's kinetic playground sculptures carry human freight orbiting to delight (Figs. 443, 444).

Pushing the frontiers of musical sound, and visually superb, are the sonant sculp-

434 Hans Haacke with *The Wave*

435 Mack: *Light, Wind, Water* 1959

tures called *structures sonores* by the brothers who create them, François and Bernard Baschet (Fig. 445). Ranging from the exquisite to the monumental, musical instruments that are equally sculptures, the *structures sonores* pertinently point up the ambiguity of the old art pigeonholes.

A far different sort of musical instrument is Tinguely's *M/M Sculpture-Radio,* a perverse, feathered little demon, a robot-radio that oscillates forever between stations and can only be turned off, not tuned in (Fig. 446). With this imp as, in fact, with Rauschenberg's combine-painting *Broadcast* (Fig. 406), and with or without McLuhan's blessing, the medium *is* the message.

Among other apparitions in this recent field of kinetic-phonetic sculpture are the anti-anthropomorphic electronic wood *assemblages* of Pol Bury (Fig. 447). Tame and docile-looking like enlarged educational toys, they are not musical instruments but furniture for a Charles Addams nursery, art with an unrationale. They move with furtive stealth; hum, rustle, click with faint, disquieting sounds. Poe would have loved them, and it is with affection that Ionesco describes them:

Now, watch how this thing moves and that bends; listen to how this grinds, that growls and grunts, listen carefully and watch how it moves, not much, just a little, this one hardly stirs and that one stops and this one starts again. . . . Thus . . . for Pol Bury the concrete world exists, the world of immediate facts has a heavy, oppressive reality. And . . . if this world has any reality, if it is at all tangible, it is because danger makes it so.[1]

Enrique Castro-Cid's programed constructions are grim robots, such as transparent cases holding sketched skeletons with electronic heads, that perform their

[1] Written by Eugène Ionesco for a Pol Bury exhibition, in 1966, at the Lefèbre Gallery, New York.

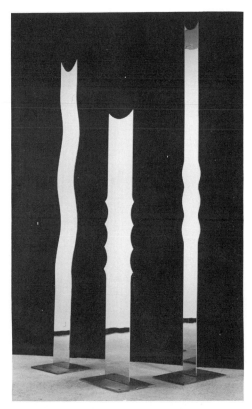

436 Mack: *The Three Graces* 1966

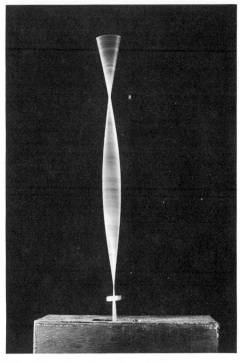

437 Gabo: *Standing Wave* 1920

438   Tinguely: *M.K. III*   1964 (stationary)

439   Tinguely: *M.K. III*   1964 (in motion)

290

440 Lye: *Loop* 1963 (stationary)

441 Lye: *Loop* 1963 (in motion)

442 Lye: *Fountain* 1963 (in motion)

443 Di Suvero: *Kinetic Playground Sculpture*
(stationary)

444 Di Suvero: *Kinetic Playground Sculpture*
(in motion)

445 François Baschet with
*French Monument
Born on 57th Street*
1965–1966

446 Tinguely: *M/M Sculpture-Radio* 1962

447 Bury: *19 Balls in an Open Volume* 19

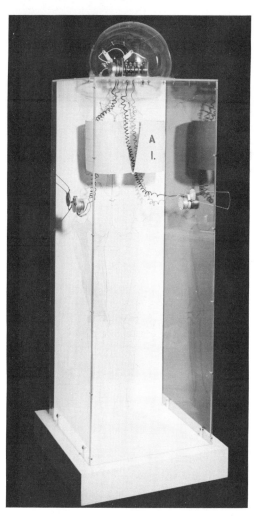

448   Castro-Cid: *Anthropomorphical I*   1964

useless tasks over and over forever, actors in an electronic theater of the absurd (Fig. 448).

Eerie and dehumanized is the electronic construction called *The Watcher*. James Seawright deserted abstract sculpture in bronze to devote several years to creating this single work. It must have hypnotized him. It hypnotizes all who watch it at work. Exceedingly delicate, exceedingly complex, exceedingly beautiful in the manner of machines, it begins as slow as the dawn. A nine-tiered bank of lights slowly activates the tentacular photo-electric cells and sets into sweeping, scanning motion the "head" or monitor. Just as slowly, out of silence, begins a high-pitched haunting little refrain, over and over, like faraway pigmy marimbas in the Congo rain forest. The slow, enigmatic, beautiful movement, the hypnotic lights, the droning atavistic sound—it becomes an enchanting, brain-washing little machine. Yet, faint as the sound, there is menace behind the magic. This is the sort of form that Big Brother might actually take (Fig. 449).

The Watcher is nonspecific yet pointed. However softly, it speaks of, and to, our time. Far more open and frank is the work of Bruce Lacey. Like an English Kienholz, Lacey is clearly concerned with the problems of society, many of which parallel his own. The key to his savage, brooding humor and the immanent horror of his work is to be found in the terse chronicle of an exhibition catalog: [2]

BRUCE LACEY

1927	Born in Catford, London
1938	At age of 11 started to collect junk
1942–43	Worked in explosives factory
1943–45	Worked as bank clerk
1945–47	Electric mechanic in Royal Navy
1946–48	In Hospital Unit with T.B. where he began painting as occupational therapy
1948–51	Studied painting at Hornsey School of Art
1951	Won Knapping Prize
1951–54	Studied painting at Royal College of Art
1956–60	Made trick props for T.V. shows. Became comic cabaret performer.
1963	Presented two electric actors in "An Evening of British Rubbish."

Despite Lacey's cabaret performances with his "electric actors," the real stage of his sardonic little vaudeville turn was the one that Poe referred to as "the Tragedy called Man." The true irony of their lines (and action) is that, electronically programed by society, they do not protest. They do only the right things. They browse the supermarkets of food, gadgets, and sex, while exclaiming, "Boy, oh Boy, am I living!" Built of machinery, plastic, prosthetic human limbs, artificial organs, wheels, and motors, they are, as an English critic observed, "odes to plastic surgery that envision a situation whereby man slowly becomes a machine [with] a major part of the machine's functions . . . concerned with giving [it] the illusion that it is human" (Figs. 450–453).

From 1964 to 1966, kinetic constructions all but dominated contemporary sculpture. But nowadays to name a movement seems the kiss of death; the first definitive exhibition becomes a retrospective; wide acceptance engenders rejection; to succeed makes the avant garde the academic. Also, on the creative side in art—as with energy in physics—action begets reaction. So, ushered in by a large exhibition at the Jewish Museum in New York early in 1966, there came a sculpture devoted to purism, to the image of Mathematics rather than Man, and concerned only with the indubitably esthetic but rather ivory-tower problems of the plasticity of abstract geometric form.

The new Primary Structures have, to be sure, a contrary mythos, claiming deep involvement with humanism, as

449 Seawright: *The Watcher* 1965

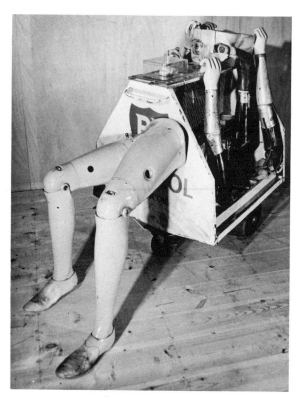

450 Lacey: *Supermarket* 1964

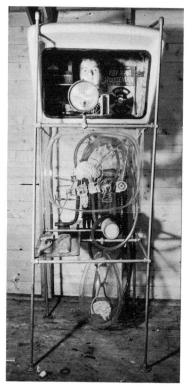

451 Lacey: *The Brain Machine* 1964

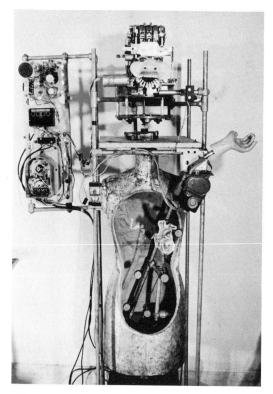

452 Lacey: *Old Money-Bags* 1964

453 Lacey: *Superman 2963 A.D.* 1963

454   Marisol with *The Party*   1966

exemplified by the movement's patron saint, painter Barnett Newman. Newman named a series of his large canvases, each cleft by a single vertical line, the *Stations of the Cross,* and proposed that they are universal symbols of human sorrow. This, of course, effectively reduces symbolism to a fundamentally noncommunicative, personal, arcane hieroglyph. No purist art needs such an apologia, any more than Mondrian did, and it simply confuses an otherwise clear issue. In any event, this new sculpture, mainly concerned with pure archetypal forms disposed in free arrangements, bears little or no relation to collage or the collage idea. Anyhow, primary form was definitively ushered in for our time by Saarinen's simple steel arch towering, modest and magnificent, above the Mississippi River in St. Louis.

Although our time is obsessed with the machine, it is also obsessed with its own human feelings, and purism (except, perhaps, Op art) seems little likely to long engage more than a few. This dual obsession with machine and ego is why the mechanical, amplified by motion, has proved so powerful a way of expressing man's dilemmas. At another extreme is Pop art's packaging-supermarket motifs, while in between is a small area of static and rather strange sculpture that, if far from Carel Kapek's robot world of *R.U.R.,* is close to the sad, mad absurdities of Ionesco's *The Rhinoceros.*

297

455   George Segal's studio, August 1965

A beautiful, silent, enigmatic Vene-
zuelan, Marisol (Escobar), with a just
but merciless eye, balances pity and
cruelty in construction-box-sculpture-
paintings that are documents of human
folly, a kind of psychological packaging,
sinister life-size dolls, totems designed
by a philosopher for an amusement arcade. A gallery full of them, as in the
1966 exhibition of fifteen figures called
The Party, creates a sculptural space
(echoing with sardonic laughter) in
which the gallery-goers, not the coffined
manikins, are the unreal interlopers
(Fig. 454).

Only silence sounds in the strange

space filled with George Segal's ghostly,
bandaged, white figures, No-Man's-Land
environments where everything has already happened and will never happen
again and dust will settle forever over
the motionlessness. Cast like death masks
on real living human bodies (the band-
aging is to protect the flesh from the
hot, solidifying plaster), Segal's plaster
personages are combined with real artifacts—an old woman at a real window,
a man and nude woman on a real bed,
a girl in a real doorway. Here datum
meets dream (Fig. 455).

Far more disquieting than Marisol's,
these Segal personages, these apparitions

298

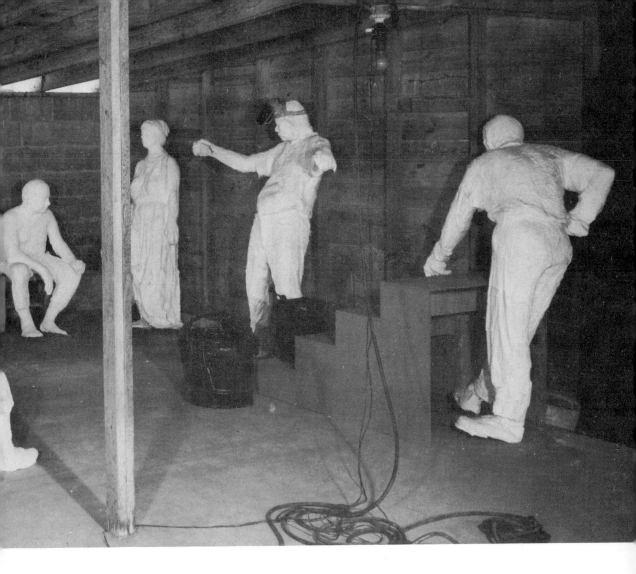

that are neither dead nor alive, are altogether repulsive and horrifying. Why then do silent, teeming crowds go to see them? Today's phenomenal public response to fine art is called by some the "art boom," and is supposed to indicate vulgarization, commercialization, and lowered standards. On the contrary, it might mean that art is realistic, serious, and meaningful again, that it shows us ourselves and our world (and keeps pace with that changing world), that the artist is fighting his way back into the world as a useful member of society.

Beyond any question, the best of today's art speaks directly to people (in their language) and is no longer to be understood, appreciated, and owned only by the few. And above all, at its most cogent, it possesses a power of impact, both emotional and revelatory, that art has not shown for many decades.

This power is perfectly exemplified in the mummy-men (and women) of Segal. It is a power perhaps explicable only in terms of a final, decisive confrontation between the true and the false, the real and the unreal, a confrontation in which neither wins, and all the certainties finally dissolve. It is a confrontation on art's terrain. But well we know, it may shift to ours.

17

THE ENVIRONMENT
IS THE HAPPENING
IS THE MESSAGE

Cows in the meadow, though once a fairly common sight, did not—even in 1844—enthrall Turner, who turned instead to a fiery, smoking locomotive in the painting *Rain, Steam and Speed*. Even then the city was the real human environment, for the city is the world that man makes for himself. No matter that he dreams at times of other worlds . . . nymph-haunted groves from which even cows are barred and only Pan may bring his goats.

A plate-glass canyon in the Manhattan of the 1960's is in essence the same thing as a street in the Bronx yesterday and today. It is our own: the mechanical landscape. It is the collage-construction-environment that is man's real habitat despite his two summer weeks in a national park. With lights blinking on and off, people swarming on sidewalk and cars swarming on asphalt, the environment becomes the happening. This is the Pop art world. Its innocent Eden was a Times Square where once a billboard blew smoke rings across Broadway (Fig. 458).

This has been a tough century for art critics. With Pop art it became unbearable for those trying to appraise a Pop painting by the "eternal" esthetic canons that, on the whole, reach back to medieval Italy and, through the Renaissance, on back to Greece. Mentally, they hang a Warhol *Campbell's Soup Can* beside the *Mona Lisa* and are very unhappy. Actually, it's a minor confrontation, an odious comparison, and one without point.

Pop's origins may well be far less art and far more non-art, and its patron saints not Giotto and Michelangelo at all, but Henry Ford and Foster & Kleiser. Perhaps Pop is not out of Greece by Rome, but out of Detroit by Madison Avenue.

If it is, so is junk sculpture and so is kinetic sculpture, and much collage from at least Schwitters on. And this makes them, if so, as realistic and as contemporary as any arts have ever been. In Allan Kaprow's definitive words, *They accept whatever is here*.

One feels like saying: After all your hue and cry for a realistic art, gentlemen, here it is. Here is the twentieth century where the action is. Here is *our* Environment. Here is *our* Happening. To question the esthetic value of so much of today's art is actually to ques-

456 Corot: *The Sleep of Diana* 1868

457 Street scene in the Bronx 1966

458 Smoke rings over Broadway 1945

tion our criteria. We may need to find new ones, as we finally did for jazz. Critics do not have the last say. Artists who are firmly in their own time do. Besides, like the hen, they make the product.

Perhaps instead of truth we now have datum; for meaning, any proven existence; for permanence, the "open end"; for life, movement; for form, process; instead of beauty, the thing-in-itself. If so, these must be the criteria of today. And today's art, then, is the triumph of environment over heredity.

And what an environment! Just look around. To paraphrase both Marshall McLuhan and Gertrude Stein: The environment is the happening is the message.

The environment *is* the happening. Wherever it is on the move, especially in the streets and on the superhighways, it is the biggest, most dynamic happening short of war, and its central fact is

the automobile, that fruit of America's bumper-to-bumper crop. In America you can get away from almost anything, but you have to take an automobile to get away.

The automobile amuses us, bemuses us, confuses us, abuses us. It is the Dream Boat of the American Dream. It fills our libidos and drains our budgets. A purring, rubber-footed, chromium supercat, it carries us on six-lane superhighways from Nowhere to Nowhere Else.

And it kills a lot of us, halfway there.

The twentieth-century artist's ivory tower has picture windows scanning the superhighway, and a three-car garage in its basement. Even before this century dawned Toulouse-Lautrec was turning his notably factual eye on the new horseless carriage. And artists ever since have got the automobile's message. For seven decades since Lautrec it has, in fact, been a kind of Auto-Motive in art, as the fold-out pages will show.

469 Picasso: *Baboon and Young* 1951

470 Frazier: *Scout* 1962

471 Frazier: *Stutz Bearcat Pre-World War I* 1962

477   Larkin: *Motorcyclist and Girl Friend*   1966

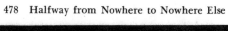

478   Halfway from Nowhere to Nowhere Else

Although not named until recently,[1] Pop art has been with us for a long time. Its roots go back at least to the 1830's when Stephenson's locomotive began carrying the new mechanistic city into the country. Actually, if established categories—like *l'Art Nouveau*—did not inhibit our thinking, we would see Pop in a Toulouse-Lautrec poster. With less difficulty we can sense Pop in much of Duchamp—his *Pharmacie* for example (a sentimental calendar landscape altered ironically by the artist), or, pre-eminently, the paint advertisement he altered to read "Apolinère Enameled."

By the 1920's the Pop idea settles firmly into the American modern concept with a 1921 painting like Stuart Davis' *Bull Durham* (Fig. 479), and Gerald Murphy's *Razor* (Fig. 480). In such works as these, the shoeshine boy or the blacksmith of nineteenth-century genre painting is replaced as hero by cigarette tobacco, safety razor, matches, and fountain pen. From there to the 1960's and Andy Warhol's "portraits" of Campbell soup cans (Fig. 481) requires no leap of imagination, only an arbitrary one in time.

With this lineage, it is difficult to justify the summary rejection by many critics of this realistic, generally non-judicative, and open-eyed look at the Great Society of Goods.

Pop reports our whole subliminal, brain-washing environment: billboards and beer cans by the highway, never-ending audio-visual chatter of the television commercials, traffic jam of food carts in the supermarket. Yet critics who presumably live comfortably with this environment are shocked by the art that reports it! Henry McBride, a great critic of an earlier generation, reviewing the Armory Show in 1913, put it straight. "To be shocked," he wrote, "says well for the power of any painting."

As usual, of course, terminology began

[1] By Lawrence Alloway.

479 Davis: *Bull Durham* 1921

immediately to confuse matters by embracing as Pop everything from Warhol to Segal. The apt three-letter word, applied wholesale, concealed crucial differences. Intentionally or not, Rauschenberg, Jasper Johns, and Oldenburg, for example, are commentators. They accept but do not surrender. Some, like Warhol, seem to surrender all judgment. Actually, the artist's selection is involved as much as it was in Duchamp's Ready-Mades. Still others, like Kienholz, Marisol, Lacey, and Segal, are seriously misrepresented by the term "Pop." They are in no real sense pop artists at all any more than a deepwoods Mississippi

480 Murphy: *Razor* 1922

blues is a pop tune. They are, instead, artists who project the wounds-and-death theme that darkly counterpoints the hurdy-gurdy tune of their time.

Apart from content, Pop art has helped to keep alive the tradition of easel painting at a time when a metropolitan art critic could seriously refer to it as an "all but antiquarian pursuit." [2] So, too, has Op, or optical, art, the other main painting tendency of the 1960's. Christened by a magazine art editor,[3] Op is no frank confrontation of our environment. Yet, though a purist art, it is not wholly one of escape. Op is intellective in several ways: first, in its rigorous cleaving to geometrics often as ascetic as those of Mondrian; next, in its recourse to science for new visual-perceptive methods; and last, by the fact that its kinetics or movements are not in the Op pictures at all, but in the perception-train of the beholder. Itself static, Op precipitates movement, not in real, but in psychological, space, thus satisfying a generation interested in both fact and feeling, and one obsessed by movement.

[2] Hilton Kramer, New York *Times,* July 9, 1966.
[3] Jon Borgzinner, in *Time.*

This generation is also interested in illusion, in the special sense of false interpretations of data—the psychic subjective drama of the true and the false. Certain Op art is addressed to this interest, in paintings that, by manipulating either the relative scale and position of objects or the perspective of surface topography, seemingly alter the indubitable flatness of the picture plane, or canvas. Paintings of this kind (Figs. 492, 493) are True or False questions to quiz the spectator, as he tries correctly to interpret figurations that actually indicate nonexistent configurations.

Sidney Janis has aptly named all of this geometric hocus-pocus "abstract *trompe-l'oeil,*" and it is, in fact, the contemporary, psychologically oriented phase of a tradition that goes back through Dali to Arcimboldo and unites it with the purism of Mondrian and De Stijl. The marriage took place, actually, early in this century. As early as 1912, the futurist Balla was painting visual color-form kinetics that he called "Irides-

481 Warhol: *Campbell's Soup* 1966

482   Lichtenstein: *I Can See the Whole Room and There's Nobody in It*   1961

cent Compenetrations" (Fig. 490). Even
Kandinsky, essentially expressionist, was
occasionally interested in visual distortions of form-on-surface that assault the
eye, disturb the equilibrium, and falsely
report topology (Fig. 491). And, as already noted, Marcel Duchamp heralded
both Op art and kinetic sculpture in his
Rotary-Demisphere of 1925 (see pages
133, 134).

By the 1920's Josef Albers became interested in this visual magic, especially
in black-and-white linear schemata that
produce spatial contradictions, or else
not only induce visual vibrations be-

tween parallel lines but also create illusions of rainbow colors. Quite literally
spectral, these rainbows seem to inter-
weave with the black and white (Fig.
494).

All Op art, then, aims at psychological
effects, but these effects divide into two
kinds: one, effects that are seemingly
external and nonsubjective, and two,
those that are easily recognizable (by
the subject himself) as subjective. Seemingly external are the various topologi-
cal distortions, the waverings and blur-
rings, and the phantom rainbows or
spectra. All of these exploit our uni-

483 Wesselmann: *Still Life No. 17* 1962

484 Rosenquist: *F-111* 1965

485 Warhol: *Coke Bottles* 1963

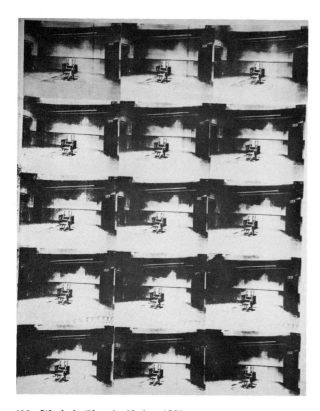

486 Warhol: *Electric Chairs* 1965

versal spatial illusion that retinal images decoded in the brain are actually outside us in real space. We stubbornly believe that the image is the object.

Recognizably subjective, on the other hand, is the whole gamut of emotional disturbance when the eyes' report and its decoding are interfered with or tricked. Vertigo and headache are apt to be actually less disturbing than to be forced to admit that seeing is *not* believing.

In practice, some Op art, both pictures and constructions, is operative on the retina of a stationary viewer, while in others the kinetic or chromatic illusions are created by the viewer's moving —in other words, the viewer becomes kinetic agent. Certain relief paintings in the Op art category develop into three successive pictures as the spectator moves past. The Israeli artist, Agam, has successfully exploited this nineteenth-century advertising device, in which different pictures are placed, respectively, on the picture plane proper, and on the two different sides of projecting, parallel, vertical fins.

Veterans active in today's Op group include the French artist Victor Vasarely and the American Ben Cunningham. Vasarely, working both in monotones or gold and in three-dimensional Plexiglass enclosures, sometimes uses shifted forms that seem to be in actual process of being displaced (Fig. 495). At other times, in single-color canvases, Vasarely creates the glare and stop-and-go of the lights in our nocturnal urban environment.

Cunningham, as we have seen (Fig. 493), creates intricate *trompe-l'oeil* topographies by carefully shifted, twisted, and gradated checkerboards of color. A Cunningham canvas is tantalizing rather than disturbing, inviting the viewer to come in and explore a strange and interesting, but not inhospitable, space.

Among those using three-dimensional transparencies with strong optic effect is

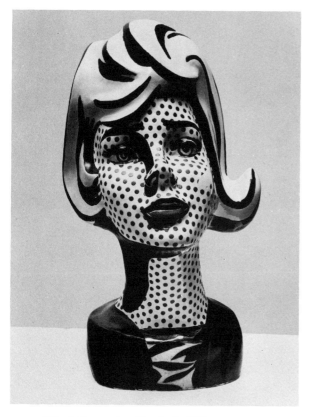

487 Lichtenstein: *Blonde I* 1965

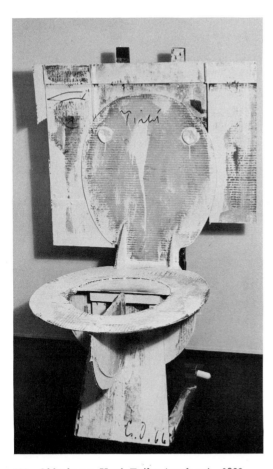

488 Oldenburg: *Hard Toilet* (mock-up) 1966

489 Oldenburg: *Soft Toilet* 1966

Josef Levi, who combines liquitex paint, perforated metal screens, and fluorescent light with its marked cyclic pulsation (Fig. 496). Levi's work, like that of others, explores the shifting retinal illusion, strongly three-dimensional, known as the "moiré" effect. The scientist Gerald Oster is credited with introducing the moiré effect to the art world through constructions he presumably planned more as theorems than as art works.

Among the many other Op artists working today are two who are primarily painters, a young American, Richard Anuszkiewicz, and a young English woman, Bridget Riley. Anuszkiewicz frequently uses strong complementary colors juxtaposed to excite, weary, and confuse the optic nerves. In other paint-

ings, through geometry, he sets up an eerie, tilting, topsy-turvy space that advances and retreats (Fig. 492).

Miss Riley has been especially adroit in black-and-white paintings so dazzling as to produce acute vertigo in some viewers, and so productive of rainbow superimpositions that it is difficult for some spectators to believe that the artist has used only black paint on white canvas (Fig. 497).

Where Pop reports illusory facts, Op reports factual illusions. One runs from gay to grim, the other from visual gadget to a profound purism fired with the drama of each individual consciousness. Together, they comment (with or without intent) on our ambivalent world.

Altogether, today's art is truly of our time. Like a burning-glass it focuses

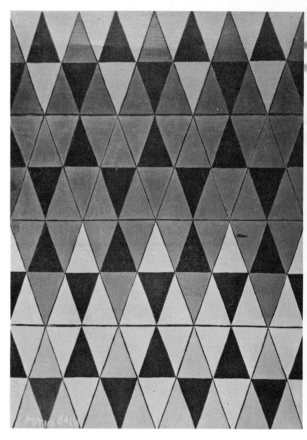

490   Balla: *Compenetrazione Iridiscente No. 3*   1912

491   Kandinsky: *Square*   1927

492   Anuszkiewicz: *Knowledge and Disappearance*   1961

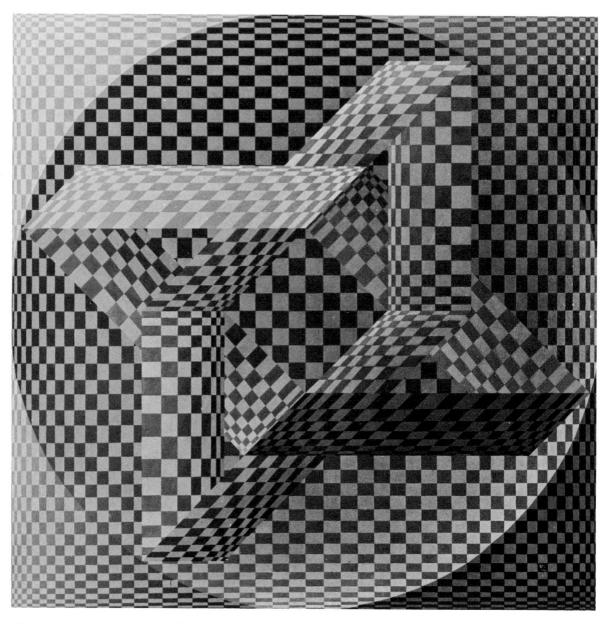

493 Cunningham: *Equivocation* 1964

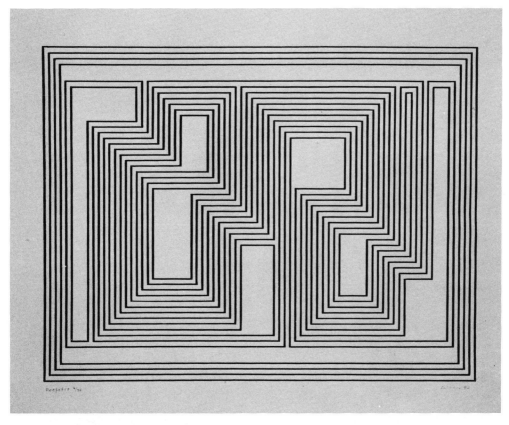

494 Albers: *Prefatio* 1942

meanings in symbols as concentrated as lasers. It does not warn, plead, argue, or sermonize. It is unpretentious, anti-didactic, and ironic with understatement. It reports the world the artist sees.

Yet, it encompasses it all: the vacant, voracious, insatiable smile, the alienation, the lost capacities to feel; all the vain laws and faded values; the mechanized men and the machines that "think"; all the precarious balances and explosive mixtures—wealth and destitution, freedom and bondage, satiated peace and each new "dirty little war."

Artists and art—they bait us with our own idiocy, ambush us with the terrors we hide from. With philosophers paralyzed, poets mute, priests palsied, and statesmen benumbed, only the artists still try to make us face ourselves and the world we have built, a world (like the music that Arthur Symons heard) truly made for all passionate, wounded, capricious, consuming hearts.

Fact has become art and at last is its own commentary. Is this truth, free alike from philosopher and fool—truth the true object, the naked thing-in-itself?

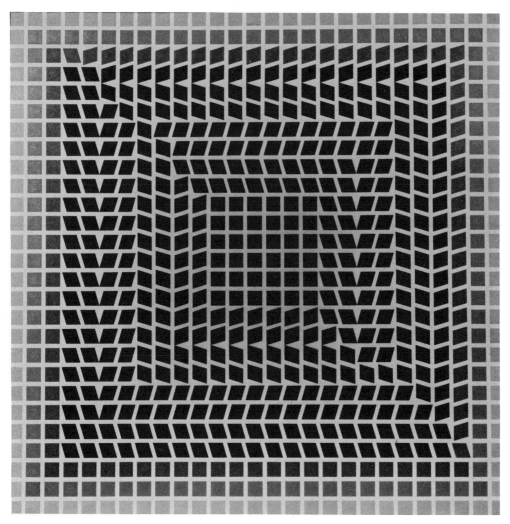

495 Vasarely: *Tau-Ceti* 1956–1965

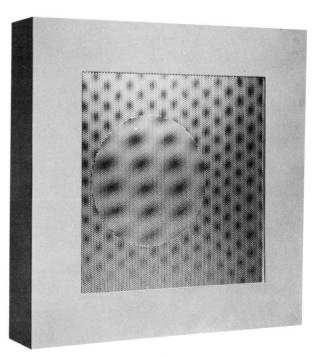

496 Levi: *Nyctitropic* 1965

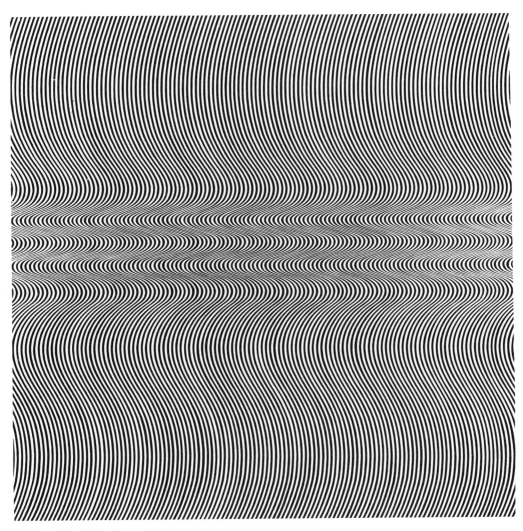

497 Riley: *Current* 1964

GLOSSARY

TECHNICAL TERMS AND PROCESSES

affiches lacerés, s.m.—torn posters.

assemblage, s.m.—the act or the product of assembling parts.

boardism, s.—the act or the product of making reliefs or constructions from wooden boards.

brûlage, s.m.—burning or scorching, or the artistic product.

cementing, v.—assembling collage parts with cement, especially plastics and synthetic resins.

collage, s.m.—pasting; specifically, pasting paper, cloth, etc. into pictures or objécts, or the artistic product. (Secondary French meaning: cohabiting without marriage.)

colle, s.f.—paste, glue, gum, gum-arabic. (Secondary French meaning: a sham, a fib.)

collé, v.—pasted, glued, etc.

combine-paintings, s.—an artist's special term for oil paintings embodying ready-made objects.

coulage, s.m.—leaking. By extension, dripping of wet paint as an art technique.

décalcomanie, s.f.—decalcomania in art: patterns left by wet paint in a certain process.

déchirage, s.m.—tearing. In collage, tearing paper.

déchirage mouillé—tearing wet paper.

décollage, s.m.—ungluing, unpasting, etc. In collage, partially pasting.

découpage, s.m.—cutting out, cutting up. In collage, whatever is cut with scissors, knife, etc.

dépouillage (*dépouillement*), s.m.—stripping, peeling.

éclaboussage (*éclaboussement*), s.m.—splashing, spattering. In art, explosive splashes of wet paint.

flottage, s.m.—floating. In art, floating paint on water to deposit it on paper or canvas.

froissage (*froissement*), s.m.—crumpling, creasing, crushing, as paper.

frottage, s.m.—rubbing. In art, transferring a relief pattern by rubbing.

fumage, s.m.—smoking. Creating patterns or tones by smoking the surface.

grattage, s.m.—scratching, scraping. A pattern made by this process.

laceré anonyme, s.m.—in art, a torn poster unaided by artist, presented as an unsigned *objet trouvé*.

Merzbild, s.m.—Schwitters' term for his collages.

montage, s.—combining pictorial elements from several sources so that elements are both distinct and blended into a whole.

objet trouvé, s.m.—a found object presented as a natural work of art.

papier collé, s.m.—pasted paper; a collage of pasted paper.

papier déchiré, s.m.—torn paper; a collage of torn paper.

papier découpé, s.m.—cut paper; a collage of cut paper.

photomontage, s.—photographs joined whole or in parts; especially when joined or superimposed as negatives prior to printing.

sewing, v.—in collage, sewing together in lieu of pasting.

sgraffito, s.m.—making patterns by scratching. (see *grattage*.)

welding, s.—fusing metal parts with heat. In art, the technical equivalent of pasting paper.

SELECTED LIST OF EXHIBITIONS

1912 *Braque, Picasso.* Collages introduced in the continuous changing cubist exhibition at Kahnweiler's gallery, Paris.

1912 *Futurist Exhibition.* Galerie Bernheim Jeune. Traveled to London, Berlin, Amsterdam, Vienna, and many other European and American cities.

1917 *Duchamp Ready-mades* included in a group show at Bourgeois Gallery, New York.

1920 *First International Dada Fair.* Burchard Gallery, Berlin. July–Aug.

1920 *Kurt Schwitters.* Der Sturm, Berlin.

1920 *Arp, Baargeld, Ernst—dada exhibit.* Cologne, April.

1920 *Max Ernst—Au-delà de la peinture.* Au Sans Pareil, Paris. May 3–June 3.

1920 *Schwitters Merzbilder* included in 5th exhibit of Société Anonyme; his first formal institutional recognition in the United States. 19 E. 57 St., New York. March. (From 1920 to 1942 the Société Anonyme included Schwitters in 27 exhibits at 20 different institutions.)

1921 *Ivan Puni.* Walls arranged as collages of pictures. Der Sturm, Berlin.

1923 *Ivan Puni.* Above exhibit repeated at Winterpalais, Leningrad.

1926 *Man Ray.* Exhibit including "island objects." First surrealist exhibition at the Galerie Surréaliste, Paris.

1927 *Calder's Circus.* Wire constructions. Salon des Humoristes, Paris.

1930 *La peinture au défi.* Foreword by Luis Aragon. Gallery Goemans, Paris.

1932 *Joseph Cornell's* first collages included in an exhibition of surrealism. Julien Levy Gallery, New York.

1936 *Exhibition of Surrealist Objects.* Charles Ratton, Paris. May 22–May 29.

1936 *International Surrealist Exhibition.* New Burlington Galleries, London.

1943 *Exhibition of Collages.* Peggy Guggenheim's Art of This Century, New York. April 16–May 15.

1944 *Schwitters.* Modern Art Gallery, London. December.

1948 *Kurt Schwitters.* Memorial Exhibition. Rose Fried's Pinacotheca, New York. January 19–February 29.

1948 *Collage.* Museum of Modern Art, New York. September 21–December 5.

1949 *Robert Motherwell: Collage Retrospective, 1941–49.* Kootz Gallery, New York.

1952 *Faschings-Dekorationen* (Environments). Walter Gaudnek and group. Haus der Kunst and Hotel Regina. (These exhibits began c. 1938–39, became Environments in 1952, and still continue).

1953 *Dada.* Sidney Janis Gallery, New York. April 15–May 9.

1954 *Art versus Machine.* Building Centre, London.

1954 *Schwitters.* Kestner-Gesellschaft, Hanover.

1955 Gutai Association with others (Environments). Ashiya City, Japan.

1955 *International Collage Exhibition.* Arranged by Herta Wescher. Galerie Arnaud, Paris.

1955 *Arthur B. Dove Collages.* Downtown Gallery, New York.

1956 *International Collage Exhibition.* 85 artists exhibited. Rose Fried Gallery, New York. February 13–March 17.

1956 *First Gutai Exhibition* (Environments). Ohara Hall, Tokyo.

1956 *Penny Arcade.* Allan Kaprow Environment. Hansa Gallery, New York. November 30–December 24.

1956 *Second Gutai Exhibition* (Environments). Ashiya City, Japan.

1956 *This is Tomorrow.* Whitechapel Art Gallery, London.

1957 *Statements.* Arranged by Lawrence Alloway. Institute for Contemporary Arts, London.

1957 *18 Happenings in 6 Parts.* Allan Kaprow Happening. Rutgers University.

1957 *Dimensions.* O'Hana Gallery, London.

1957 *Third Gutai Exhibition* (Environments and Art on the Stage). Sankei Hall, Tokyo.

1957 *Aktiv-Abstrakt.* Munich.

1957 *Otro Arte.* Barcelona and Madrid.

1957 *Collages by Kurt Schwitters.* The Phillips Gallery, Washington, D.C. January 6–February 25.

1957–58 *Collage in America.* Zabriskie Gallery, New York. December 16, 1957–January 4, 1958.

1958 *Fourth Gutai Exhibition* (Environments). Osaka Festival.

1958–59 *Collage in America.* Zabriskie show with deletions and additions, and with dada and surrealist inclusions. Circulated by the American Federation of Art to 9 American colleges and museums.

1958 *Collage International.* Arranged by Dr. Jermayne MacAgy. Contemporary Arts Museum, Houston. February 27–April 6.

1958 *Exposition of the Void.* Yves Klein. Galerie Iris Clert, Paris. Opened April 28.

1958 *Three Collagists.* Institute of Contemporary Arts, London. November.

1958–59 *Dada—The Documents of a Movement.* Kunstverein, Düsseldorf; Stedelijk Museum, Amsterdam.

1958–59 *Beyond Painting.* Arranged by Howard Rose. The Alan Gallery, New York. December 29, 1958–January 24, 1959.

1959 *Collages by E. L. T. Mesens.* Palais des Beaux-Arts, Brussels. April 25–May 13.

1959 *International Collages.* Hessenhuis, Amsterdam. May 23–June 13.

1959 *Exhibition Lacéré Anonyme.* Included in *Première biennale de Paris; Manifestation biennale et international des jeunes artistes.* Musée de l'art Moderne, Paris.

1959 *Out of the Ordinary.* Arranged by Robert Morris. Neodada collages and objects, with dada and surrealist inclusions. Contemporary Arts Museum, Houston. November 26–December 27.

1959 *An Apple Shrine.* Allan Kaprow Environment. Judson Gallery, New York. November 30–December 24.

1959 *Arte Nuova.* Turin.

1960 *Ray Gun.* Dine-Oldenburg Environment. Judson Gallery. February–March.

1960 *Collages.* Area Gallery, New York. March 6–26.

1960 *Tseng Yu-Ho.* Downtown Gallery, New York. April 19–May 7.

1960 *Collage: Art in Scraps and Patchwork.* Newark Museum, Newark. April 28–June 12.

1960 *Eléménts Botaniques* by Dubuffet. Arranged by Lawrence Alloway. Arthur Tooth & Sons Ltd., London. May 31–June 18.

1960 *Retrospective, Kurt Schwitters.* 30th Venice Biennale.

1960 *New Forms—New Media I.* Martha Jackson Gallery, New York. June 6–24.

1960 *New Forms—New Media II.* Martha Jackson Gallery. September 27–October 22.

1960 *Car Crash.* James Dine Happening. Reuben Gallery, New York. November.

1960 *The American Moon.* Robert Whitman Happening. Reuben Gallery. November.

1960 *The Shining Bed.* James Dine Happening. Reuben Gallery. December.

1960 *Manifestation de Tripaille* (Garbage). Arman Environment. Galerie Iris Clert. Paris.

1960 *30 Collages, 30 Artists.* Mayer Gallery, New York.

1960–61 *Taller Torrés-Garcia.* New School for Social Research, New York. December 12, 1960–January 9, 1961.

1960–61 *Contemporary Collage.* Arranged by Bertha Schaefer. Toured U.S. colleges.

1961 *Unlimited Dimensions.* Walter Gaudnek Painted Environment. 10/4 Gallery, New York. January 17–February 14.

1961 *Ironworks-Fotodeath.* Claes Oldenburg Happenings. Reuben Gallery. February 21–26.

1961 *Max Ernst.* Retrospective: 1916–1960. The Museum of Modern Art, New York. February 27–May 7. This exhibition was shown at the Art Institute of Chicago, June 14–July 23, 1961.

1961 *A Spring Happening.* Allan Kaprow Happening. Reuben Gallery. March.

1961 *Collages: Franz Roh.* Otto Stangl Gallery, Munich. March 23–April 21.

1961 *Mouth.* Robert Whitman Happening. Reuben Gallery. April 18–23.

1961 *Construction: England, 1950–61.* Drian Gallery, London.

1961 *Environments-Situations-Spaces.* Martha Jackson Gallery. May 25–June 23.

1961 *British Constructivist Art.* Arranged by Lawrence Alloway. Toured by American Federation of Arts. September 1961–September 1962.

1961 *The Art of Assemblage.* Arran William Seitz. The Museum of Modern Art, New York. October 2–November 12.

1961 *Joseph Stella.* Collages. Zabriskie Gallery, New York. October 2–October 28.

1961 *Max Ernst.* Bodley Gallery, New York. October 30–November 25.

1961 *Robert Rauschenberg.* Combine-paintings. Leo Castelli Gallery, New York. November 7–December 1. (Because of its progressive day-by-day installation and corresponding dé-installation, this exhibition became a Happening.)

1962 *The Art of Assemblage.* The 1961 Museum of Modern Art show scheduled for Dallas Museum for Contemporary Art, January 9–February 11; and for the San Francisco Museum of Art, March 5–April 15.

1956 *George Segal.* Hansa Gallery, New York.
1958 *Marisol.* Leo Castelli Gallery, New York.
1962 *Contemporary Society.* Art Institute of Chicago.
1963 *Contemporary Society.* Art Institute of Chicago.
1963 *Robert Rauschenberg: Retrospective.* Jewish Museum, New York.
1963 *Art 1963: A New Vocabulary.* Arts Council of YM/YWHA, Philadelphia.
1963 *An American Viewpoint 1963.* Contemporary Arts Center, Cincinnati.
1964 *Four Environments by Four Artists.* Sidney Janis Gallery, New York.
1964 *The Atmosphere of '64.* Institute of Contemporary Art, University of Pennsylvania, Philadelphia.
1964 *The Artist's Reality.* New School Art Center, New York.
1964 *Recent American Sculpture.* The Jewish Museum, New York.
1964 *Boxes.* Dwan Gallery, Los Angeles.
1964 *The New Art.* Davison Art Center, Wesleyan University, Connecticut.
1964 *Annual Op Festival.* East Hampton Gallery, New York.
1965 *Abstract Trompe L'Oeil.* Sidney Janis Gallery, New York.
1965 *Color-Motion in Op Art.* Brookhaven National Laboratory, Long Island.
1965 *The Responsive Eye,* Museum of Modern Art, New York; City Art Museum, St. Louis; Seattle Art Museum; Pasadena Art Museum; Baltimore Museum of Art.
1965 *The Great Society: A Sampling of Its Imagery.* Arts Forum, Haverford, Pa.
1965 *Rêves Réalistes.* Galerie Saqqârah, Gstaad.
1965 *Ben Cunningham: Optical Paintings.* East Hampton Gallery, New York.
1965 *Annual Op Art Festival.* East Hampton Gallery, New York.
1965 *François and Bernard Baschet: Structures Sonores.* Moderna Museet, Stockholm; Museum of Industrial Art, Oslo; Kunsthalle, Bern; Palais des Beaux-Arts, Brussels; Museum of Modern Art, New York.
1965 *Bruce Lacey: Kinetic Sculptures.* Marlborough, London.
1965 *George Segal.* Sidney Janis Gallery, New York.
1965 *New American Realism.* Worcester Art Museum, Worcester.
1966 *Max Ernst.* Jewish Museum, New York.
1966 *Heinz Mack: Lights of Silver.* Howard Wise Gallery, New York.
1966 *Marisol: The Party.* Sidney Janis Gallery, New York.
1966 *F. and B. Baschet: Musical Sculptures.* Grippi and Waddell, New York.
1966 *Primary Structures.* Jewish Museum, New York.
1966 *Around the Automobile.* Museum of Modern Art, New York.
1966 *Marcel Duchamp: Retrospective Exhibition.* The Tate Gallery, London.

1966 *Ben Cunningham: Optical Paintings.* East Hampton Gallery, New York.
1966 *Annual Op Festival.* East Hampton Gallery, New York.
1966 *Claes Oldenburg: Soft and Hard Constructions.* Sidney Janis Gallery, New York.
1966 *Multiples in Op.* East Hampton Gallery, New York.

POP ART: SELECTED EXHIBITIONS

1962 *New Painting of Common Objects.* Pasadena Art Institute.
1962 *Image in Progress.* Grabowski Gallery, London.
1962 *New Realists.* Sidney Janis Galley, New York.
1962 *Pop Art.* Pace Gallery, Boston.
1962 *My Country 'Tis of Thee.* Dwan Gallery, Los Angeles.
1963 *The Popular Image.* Institute of Contemporary Arts, London; Washington Gallery of Modern Art.
1963 *Pop Goes the Easel.* Contemporary Arts Association of Houston.
1963 *Popular Art.* William Rockhill Nelson Gallery, Kansas City.
1963 *Pop Art U.S.A.* Oakland Art Museum.
1963 *Mixed Media and Pop Art.* Albright-Knox Art Gallery, Buffalo.
1963 *Nouveau Vulgarians.* Galerie Saqqârah, Gstaad.
1963 *Pop Art.* Jerrold Morris International Gallery Ltd., Toronto.
1963 *Banners.* Graham Gallery, New York.
1964 *12 Contemporary Pop Artists.* Des Moines Art Center.
1964 *The Supermarket.* Bianchini Gallery, New York.
1964 *American Pop Art.* Moderna Museet, Stockholm; Louisiana Museum, Copenhagen; Stedelijk Museum, Amsterdam.
1964 *Slip It to Me.* Hanover Gallery, London.
1964 *The New Generation.* Whitechapel Gallery, London.
1964 *The New Realism.* Gemeente Museum, The Hague.
1964 *Four Germinal Painters [and] Four Younger Artists.* American Pavilion, XXXII Biennale, Venice.
1965 *Pop Art and the American Tradition.* Milwaukee Art Center.
1965 *Pop Art.* City Gallery, Zürich.
1965 *Pop Art—Nouveau Réalisme.* Palais des Beaux-Arts, Brussels.
1965 *Pop Art aus USA.* Hans Neuendorf, Hamburg.

KINETIC ART: SELECTED EXHIBITIONS

1955 *Le Mouvement.* Galerie Denise René, Paris.
1959 *Biennale,* Paris.

1960 *Kinetische Kunst.* Kunstgewerbe Museum, Zürich.

1961 *Tangible Motion: Sculpture by Len Lye.* Museum of Modern Art, New York.

1961 *International Kinetic Art.* Stedelijk Museum, Amsterdam; Moderna Museet, Stockholm; Louisiana Museum, Copenhagen.

1961 *Movement in Art.* Howard Wise Gallery, Cleveland.

1963 *Bewegte Bereiche der Kunst.* Kaiser Wilhelm Museum, Krefeld.

1964 *On the Move.* Howard Wise Gallery, New York.

1964 *XXXII Biennale,* Venice.

1964 *Documenta III,* Kassel.

1964 *Group Zero.* Howard Wise Gallery, New York.

1965 *Mouvement 2.* Galerie Denise René, Paris.

1965 *Movement.* Hanover Gallery, London.

1965 *Len Lye's Bounding Steel Sculptures.* Howard Wise Gallery, New York.

1965 *Group Zero.* Gallery of Modern Art, Washington, D.C.

1965 *Aktuell 65.* Aktuell Gallery, Bern.

1965 *Progression.* Manchester College of Art and Design, Manchester, England.

1965 *Bruce Lacey.* Marlborough, London.

1965 *Kinetic and Optic Art Today.* Albright-Knox Gallery, Buffalo.

1965 *Art and Movement.* Royal Scottish Academy, Edinburgh; Glasgow Art Gallery.

1965 *Kinetic and Object.* Staatsgalerie, Stuttgart; Kunstverein, Karlsruhe.

1965 *Nul 1965.* Stedelijk Museum, Amsterdam.

1965 *Art et Mouvement.* Musée de Tel Aviv.

1965 *Kinetic Art from Krefeld.* Gemeente Museum, The Hague; Stedelijk-van-Abbe Museum, Eindhoven.

1965 *Licht und Bewegung.* Kunsthalle, Bern; Palais des Beaux-Arts, Brussels; Staatliche Kunsthalle, Baden Baden.

1965 *Zero Avantgarde.* Galleria del Cavallino, Venice; Galleria il Punto, Turin; also to Stockholm and Göteborg.

1965 *De Nieuwe Stijl.* Galerie Orez, Amsterdam.

1965 *Kinetic Art.* Gallery 20, Arnhem and Rotterdam.

1965 *Nove Tendencije III.* Zagreb, Yugoslavia.

1965 *Two Kinetic Sculptors: Schöffer and Tinguely.* Jewish Museum, New York.

1965 *Art Turned On.* Institute of Contemporary Art, Boston.

1965 *Castro-Cid: Robots.* Richard Feigen Gallery, New York.

1966 *Directions in Kinetic Sculpture.* University Art Museum, University of California, Berkeley.

1966 *Pol Bury: Moving Sculptures.* Lefebre Gallery, New York.

1966 *Castro-Cid: Compressed-Air Sculpture.* Richard Feigen Gallery, New York.

INDEX OF
ILLUSTRATIONS

NOTES: Nationality and/or permanent residence shown by symbol following first entry of each artist's name:

AM = American	CU = Cuban	HU = Hungarian	RU = Russian
AR = Argentine	DU = Dutch	IC = Icelandic	SP = Spanish
BE = Belgian	FR = French	IT = Italian	SW = Swiss
BR = British	GE = German	JA = Japanese	UR = Uruguayan
CA = Canadian	GK = Greek	PO = Polish	

Dimensions are in inches unless otherwise indicated. Height precedes width. First number (at left) = serial number of illustration. Final number (at right) = page where illustration appears. Ph = photograph. CU = collection unknown.

329

335

SUBJECT INDEX

(Folios set in **boldface** refer to illustrations)